What is slavery to me?

POSTCOLONIAL/SLAVE MEMORY IN POST-APARTHEID SOUTH AFRICA

Pumla Dineo Gqola

WITS UNIVERSITY PRESS

Published in South Africa by:

Wits University Press
1 Jan Smuts Avenue
Johannesburg
2001
http://witspress.wits.ac.za

First published 2010

ISBN 978 1 86814 507 2

Cover art courtesy Berni Searle:
Details of 'Girl', From the 'Colour Me' series, 1999 (see page 176).

Edited by Lee Smith
Indexed by Margie Ramsay
Cover design and layout Hybrid Design

CONTENTS

For

Nkcithakalo and Nototose Rasoyi (neé Gqola)

Sakiya and Sebabatso Gugushe (neé Ramapepe)

Mabusetsa Gugushe

ACKNOWLEDGEMENTS

My birth family, who have always supported and loved me, are truly Qamata's greatest gift. My parents, Dambile and Thato, insisted that intellectual independence, generosity and living with integrity are standards worth living by. Lebohang, Vuyokazi and Melisizwe, my siblings, are 'my constant': they celebrate my triumphs, apparently know 'everything' about me and teach me humility. Graham Huggan, my doctoral supervisor, read several drafts in this book's earlier lives. I am grateful for his humour, time and vision. Graham and Stephan Klasen provided fine intellectual leadership at the first International Interdisciplinary Postcolonial Studies Graduirtenkolleg, which allowed for exchanges that would not have happened otherwise. Desirée Lewis and David Dabydeen inspire me and broaden my world in more than a million ways. The financial support of the Deutsche Forschungsgemeinschaft (DFG) and the Bavarian government is hereby acknowledged for enabling the original study. Antje Schuhmann, Rumana Hashem, Fatmata Lovetta Sesay, Nina Engelhard, Thulani Khanyile, Tirop Simatei, Helene Strauss, Zine Magubane, Zimitri Erasmus, Yvette Abrahams, Vanessa Ludwig all went well beyond the call of collegiality, friendship and kinship. They shared their own work, time and much more. Marion and Peter Schuhmann became my family in Munich, and I owe Antje a debt of gratitude I can never repay for sharing them with me. Angelo Fick, Christopheros Campbell, Pandora Ndungane, Putuma Patrice Gqamana and Kaizer Nkosi allowed me to feel connected to something bigger and more beautiful all the time. Oya and Ajda Ataman, Kimberley Yates, Jane Poyner, Michele Barzey and Jo-Anne Strauss offered much needed diversions. This book benefited tremendously from Thembinkosi Goniwe's and Gabeba Baderoon's insights, comments and criticism, without which this would be a much poorer book. Its weaknesses are all mine. I am grateful to my teachers who affirmed that literature is not a luxury, that language always matters and that women should own their minds. They were the kinds of thinkers, teachers and women I wanted to grow up and be like: Nomntu Mali, Fatima Dada and Carli Coetzee. Angelo Fick, Nomboniso Gasa and Gail Smith, thank you for everything: your breathtaking courage, unwavering support, the gift of letting me share in your own work, your generosity, and telling me when I am wrong. Thank you to Ncumisa Mnyani, Barbara Keitumetse Mashope, Nokuthula Mazibuko, Jaysveree Louw, Chijioke Uwah, Derilene Marco, Ange Khumalo, Nthabiseng Motsemme, Dina Ligaga and Sarah Chiumbu for things too numerous to mention. The wonderful Berni Searle gave permission for her work to be used on the cover of this book, which gave me additional pleasure, given my analysis of her work within its pages. I am most thrilled to have a Searle artwork on the second cover of my work, the first having been a journal special issue I edited in 2005. My colleagues at the University of the Free State offered stimulating conversations and growth opportunities on an unpredictable university campus. This is especially true of Engela Pretorius, Susan Brokensha and Mariza Brooks. Other colleagues in the Department of English and Classical Culture took on larger duties during my stints at the Universities of Warwick and Munich: Pat Minaar, Patsy Fourie, Willfred Greyling, Humaira Ahmed, Margaret Raftery and Arlys van Wyk. Team Wits University Press have been incredible. Thank you especially to Veronica Klipp and Julie Miller. Melanie Pequeux and her production team were available for extended consultations over the book's positioning. Lee Smith has been the kind of editor that writers dream about: attentive, graceful and patient.

Finally, my deepest gratitude goes to Thembinkosi who has had to live with the many lives of this project, whose artistic genius and intellect are a great gift for me to witness daily. The joy, encouragement and laughter he and Yethu bring to my life are the magical beat in my spirit. With them, I grow, play and love.

Earlier versions of chapters appeared in various guises, and appear in revised form in this book. Gqola (2005) contained parts of Chapter 5; an earlier version of Chapter 2 was published as Gqola (2008); ' "Slaves don't have opinions": Inscriptions of slave bodies and the denial of agency in Rayda Jacobs' *The Slave Book*', in Zimitri Erasmus (2001c), has an early exposition of some of the ideas in Chapter 4.

ACRONYMS

ATR	African Traditional Religion
AWB	Afrikaner Weerstandsbeweging
!HCM	!Hurikamma Cultural Movement
KWB	Kleurling Weerstandsbeweging
NNP	New National Party
TRC	Truth and Reconciliation Commission
WOAC	Work of Art Committee

INTRODUCTION

TRACING (RE)MEMORY, THINKING THROUGH ECHOES OF COLONIAL SLAVERY IN CONTEMPORARY SOUTH AFRICA

Meaning is constructed out of [a] multiplicity of voices and positions. (Boyce Davies 1994: 162)

When they ask of you tomorrow
I will tell them that you are alive
   everywhere inside of me
especially where I love myself
   more than you did
where I love myself
   almost as much as you did (Mashile 2008: ll. 25–31)

I have a multiple identity. There is no crisis. There is a kind of delight as well as a kind of anguish in jumping from one identity to the next. It's like electrons which have their own energization circles. Sometimes they jump from one to the next and release an enormous amount of energy; then jump back to another circle: little electrons jumping. That is not a crisis. That is a delight and poignancy, and hopefully a release of energy. (Dabydeen in Birbalsing 1997: 195)

This book goes to print on the eve of South Africa's sixteenth democratic anniversary. *What is Slavery to Me?* examines how the South African imagination conceives of, constructs and interprets itself at a time of transition, and how slavery is evoked and remembered as part of negotiating current ways of being. The new dispensation came to symbolise the promise of freedom and multiple beginnings: individually and collectively, 27 April 1994 was an invitation to envision ourselves differently than we had up until that point.

The three quotations with which I begin this chapter, and book, capture some of the complexities that accompany being invited to imagine ourselves anew. Carole Boyce Davies conceives of meaning as weaving together layers and moving targets at the same time, something she also refers to as 'migratory subjectivities'. Rhyming with Boyce Davies, the extract from Lebogang Mashile shows how a sense of self is shaped from dealing with abstraction and remnants in the psyche which ensure that yesterday lives in tomorrow, whilst the fantasy of the future shapes what is possible today. Finally, David Dabydeen's statement stresses the work inherent in identity: energetic, creative, playful and difficult at the same time.

The three quotations capture what Thembinkosi Goniwe (2008) means when he invites us to think about apartheid and post-apartheid as simultaneously connected and oppositional. Such an approach allows us to see the shifts between apartheid and post-apartheid realities not in terms of rupture – even as we recognise what has changed – but also in terms of association. Put simply, we are both free and *not entirely* free of apartheid. These meanings rub up against each other and inflect our lives in material ways.

This new country, post-apartheid South Africa, is a site of affirmation, where speaking begins and silencing ends. It is also marked by contradictions where the textures of this newness remain contested, questioned and are constantly being refashioned. Contradiction is complexity, creative inflection, play and newness; it is akin to Dabydeen's 'delight and poignancy'.

In the public imagination, this opening up of identifications and imagination on future selves was tied to the proceedings of the Truth and Reconciliation Commission (TRC) as well as to the rainbow nation metaphor (Gqola 2001a). Dorothy Driver has observed that, 'South

Africa's entry into democracy at the end of the armed struggle against apartheid (this had involved all Southern African countries in one way or another) meant new geopolitical identifications became possible' (2002: 155). Shortly after the advent of the new democracy, the much written about TRC was inaugurated as a forum to decipher the immediate past under apartheid, and to mark the beginning of a process of shaping a new democracy. An explicitly mnemonic exercise, the TRC was a response to the invitation to imagine ourselves anew posed by the first democratic election. As Kader Asmal (1994: 5) reflected about the imperfectly inventive TRC process:

> [n]o international models were relied upon in South Africa, because there were none that could apply. Each mode of negotiations had to be invented at each stage. This took time but towards the end had been pretty well developed. It was a case of learning on the job.

As explicit processing of the apartheid past took shape through the valuation of narrative, we saw the inauguration of what Sarah Nuttall and Carli Coetzee (1998) would later describe as the memory industry in South Africa.

In late apartheid, Njabulo Ndebele (1990a) commented on the challenges facing South Africans as we prepared for a democratic order. He had suggested that these difficulties would pertain specifically to dialogue on relationships with the past, and would engender new valuation and valuable systems, especially in the arena of narrative and the mind's eye. The power differentials which were given structural legitimacy under apartheid would influence the ascendant tendencies of compromise, crises of culture, and emergent responsibilities. In other words, Ndebele pre-empted what Goniwe would observe post-apartheid. Using a series of examples from media coverage that year, Ndebele suggested that in 1990 the tone being set was one predicated on a facile negotiation in the terrain

3

of economics, where white business would make certain declarations which would then be seen to work as actualisation of equity, resulting in what he called 'epistemological confusion'. Further, the roles of the imagination in the era immediately after apartheid would doubtlessly explore some of the stickier parts of these processes.

WHAT IS SLAVERY TO ME?

This book presents the findings of the first full-length examination of slave memory in South Africa, drawing on the current vibrant discourse on memory started by examinations of the TRC and overall transition in South Africa, most notably Sarah Nuttall and Carli Coetzee's *Negotiating the Past: The Making of Memory in South Africa* (1998). While the bulk of memory studies in South Africa have focused on apartheid – and within that, specifically on the TRC proceedings – and a few have ventured into late colonialism, this study departs significantly from this trend by focusing specifically on slave memory and the uses of evoked slave pasts for post-apartheid negotiations of identity.

Zoë Wicomb (1996, 1998), the celebrated writer and scholar of South African literature and culture, lamented the absence of folk memory of South African slavery even in the Western Cape, where the bulk of the slave population lived between 1658 and 1838, and where the majority of their descendants continue to live. Historian Robert Ross (1983) questioned the same when he noted that the only residue of this era in South African history lies in court records. These court records offer us a mere glimpse of what slave life was like for the enslaved. As I have argued elsewhere (Gqola 2007), thinking about such lives in academic memory studies today requires a multilayered approach to the fragments that survive. It also necessitates tracing some of the inheritances that remain in our societies from theirs, even if such traces reside in 'modes that do not easily give up the stories' (Nzegwu 2000: n.p.), where historical consciousness is masked by later generations as a matter of survival. This is how it is possible for Wicomb (1996, 1998) to lament the absence of slave memory among ordinary people. At the same time, my initial study (Gqola 2004), which this book extends and revises, as well as Gabeba Baderoon's (2004) doctoral work make the argument that slave memory is evident in various sites in post-apartheid South Africa.

This book is interested in tracing the processes through which South Africa's slave past moves from the obscured to the well recognised. It is important to analyse the specific manifestations of such a consciousness of the past and the uses to which such collective memory is put.

Later in the same year (1998) of Wicomb's lamentation, the South African Cultural Museum, close to Parliament and surrounded by monuments, would attract attention which led to its renaming as the Slave Lodge. The plaque in front of this building which marks the historic location of the slave tree would become more visible. This part of Cape Town would also be the site of Gabeba Abrahams's archaeological dig in April 2000, a collaboration between academics and public institutions which welcomed and, at times, invited the participation of the public. However, as Gabeba Baderoon (2003), Capetonian poet and scholar of Muslim identities, has subsequently observed,[1] while many people knew that they were of slave descent, the particularities of this were unknown, so that it is only 'recently, intersecting with international dynamics about slave histories, reparation, slave routes' that they could surface. It is possible, for example, that only then did many of the artists exhibiting at the renamed museum themselves recognise the significance of their surnames being 'January' or 'Jacobs'.

My book title paraphrases the first line of Countee Cullen's much analysed poem, 'Heritage'. In that poem, Cullen seeks to make sense of the conflicting ways in which Africa has relevance for him as an African American, descended from enslaved Africans. The poem's speaker makes sense of the various ways in which Africa remains both important to his politico-psychic identity and elusive mythologised site. There are many

5

ways in which the questions posed in my book both link with and diverge from those of Cullen's speaker. Like Cullen's persona, I am interested in how the languaging of historic slavery in at once intimate and overtly political ways functions in the post-apartheid imagination. In other words, I am concerned with the textures of the imaginative project of claiming slave ancestry in an era long after slavery's end.

Unlike Cullen's speaker, I also want to probe the extent to which any memorying of slavery needs to be an engagement with the multiple shifts which accompanied enforced, and self-proclaimed, identities under and following on from conditions of enshacklement. Self-definition, and an ongoing attempt to refashion ways of dealing with the historical consciousness of the past, remains tricky. Where Cullen's speaker is a 'me' clearly descended from slaves, I am also concerned with how claiming slave ancestry matters today for white communities whose identities were predicated on disavowal of such ancestry.

Uncovering memory and history demands a critical attentiveness to the uses of the past to negotiate positions in the present. In this regard it is inseparable from postcolonial debates. The absence of published slave narratives by Dutch and British slaves was seen to confirm the slaves' inadequacy. Further, studies of South African slavery within the discipline of history are as recent as the 1980s (Worden & Crais 1994) and this has contributed to the general disregard demonstrated for that particular moment in history, until recently.

Slavery was practised in the Cape between 1658 and 1838. The Dutch, and later the English, transported slaves from South East Asia, East African islands (such as Mauritius and Madagascar), as well as the East African and southern African hinterland. The descendants of these enslaved people would later officially be classified 'coloured' in apartheid South Africa. For the purposes of this book, slavery, colonialism and apartheid are seen as moments along a continuum, and not as separate, completely distinct, and mutually exclusive periods. However, a continuum suggests linearity, which is undermined by the working of memory and ideology. In order to capture both the linkages across time suggested by the image of a continuum, as well as to complicate the ways in which these periods are embedded in each other and beyond, other models for thinking about memory are discussed in detail later in this chapter.

I am concerned in this book with expressions of this slave memory as recent phenomena, enabled in part by the onset of democracy, and therefore the end of the repression which started with slavery. Questions are asked about the relationships of entanglement between the forms of memory found and the timing of their public rehearsal. Some of the practices examined pre-date the onset of democracy but undergo some form of alteration during this moment, which I read as significant. It is important that the implications and nuances of these alterations be unpacked.

My analysis draws extensively from postcolonial theories on race, identity, diaspora, subalternity and hybridity. It is indebted to African studies debates, postcolonial theorisation on identity and is grounded in feminist theory. Theoretically, it engages closely with the vast terrain of memory studies which currently traverses academia in interdisciplinary ways. This study, then, is in conversation with various strands of academic research on South African identities: historical research on slavery; sociological and interdisciplinary explorations of racialised identities in South Africa; the processes of memory and narratives of nation; and interdisciplinary research on the clustering of race and gender identities historically.

The debate on the meetings and divergences of history and memory has grown increasingly interdisciplinary,[2] and perhaps it is less urgent to rigidly establish a distinction between history and memory than it is to participate in locating and distinguishing between different sources and modes of historical authority.

The relationship of historiography to memory is one of containment: history is always part of memory whilst history delineates a certain kind of knowledge system within the terrain of memory. Put differently, whereas memory is a shadow always hovering and governing our relationship to the present and the future, history is the art of recording and analysing this consciousness of the past (Anthony 1999). Memory resists erasure and is important for the symbols through which each community invents itself. It requires a higher, more fraught level of activity to the past than simply identifying and recording it (Poitevin & Bel 1999). The latter is especially true when related to slave and colonial memory, and is best formulated by Toni Morrison's wordplay with activity and reassemblage in her 're-memory' or 'memorying', where events and knowledge are 'memoried', 'memoryed', 'remembered' and 're-memoried'. Morrison's word range implies a much wider field than simply collection, recollection and recalling, and is itself a commentary on the (dis)junctures between memory and history, working as it does not only against forgetting but also what I call 'unremembering'. Whereas both forgetting and unremembering are inscribed by power hierarchies, unremembering is a calculated act of exclusion and erasure. Forgetting, on the other hand, is the phenomenon lamented by Wicomb.

Toni Morrison (1987) evokes 'literary archaeology' as a way of speaking about her work, especially *Beloved*, in her essay 'The Site of Memory'. Morrison explains that this calls for 'imagining the inner life' of a slave and conceptualising 'history-as-life-lived', which is about 'giving blood to the scraps ... and a heartbeat' (1987: 112; see also *City Limits* 31 March–7 April 1988: 10–11[3]). This is the work she refers to as 'rememory'. Recognising that history is always fictional, Morrison's rememory is a reminder that it is not over for those 'who are still struggling to write genealogies of their people and to keep a historical consciousness alive' (Chabot Davies 2002: n.p.).

Rememory invites the creative writer or artist to 'journey to a site to see what remains were left behind and to reconstruct the world that these remains imply' in order 'to yield up a kind of a truth' (Morrison 1987: 112). This filling in, recasting, relooking, reformulating (both of memory and history) outside historiography is Toni Morrison's rememory. It is a necessary project because '[t]he past is only available through textual traces' and these are necessary in order to re-humanise the 'disremembered and unaccounted for' (Chabot Davies 2002: n.p.).

In line with Morrison's theorisation above, much academic writing on memory focuses on precisely its refusal to remain distantly in the past; such scholarship insists instead that memory has an ever-presence which is mutable. The refusal to stay in one place suggests roaming qualities closer to a cyclical model than the linear one conventionally conjured up by continuum. Patricia J. Williams (1991) had conceptualised slave memory as a shadow which hovers above the present and influences it in unpredictable ways (also see Anthony 1999); Nkiru Nzegwu (2000) has theorised memory's mobility since it is always open to relocation across aesthetic and temporal planes; Guy Poitevin and Bernard Bel (1999) write of memory as somewhat cyclical; and Tobias (1999) insists on viewing memory as not only differentiated but also fragmentary.

Even more beneficial to a visual imagination of memory is Dorothy L. Pennington's (1985) conceptualisation of memory as a helix. She noted:

> those whose egos extend into the past for a sense of completion emphasize the importance of the ancestors or those of the past who are believed to give meaning to one's present existence. This view may be likened to a helix in which, while there is a sense of movement, the helix at the same time, turns back upon itself and depends upon the past from which it springs to guide and determine its nature; the past is an *indispensable part of the present which participates in it, enlightens it, and gives it meaning.* (Pennington 1985: 125, emphasis added)

In other words, memory resists the tenet of much academic history that the past is complete and in need of analysis, contextualisation and explanation because 'in order to use the past in their daily lives [people]

9

must create and recreate open-endedness in their experiences' (Thelen 2002: 5). The South African context has an active tradition of probing the relationships between memory and history, within the academy, the heritage sector and in public discourse.[4]

Studies focusing on texts charged with the project of creatively rendering a slave past that cannot physically be remembered entail an analysis of how memory is negotiated in artistic production and other imaginative spaces, such as that of explicitly recasting identity. Paying particular attention to the language and structure of the texts, these studies examine the stylistic and ideological representation of slave characters and of the institution of slavery itself. Necessary questions about the choice of memories re(-)presented and the manner of this portrayal are foregrounded. Some of the loci for the production of memory in the representations of the slave psyche are probed, where memory is understood as a collective process, paying attention to creative engagements with this space. Furthermore, given the theorisation of multiplicity as complexity within postcolonial discourse, the role of contradiction within this exercise of memory needs unpacking.

The project of memory creates new ways of seeing the past and inhabiting the present. When slavery is 'forgotten' or unremembered, the connections between slavery and current expressions of gendered and raced identities are effaced (Hesse 2002). Slave memory studies 'invite a questioning of the relations between what is forgotten and what is remembered' (Hesse 2002: 164).

Postcolonial memory recognises that slave pasts cannot only be addressed through 'abolitionist, curatorial, or aesthetic memories' (Hesse 2002: 165) since it is not concerned with slavery in the past, but with the ongoing effects and processing of that historical consciousness. It is concerned with how the haunting shadow of the past conceived by Williams, and the helix-shaped memory Pennington writes about, shape today's experiences. Like Hesse, then, '[w]hat I call postcolonial memory takes the form of a critical excavation and inventory of the marginalized, discounted, unrealized objects of decolonization and the political consequences of these social legacies' (Hesse 2002: 165).

Postcolonial memory as critical activity recognises that imaginative forms partake in a general landscape of cultural production constituted in and through language. It is the nuances of such narratives that I am interested in reading here as slave memory increases in visibility in post-apartheid South Africa. Like the broader field of postcolonial studies, postcolonial memory assumes that all production is permeated by and implicated in relations of power, and investigates the articulations of this power as well as the ways in which it is negotiated through various texts. These critical tools are used to read public cultural, literary, televisual, filmic and visual material against the larger debates they are shaped by, and which they in turn shape.

Postcolonial and revisionist representation engages analytical tools which are attentive to the networks of repressive depiction since they are methodologically disposed to probe the historical and social specificities of oppressive definitional structures. This is because:

> [p]ostcolonial theory has emerged from an interdisciplinary area of study which is concerned with the historical, political, philosophical, social, cultural and aesthetic structures of colonial domination and resistance; it refers to a way of reading, theorising, interpreting and investigating colonial oppression and its legacy that is informed by an oppositional ethical agenda. (Low 1999: 463)

The imperative of postcolonial memory studies is to recognise heterogeneity in the concrete historical subjects who were enslaved, rather than confining them to sameness and anonymity, in keeping with colonial epistemes. It thus becomes possible to resist participation in 'an epistemology ... conceived purely in terms of a total polarity of absolutes' (Ndebele 1994: 60; see also Figueroa 1996).

GENDERING POSTCOLONIAL MEMORY

David Dabydeen reminds us that the 'Empire was a pornographic project; it wasn't just economic or sociological or a political project, it was also a project of pornography' (in Dawes 1997: 220). Yvette Abrahams (1997), too, has posited that the 'great long national insult' was a gendered corporeal project. Dabydeen's and Abrahams's cues are of utmost importance because apartheid and slave memory are often considered engagements with race. Although feminist scholarship has challenged this assumption successfully, such scholarship has often been as response to initially muted explorations of how pasts are gendered. Feminist historians of colonial and slave eras in southern Africa continue to challenge the erasure of women slaves, but also how slavery was a gendered project (Y. Abrahams 2000; Bradford 1996; Magubane 2004; van der Spuy 1996).

What might it mean to chart a field from the onset in ways that critically engage with how gender works alongside other axes of power? I am concerned with what new meanings are inevitably covered when we ask questions differently, as are the central tenets of postcolonial (and) feminist scholarship (Gqola 2001b). Elleke Boehmer (1992: 270) has demonstrated how representations of the slave body in colonial slavery:

> offered important self-justifications. For what is body and instinctual is by definition dumb and inarticulate. As it does not itself signify, or signify coherently, it may be freely occupied, scrutinized, analyzed, resignified. This representation carries complete authority; the Other cannot gainsay it. The body of the Other can represent only its own physicality, its own strangeness.

Thus locked into bodily signification, Others were not 'merely emblematic representations of the [Empire's] most cherished ideals but also actively deployed as *somatic* technologies' of patriarchal empire building (Ramaswamy 1998: 19). Using Saul Dubow's (1995) earlier work, Cheryl

12

Hendricks (2001) has argued that the status of the Khoi as 'the missing link' between animals and people was not a separate project from the one which saw Sarah Bartmann put on display in Europe in the nineteenth century. For Abrahams, the fascination with Khoi women's genitalia, more specifically the fabrication of 'the Hottentot apron', was central to the development of scientific racist discourses. The work of these three scholars further demonstrates the direct links between the Khoi body generally but, more specifically, the Khoi woman's body and the language of scientific racism (Abrahams 1997).

There is a large volume of work which further explores the connections between slave women whose bodies were inscribed in terms of 'miscegenation' and 'racial mixing' and who were represented as deviant, contagious and shameful. Male slave bodies were further rendered in terms of the dangerous, ravenous male phallus when they were of African origin, or as volatile noble savages capable of great violence if they were of Asian origin. Vernie February's (1981) study established the links between the literary stereotypes of coloured characters and the ways in which Khoi and slave bodies were inscribed during British and Dutch colonialism in South Africa. The connections between the bodily branding of these historical subjects and some of the associations of shame for their coloured descendants were later developed by Zoë Wicomb. Wicomb's theories in this regard have been engaged in multiple ways and responded to variously, as will become clear in Chapter 1.

Attitudes to the 'mixed-race' slaves were recorded by historians such as G.M. Theal on the eve of manumission; he argued that these were 'deserving of freedom, but the change was not beneficial to "pure blacks"' (in Saunders 1988: 27). Later, the descendants of these slaves were to be the 'beneficiaries' of Coloured Preferential Employment policies in the western Cape because apartheid positioned them in terms of an in-between identity, a biologically based hybridity which at once made them superior to blacks and inferior to the same because of their 'lack of culture'.

DEPARTURES: IMAGINING SLAVE MEMORY

The excavation of slave memory and spaces seen as the repositories for such memories is part of the general project of memory-making in South Africa. It is implicated in some of the shortcomings of the greater effort even as it forces the analysis of the terrain to engage with the past in more complex ways. This is evident in the various explicit links between public memory rehearsal and the making of nation. Yet the segment which deals with the rendering visible of slavery and colonial history questions some of the tools used to interpret and shape the new nation. It draws attention to the contestation of race, identity and language in the contemporary South African topos by opening up many of the taken-for-granted categories for revision. There have been shifts from initially rare examinations of a past of enslavement as integral to memory in South Africa to a flourishing exploration of this phenomenon in literary texts. Thus, slave rememorying is entering the terrain of nation-building and therefore the consciousness of the larger South African populace.

Laura Chrisman (2000) has noted and demonstrated, with outstanding dexterity, the manner in which, although helpful, many of the core theoretical concepts in postcolonial literary studies are inadequate when reading the nuances pertaining to literary imaginative projects which address colonial south(ern) Africa. For Chrisman, ' "writing back to the centre," "mimicry," or "hybridity" do not adequately account for the formal, linguistic and ideological textures' of some of the literature under study, and this is particularly so when the texts are treated as 'historically specific' (2000: 208).

Language then becomes a challenge in the crafting of memory and the creation of a future, more equitable country at every level beyond the legislative. Neville Alexander further suggests that the only plausible way out is possible when there is an effort to 'invent a new discourse involving a new set of concepts that is more appropriate to the peculiarities of South African history, seen in the context of world history' (2001: 83).

14

The unpredictability of memory, and the ambiguities of a conceptual vocabulary that functions well elsewhere, are central to the exploration of representations of slave memory. It links with Pennington's helix model in its emphasis on movement and many possible directions. Another similarity pertains to its ability to move in several directions at once, turn upon itself, a living organism influenced by forces in its environs. These forces shape direction, speed of movement, and growth. Pennington offers refreshing perspectives on the dynamic movement within memory politics and the identities which stem from those processes.

A NOTE ON TERMINOLOGY

There are growing discussions within South African historical studies on whether the distinctions made by the VOC (Vereenigde Oost-Indische Compagnie) between forms of unfree labour (slavery versus indentured servitude) had any materiality beyond the law books. My approach is informed by the work of historians such as Yvette Abrahams (1997, 2000) who have demonstrated that, legal definitions notwithstanding, the conditions of the Khoisan were very similar to those of legally called slaves. The same applies to definitions of Bartmann as slave rather than as contracted worker. In this book, I read Krotoä and Sarah Bartmann as slaves both because of such scholarship, but also because the bulk of the primary texts under analysis represent them as such.

Secondly, the differences between 'native', 'slave' and 'Khoi' were significant in the past, and these categories only appear similar after the benefit of various political developments, among them the Black Consciousness Movement. Since my concern is with how the past is made sense of in the present, I am less concerned with the detailed nuances of their differences historically, than with the fact that memory uses the lens influenced by a range of political movements and insights. Therefore it is memory that blurs what would have been sometimes stark differences a few centuries ago, because memory operates now and not in the past.

Thirdly, the label 'Cape Malay' is not without problems/limitations when used in the context of the descendants of slaves living in the Western Cape of South Africa. Some of the problems which attach to this terminology are discussed later in this book. I retain its usage here for an assortment of reasons. I find it more useful than 'Muslim' for clarity, given that all large Muslim communities in South Africa are diasporic and participate in diaspora in ways which do not necessarily have to do with the *particular* slave trade I discuss here. I use 'Cape Malay' and 'Capetonian Muslim' interchangeably, after Baderoon's (2004) introduction of the latter into academic discussions of historic formations of such identities. The inaccuracies which remain after my retention of the marker 'Cape Malay' notwithstanding, it is one of the clearest referents available to discuss the section of the population whose artistic and cultural production I am concerned with here.

In a linked manner, I use a capitalised 'Black' to refer to the anti-apartheid definition of Blackness which emerges out of the Black Consciousness Movement. In other words, the capitalised Black refers to those people who would have been classified 'Indian', 'coloured' and 'black' under apartheid. I retain the small caps 'black' to refer to Black people sometimes codified as 'African', racially speaking, in South Africa.

While it has become customary to insist that we need to move beyond race markers in South Africa, I see this project as premature given the continued ways in which race continues to matter in South Africa in social, political and economic ways. Identities marked as race have also taken on added meanings in addition to, and other than, those bestowed through slavocracy, colonialism and apartheid. Part of the anti-racist and postcolonialist critical project needs to take these meanings seriously rather than placing them under erasure and denying the agency with which they were invested with new, conflicting meanings by subjects thus classified, and self-identifying, over 350 years. To identify as Black in its various gradations, therefore, is always more than simply rehearsing 'an archive of one's victimisation', to borrow Dabydeen's formulation (in Binder 1997: 172).

Chapter 1 enters into this debate by examining the ways in which coloured and Khoi identities, as formulated in recent years, are an engagement with a slave history. The chapter investigates the implications of colonial and slave rememory for racialised identities among the descendants of slaves, in South Africa specifically. I explore how this activity within the 'rememory landscape' works to disrupt some official national and historical narratives. It focuses specifically on debates around coloured identities and Khoi self-identifications. Reading coloured articulations alongside their Khoi counterparts, the chapter analyses the manner in which slave foreparentage is used to fashion a variety of positionings in relation to a history which classified the descendants of slaves 'coloured'. Finally, it suggests ways in which readings of Khoi self-identification and some articulations of coloured identity may be seen as complementary and as partaking in related projects.

The second chapter explores literary representations of slaves and colonised subjects. It examines contemporary imaginative rewritings of the late eighteenth and nineteenth centuries. This examination is informed by an engagement with the centrality of southern African women's bodies in the generation of knowledge, scientific racism and sexuality, because indeed '[e]veryone knows it is virtually impossible to talk candidly about race without talking about sex' (West 1993: 120). Focusing specifically on contemporary Black feminist engagements with colonial representations of Black women from southern Africa, it analyses a series of written texts which address themselves to the difficulty of representing Sarah Bartmann. The texts include Dianne Ferrus's poem 'I Have Come to Take You Home', which ultimately convinced the French Parliament to return the remains of Sarah Bartmann to South Africa in 2002; Zoë Wicomb's (2000) refusal to represent Sarah Bartmann in her

David's Story; some of the challenges unpacked by Yvette Abrahams, pre-eminent Khoi historiographer and Sarah Bartmann's biographer; and Gail Smith's writing on the process of fetching Sarah Bartmann's remains from Paris as part of the film crew making a documentary on Bartmann's return (*Mail & Guardian* 12 May 2002[5]).

In Chapter 3, I ask questions about the effects of the claim in the case of Afrikaners to slave foreparentage, since it appears to foreground the re-evaluation and rejection of the claim to racial purity which sustained slavery and apartheid. This chapter analyses such public creative reclamations alongside two television texts which also locate Khoi and/or slave presences in Afrikaner families. Here I am interested in the effects of such invocation in as much as I analyse the language which emerges to describe, analyse and introduce such activity. I explore some of the ways in which claiming slave foreparents is used in contemporary South Africa; these are then examined in conjunction with the refashioning of some white identities, as well as the celebration of racial purity among communities previously classified coloured. What might the effects of this contested discursive terrain be for how we understand apparent shifts in the relationship of whiteness to purity and of colouredness to miscegenation?

This examination is followed in Chapter 4 by my attempt to take up the challenge thrown up by Zimitri Erasmus (2001a, 2001b, 2001c) and Muhammed Haron (2001) to envision the variety of self-identifications which attach to contemporary coloured assertions of diaspora and claims to Cape Malay identities. I read the various debates about the meanings of the Muslim/Malay diaspora and its relationships to South East Asia alongside an analysis of the meanings of Islam and Malay identities in articles published in *Sechaba*[6] and Rayda Jacobs's novel *The Slave Book* (1998). In this chapter I am also concerned with uncovering the opportunities offered by slave memory to deepen scholarly understandings of diasporas.

18

In the final chapter, I read scholarship on the meanings of Muslim food in Cape Town alongside exhibitions on memory by the award-winning artist Berni Searle. Analysing these articulations along a continuum is a strategy suggested by Carolyn Cooper (2000) as particularly valuable in making sense of the apparently simple and contradictory diasporic formations which follow from slavery. The juxtaposition of Searle's work and the genre of Malay food permits a fruitful comparison of varied sites of creativity in the service of memory. It also makes sense given the assertion of Cape Malay food as diasporic *artistic* expression, a claim that is part of the ground I analyse in this chapter.

Conceptualisations of memory in terms of Morrison's rememory, and Pennington's helix-like attributes, permit the imagination of this process of representation in terms of the slipperiness with which the lives of the disremembered can be imaginatively rendered. Such frameworks on memory stress the ongoing entanglements: remembering and forgetting always side by side. This is part of the cost of rememorying, because helix-like it changes the present as well as conceptualisation of the past. In addition, any movement of a helix causes structural change, so that it opens up an infinite number of possibilities. In this manner, the helix structure is a precise representation of Morrison's rememory and works in specifically the same way. The relationship between the past and present in/of/with the helix is unstable in exactly the same manner as the archaeological and imaginative work of rememory. Like the perpetual incompleteness of rememory, the helix constantly changes planes, re-interrogates and reshapes itself. Both are in need of re-minding as well as reminding and are generative in different ways. They generate a reading of the shifting instability of the creative representation of slave memory, whilst being involved with linking different lineages in various conglomerations of past, present and future.

CHAPTER 1

REMEMBERING DIFFERENTLY: REPOSITIONED COLOURED IDENTITIES IN A DEMOCRACY

Post-apartheid South Africa has witnessed notable shifts in the scholarly and identitiary treatment of coloured subjectivities. Such shifts challenge earlier hegemonic conceptions of coloured people without necessarily completely dislodging them. These changes in the scholarly and political understandings of what coloured identities mean make sense given the specific prominence that colouredness has taken on in a general revisiting of racial identification and its languaging in a democratic South Africa, and:

> A number of scholars of coloured identity in South Africa have suggested that the onset of democracy has permitted the creative and affirmative re-articulation of colouredness as a social identity in ways that were impossible under white supremacist rule. (Strauss 2009: 30)

In this chapter, I argue that such 're-articulations' both challenge and rhyme with postcolonial discursive phenomena from elsewhere. This is especially the case when such shifts are read as mnemonic activity related to slavery, as foregrounded in the theorisation of shame by Zoë Wicomb (1996, 1998), and creolisation by Zimitri Erasmus (2001). The interventions of both Wicomb and Erasmus, key figures in the post-apartheid shifts in understanding constitutions of coloured identities, are analysed below.

In her influential essay 'Shame and Identity: The Case of the Coloured in South Africa', Zoë Wicomb (1998) argues that shame is a constitutive part of coloured identities. This shame infuses historic inscriptions of coloured people with miscegenation, degeneracy and non-belonging. It is this shame which undergirds the absence of a slave memory among coloured people, many of whom are descended from slaves, according to Wicomb. This repression of memory:

> presumably has its roots in shame: shame for our origins of slavery, shame for the miscegenation, and shame, as colonial racism became institutionalized, for being black, so that with the help of our European names we have lost all knowledge of our Xhosa, Indonesian, East African or Khoi origins. (Wicomb 1998: 100)

For Wicomb, shame is partly constituted by the historical connections of 'colouredness' with degeneracy through associations with 'miscegenation' and its internalisation by members of the communities described as such. The additional part is linked to the devaluation of Black bodies and subjectivities under white supremacist periods. Consequently, those who are seen to embody both aspects of 'inferior' histories in the form of African ancestry *and* who are defined through discourses of miscegenation cannot avoid contamination by shame. Because shame attaches to all conditions of humiliation, a past which foregrounds precisely the debasement of the ancestry of coloured people engenders shame. This shame is therefore a response to a series of degrading periods in the past. Shame, however, is a relationship to this historical consciousness. As Wicomb theorises it, it is a collective self-protection from the trauma of slavery and successful colonisation and dispossession. It is 'easier' than remembering the complex myriad of collective traumas which precede the present. Wicomb's shame is a relationship with the past which forecloses on memory.

Coloured definitions are structured in ways that challenge postcolonial perceptions of cultural hybridity as freeing. In the case of the 'coloured', Wicomb observes, it is 'precisely the celebration of inbetweenness that serves conservatism' (1998: 102–103). This conservative impulse does not only appear in the noticeably problematic guise of 'racial mixedness', but is founded on cultural hybridity as well. In other words, when coloured South Africans are historically read as both biologically and culturally hybrid, such framing is conservative since such logic posits the cultural and biological as intertwined. It is in such light that Wicomb distances herself from Bhabha's (1994) reading of coloured subjectivity as in-between and subversive in his analysis of a South African novel, Nadine Gordimer's *My Son's Story*. Wicomb (1998: 102) notes that:

> Bhabha speaks of the halfway house of 'racial and cultural origins that bridges the "inbetween" diasporic origins of the Coloured South African and turns it into the symbol of the disjunctive, displaced everyday life of the liberation struggle'. This link, assumed between colouredness and revolutionary struggle, seems to presuppose a theory of hybridity that relies, after all, on the biological, a notion denied in earlier accounts where Bhabha claims that colonial power with its inherent ambivalence itself produces hybridization.

While postcolonial proponents of hybridity as subversion in the terrain of race see it, after Bhabha, as being able to 'provide greater scope for strategic manoeuvre' (Bhabha 1994: 145), and therefore clearly problematise the deployment of hybridisation in the discourses which transcribe 'miscegenation', cultural hybridity is not always subjected to the same rigours. Desirée Lewis (2000: 23, emphasis added) suggests that:

> [t]he fluidity suggested by hybridization is a feature of all discursively constructed subjects and cultural experiences. In *self-consciously disruptive* theoretical writing and political practice, however, hybridization becomes a response to fixed positions and binarisms.

Like Wicomb, Lewis warns against the dangerous assumption that social and cultural hybrid forms or declarations are *as a given* more subversive than discourses centred on 'miscegenation'. The 'case of the coloured' testifies to the textures of these dangers.

Coloured identities are no more stable than other (racial) markers in South Africa in the current dispensation. This is evident in the shifting, sometimes confusing uses of b/Black and C/coloured, 'coloured' and so-called coloured. Many who under apartheid rejected the label of 'coloured' wholesale, now see possibility for its reclamation in freeing ways (Ruiters 2006, 2009). However, such acceptance and/or reclamation of 'coloured' as a form of self-identification is characterised by contestation. That subjects switch back and forth across time between the various labels complicates matters even further (Kadalie 1995: 17). Noting this flexibility, Wicomb (1998: 83–84) writes:

> [s]uch adoption of different names at different historical junctures shows perhaps the difficulty which the term 'coloured' has in taking on fixed meaning, and as such exemplifies postmodernity in its shifting allegiances, its duplicitous play between the written capitalisation and speech that denies or at least does not reveal the act of renaming – once again the silent inscription of shame.

Here, Wicomb highlights the fluidity of self-identification as coloured 'undermin[ing] the new narrative of national unity' whilst showing how 'different groups created by the old system do not participate equally in the category postcoloniality' (Wicomb 1998: 94). Consequently, there are shifts in assertions of coloured identities, and mnemonic activity is a part of these turns among groups classified coloured under apartheid, just as there are for some white subjectivities, as demonstrated in the examples I examine in Chapter 3. However, the meanings and implications of shifting registers of self-identification as c/Coloured and/or Black and positioning in relation to slavery diverge.

Groups such as the Kleurling Weerstandsbeweging (KWB) call for self-determination in a separate state for the 'pure third race' of Coloureds.

The KWB, whose name translates into English as the 'Coloured Resistance Movement', echoes the right-wing, white supremacist Afrikaner Weerstandsbeweging (AWB), but it also validates the discourses of biologist notions of natural races and the appropriate positions occupied along a clearly delineated hierarchy. For Wicomb, the naming of 'black bodies that bear the marked pigmentation of miscegenation and the way that relates to culture [is linked to] attempts by coloureds to establish brownness as a pure category, which is to say a denial of shame' (1998: 92). This racial purity is named as 'Brown' within KWB discourse in ways that fix it as a 'third pure race'. It is the stress on the purity of a separate category, here coloured/brown, which forms the central organising principle of this movement. As Michele Ruiters argues, the KWB 'wish[es] to be involved in mainstream politics yet create[s] identities that partition their constituencies off from the rest of South African society' (2006: 195). According to Wicomb, this ambiguity is an engagement with shame.

Notably, shame is intractably tied to articulations of coloured identities, but is not limited to them. Wicomb punctuates her discussion of shame with references to other articulations of it in postcolonial (con)texts, such as Salman Rushdie's novel *Shame*. There are intersections between the shame she discusses in relation to 'colouredness' and its expressions elsewhere; there are also divergences.

In an interview with Wolfgang Binder (1997), David Dabydeen theorises shame through the colonised's awareness of their rejection by the coloniser and colonising culture. In this context, markers of the colonised's Otherness become constant reminders which emphasise this rejection. For Dabydeen, this is a condition of the colonised–coloniser relationship which can only be undone when the position of the Other changes. Such unravelling usually accompanies the altered status of the colonised when, for example, corporeal and cultural difference begins to signify differently in the shared society. In a society where the visibility of Otherness serves to confirm the marginality of Black bodies, one of the consequences is an internalisation of this valuation process: shame. Racist humiliation leads to a disavowal of these points of belonging and a pressure to assimilate into the values of the colonising culture. In anti-colonial movements, Otherness is often reclaimed and recast as a site of pride – the antithesis of colonial shame. Although Dabydeen is speaking specifically of the Caribbean and Black British contexts here, this conception is equally valid for other colonial contexts.

Dabydeen's is a discursive meaning of shame which has clear similarities with Wicomb's. But, like Rushdie's, it also highlights variation. In Wicomb's theorisation, shame permeates general South African society to express a variety of feelings which have nothing to do with shame. Thus, she points to the constant utterance and circulation of the word 'shame' in South African-speak which also foregrounds it without addressing or needing to acknowledge it.

Thiven Reddy (2001) argues that colouredness reveals much about the constitution of the racial categories white, Indian and black in South Africa under colonialism, slavery and apartheid. Tracing historic legal constructions of coloured people in the South African Native Affairs Commission Report of 1903–05, as well as the 1950 Population Registration Act, he uncovers how 'coloured' often works to contain the 'residue' from the other classifications: '[t]he enormous emphasis placed on "pure blood" pervades the dominant discourse as well as the all-important assumption that "pure bloodlines" actually did exist in certain "races" ' (Reddy 2001: 71). Thus, the response of the KWB critiqued by Wicomb above is to distance itself from this debasement because of 'miscegenation' through an insistence that brown people be read as racially pure. This political move attempts to intervene in colonialist and apartheid discourses by deploying the tools of that discourse. It does not question the premises through which 'race' is evaluated, given meaning and put to use. For the KWB, then, the task is not to undo white supremacist logic, or even to question it. What is focused on is the mere changing of the position of coloured/brown subjects by denying race mixing, and thereby disavowing the discursive history of 'miscegenation'. It denies 'mixing', 'left-over', 'neither-nor' discourses through an insertion of brown/coloured subjectivity at a new point along the continuum of racial valuation. The apartheid state sought to limit the ambiguities present in legislating who counted as coloured in 1959 by proclaiming that the category would be subdivided into 'Cape Coloured, Cape Malay, Griqua, Indian, Chinese, "other Asiatic", and "Other Coloured" ' (Reddy 2001: 73). Not only did the ambiguities which remained highlight the absurdities of this classifications system, they also betrayed the anxieties associated with the category 'coloured'. The KWB effort is an attempt to engage this anxiety by concretising the position of coloured through naming it via a stabilised brownness.

The increased academic scrutiny of colouredness has also been influenced by the multiple frames used to analyse various coloured locations in public discourse. In their analysis of aspects of this public discourse, and with specific reference to voting patterns in the Western Cape in 1994, Zimitri Erasmus and Edgar Pieterse (1999: 167) declare:

> we have heard that coloured people voted the way they did because they are white-identified, sharing language and religious affiliation with white voters; because they are racist towards africans and hence voted against the African National Congress (ANC); because they suffer from 'slave mentality' ... and that this voting behaviour can be explained in terms of NP [National Party] propaganda and the 'psychological damage' this has caused in coloured communities who are yet to free themselves 'from the stranglehold of psychological enslavement'.

The views explored above point to an apparent contradiction in how Black political action is made sense of in contemporary South Africa.

For those arguing along the same lines as Erasmus and Pieterse, similar questions are not asked about groups of black South Africans who were never classified coloured, and who cast their votes for political parties which have a history of collaboration with the apartheid state, such as the Inkatha Freedom Party or parties led by former bantustan leaders. Some of the respondents in Ruiters (2006) share such sentiment. They point out that there is no parallel process by which those who vote for the parties headed by previous homeland 'leaders' are denied entry into Blackness, or accused of harbouring a similar 'slave mentality'. Or, at least, where these discussions exist they are less prominent and more dismissive. In relation to the framing of coloured subjectivities, however, as Erasmus and Pieterse note, these are in the majority. Erasmus and Pieterse's paper is a challenge to these explanations as reductionist and as linked to other limited ways of thinking through coloured identity formation. The latter encompass divergent ways of essentialising colouredness, among them conservative coloured nationalism, discussed by Wicomb in relation to the KWB, and imagining that coloured subjects are overdetermined by racist apartheid naming.

The above criticisms of what is constructed as 'the coloured vote' are valid because the very discursive constitution of voting tendencies in this manner is problematic. In other words, the very language used to describe Western Cape voting patterns in the first democratic elections through primarily resorting to constructing something called 'the coloured vote' is an oversimplification that itself deserves debunking through attention to the specificities of electoral choices (Hoeane 2004; Ruiters 2006). At the same time, the conflation of 'coloured' with 'Western Cape coloured' occludes other coloured subjectivities that are constructed differently, both from within and in public discourse. This conflation is explicitly rehearsed by those who discursively construct 'the coloured vote', but it is also implicitly endorsed in Erasmus and Pieterse's (1999) critique. This is done when what happens in the Western Cape is seen to be representative of *nationwide* coloured subjectivities through the generalisation of Western Cape coloured historical specificities. Subsequent scholarship on aspects of 'coloured' identities warns against this overgeneralisation of Western Cape realities and debates (Adhikari 2009; Ruiters 2006).

Erasmus and Pieterse's paper also raised concerns about the implications of these problems for the larger national democratic project. They call for the important recognition that 'not all assertions of coloured identity are racist' because 'no identity is inherently progressive or reactionary' (Erasmus & Pieterse 1999: 178, 179). It is important to acknowledge the variety of ways in which coloured subjects shape collective identities and make meaning of their lives. This enables the understanding that coloured formulations are 'relational identities shaped by complex networks of concrete social relations' (Erasmus & Pieterse 1999: 183).

The acknowledgement of creolisation is central to this process, as is the creolisation of the Dutch language into Afrikaans by slaves and of cultural practice by these communities and their descendants. Processes of creolisation happen in proximity to and within different relations of power under conditions of slavery. This conceptualisation of creolity within recent South African studies is one of two streams. Both have moved beyond addressing only linguistic creolisation in relation to the Afrikaans language. The first, espoused by Sarah Nuttall and Cheryl-Ann Michael (2000), conceptualises creolity as any mixing of various strands to result in a hybrid formation which constantly draws attention to itself as dynamic and disruptive. The second branch is that in which Erasmus (2001a) theorises creolity under the very specific conditions of slavery and its ensuing inequalities. It draws on the extensive works of Françoise Verges and Eduoard Glissant on creolisation in the Indian Ocean Islands and Caribbean, respectively, as well as more broadly on the schools of thought on creolisation emerging from Caribbean studies. For the latter branch, not all hybrid formations are creolised. Here creolity is interpreted as encompassing a range of possibilities: creative and unstable. It is to be found in cultural practice with a slave history and is dynamic. For Erasmus's formulation of creolity, and application to the coloured historical series of experiences in South Africa, the inequity of power is paramount. Unlike the hybridity-like creolisation model adopted by Nuttall and Michael, Erasmus roots creolisation, like scholars of the Caribbean, in the specific experience of histories of enslavement. Consequently, for example, while Afrikaner and coloured experiences and identities are hybridised, only coloured identities are creolised identities. This creolisation is part of the memory project for it values the history of enslavement as a constitutive, even if not total, influence on current collective positionings within coloured communities.

Adhikari (2009) argues that Erasmus 'does little beyond proposing the idea' of creolisation to coloured identities in her introduction to her book, while Helene Strauss (2009) asks very pertinent questions in her essay on creolisation as a useful framework for thinking about contemporary coloured identities post-apartheid:

> Does creolisation help clarify processes of coloured identity formation, or does it reinforce apartheid-era essentialisms and undermine the very transgressive potential that has made it so attractive for revising cultural exclusivity? To what extent do received cultural and racial categories continue to inflect the ways in which processes of creolisation take place? (Strauss 2009: 23)

Strauss's questions can be answered obliquely through engaging with Adhikari's latest work on coloured identities in southern Africa, of which Strauss's chapter forms part. Adhikari (2009) underlines the importance of varied registers of coloured identities in South African politics and scholarship. Although he delineates four streams, two are immediately relevant for my purposes here: the 'essentialist school' and the 'instrumentalist school'. The introduction to this text is instructive, given the manner in which he reads assertions and/or definitions of coloured identities against one another, rather than solely against their perceived opposites.

Adhikari's 'essentialist school' relies on conventional colonialist registers of miscegenation and either denies the agency of coloured people in history (conservative essentialist), celebrates miscegenation as evidence that racial segregation is not preferred across history (liberal essentialist), or accepts that coloureds were a separate race that was temporarily inferior to whites (progressionist essentialist). These nuances matter for a fuller understanding of shifts and reification in how coloured identities – or, for Adhikari, identity, differentiated but in the singular – articulate themselves in contemporary South Africa.

The second stream of concern here is the 'instrumentalist school', which contains much of the anti-colonial and anti-apartheid left. Within this school, Adhikari includes movements as varied as the Non European/New Unity Movement, the Black Consciousness Movement and other parts of the non-racist and non-racialist movements, all of which see coloured identity as 'negative and undesirable but blame it on the racism and exploitative practices of the ruling white minority' (Adhikari 2009: 15). Finally, both essentialist and instrumentalist schools 'treat coloured identity as something exceptional, failing to recognise it for what it is – a historically specific social construction, like any other social identity' (Adhikari 2009: 15).

My reading of articulations of coloured identity and rejections of the label by those previously classified as such is premised on the understanding that echoes of colonial memory are complex phenomena which are not trapped in the binaries of either complicity or resistance. My exclusion of articulations such as the KWB from detailed analysis is due to the considerable attention this movement has already received from scholars of coloured identities (Erasmus 2001b; Erasmus & Pieterse 1999; Lewis 2001; Ruiters 2006; Wicomb 1996, 1998).

It is naïve to continue insisting that there is only one progressive, complex manner to be mindful of history and to make sense of a slave past, and that to do this entails theorising colouredness through first acceding to the cultures of complicity and privilege even as these were rejected (Erasmus 2001b). There are multiple progressive engagements with a past of enslavement (Marco 2009). Denying this erases the variety of ways of inhabiting colouredness and reduces the agency and choice of historical subjects classified coloured to fashion and reinvent collective identity. However, the activity evident in contemporary negotiations of coloured identities demonstrates the importance of creativity in political memory processes. To the extent that memory is an imaginative process, and not simply a recuperative one, the dynamic articulations of colouredness, along with the rejection of the identity 'coloured', bear witness to the collective reinvention of identities which is at the heart of memory. The specific foregrounding of slavery in this repositioning and re-evaluative process links the memory project directly to slavery in ways that are sometimes explicit, and at other junctures more subtle. This resonates with Carolyn Cooper's model of reading engagements with identity for creolised societies along a continuum. There are several ways in which assertions of progressive coloured identity or disavowal via the reclaiming of Khoi subjectivities reveal themselves to be along a continuum in the manner suggested by Cooper. One lens which illuminates this comparison is the theorisation of Black will and anti-will under conditions of enslavement by Patricia Williams.

Williams (1991) argues that slavery is predicated on the absence of Black will so that the perfect Black person becomes one without a will. An enslaved person is rendered object only because s/he becomes owned, therefore property, a thing. One of the basic assumptions about humanity, especially in the Judeo-Christian narrative, is the presence of spirit/intention, in other words, willpower. When the slaves are equated to other inanimate objects, or to non-human animals, this is a move which denies humanity. If what distinguishes human beings from other beings in the living world is this spirit/agency/will, the enslaved people cease to have will. This is in keeping with the construction of the enslaved as only corporeal in colonial discourse. For Williams, this leads to the conclusion that under conditions of slavery the perfect white person is the opposite of the perfect Black one: one *with* will. A reading of the variety of ways in which coloured subjects participate in an imaginative project in relation to their identity is the ultimate assertion of the presence of will and humanity in the concrete historical subjects who were enslaved, as well as those descended from them. This variety of articulations, in James Clifford's (2001) sense, testifies to the heterogeneity of the historically enslaved as well as to their survival. In other words, it testifies to the strength of this will.

It becomes important not to read these articulations as exclusively related to or overdetermined by their relationship to whiteness and discourses which sought to inscribe this in terms of 'racial purity'. A sensitive postcolonial engagement with these processes is attentive to their proximity to anti-apartheid discourses on Blackness as well. It is mindful of Zine Magubane's (1997: 17) caution that:

> [i]f we are looking at multiplicity and hybridity from a South African perspective, as important as it is to historicise, acknowledge, and celebrate our multiple identities, it is equally important to acknowledge the political gains that 'totalising discourses' like black nationalism have been able to effect. We need to understand the way in which speaking from an essentialised position can be a site of political power as well.

The recasting and meaning-making processes of Blackness in liberation movement discourses have been analysed at great length. The scholarship which has participated in this project has unearthed the ways in which discourses of Black nationalism, especially as proposed by the Black Consciousness Movement, relied on a unified Black experience rather than on physiognomy. While it is important to draw attention to the manner in which the unifying gestures of many Black nationalist and anti-colonial movements policed Blackness, and to recognise the thorny character of this monitoring, it is crucial to recognise that the effect of this unity was a direct contribution to the successes of activism.

At a time when Black people were routinely subjected to racial terror, suppressing a realistic engagement with heterogeneity within led to two contradictory effects. First, it silenced certain experiences of Blackness and was not attentive to the difference that gender, sexuality, class, 'ethnicity',[1] geographical location, and so forth, made. In this manner, it was implicated in oppressive tendencies and systems. The second effect realised the establishment, in so far as was possible under apartheid, of a 'safe' space to identify those who were in positions of collaboration with the state. Given that this was an issue of survival, the fiction that politics could be read from immediately observable behaviour meant that political affiliation was signified in a series of identifiable actions. These notions of what 'authentic' Blackness is did not successfully eliminate diversity within, but theoretically made it more possible to negotiate the delicate terrain of who could be trusted in relation to apartheid resistance and who not. They were a fiction which bore directly on imprisonment, torture and state-sponsored murder. To recognise the second as beneficial is not to justify the existence of the first impulse, nor is it to participate in the argument that discussions of gender, class, sexuality, location and so forth could be rightly postponed until the moment of liberation from colonial/slave/apartheid oppression. This argument remains nonsensical even when we recognise that the onset of democracy has enabled a different quality of exploration.

Heeding Adhikari on avoiding coloured exceptionality, what happens when we recognise that:

> Coloured identities are neither inherently progressive nor inherently reactionary. Instead articulations of coloured identity are resources available for use by both progressive and reactionary

social movements. These movements are more likely to articulate to reactionary movements under some circumstances. (Erasmus & Pieterse 1999: 184)

Erasmus has, in a variety of fora, foregrounded the possibilities which exist for claiming coloured identity and inscribing this as a progressive space. She has repeatedly suggested that to assert a coloured identity can have a variety of implications with divergent ideological impetuses. In 'Re-imagining Coloured Identities in Post-apartheid South Africa', which serves as introduction to her book on coloured identities in Cape Town, she argues in favour of reading coloured subjectivities as a dynamic presence with attendant tensions and contradictions. Locating colouredness 'as part of the shifting texture of a broader black experience' is important (Erasmus 2001a: 14). Her argument is anchored through four parts, to which I will briefly turn before I analyse their greater significance.

First, she suggests that rather than continuing to interpret coloured identities in terms of 'race mixing' or thinking of them as being invested with a special hybridity, they should be read in their own context and this is one which needs to seriously engage history. This will enable a processing and thinking of them as 'cultural formations born of appropriation, dispossession and translation in the colonial encounter' (Erasmus 2001a: 16). The presence of historical significance suggests, in Erasmus's first position, that the current assertions and activity within coloured collective subjectivities cannot be decoded with merely an eye to the present. These formations make sense, then, only when read as memory activity in conversation with, responding to and processing events of the past as a crucial part of imagining and inventing the present.

Her second pillar advances an argument for viewing colouredness through processes of creolisation where oppression was operational. This recognition will be unproductive if it then denies the agency of communities under attack to reshape and make new meanings for their lives and trajectories. Thus, although slavery, colonialism and apartheid cannot be left out of the equation, using them to assert that these systems of violence were wholly constitutive of these communities is dangerous. It is to be complicit in the denial of Black will; it is to be blind to the obvious demonstration of agency by coloured subjects.

As colouredness becomes reshaped and rethought, the discomfiting constituents of this identity need to be courageously opened up. Thus, this position requires from coloured subjects an acknowledgement of the contradictions that characterised the identity 'coloured' in colonial and apartheid discourse. Given that colouredness was framed as existing *between* white and black/African, and that subjects thus classified did not always resist this positioning, the role of complicity should be acknowledged; so too should the privilege that accorded to being coloured, especially in the Western Cape where the presence of preferential employment legislation placed certain categories of jobs outside the reach of other Blacks. Erasmus (2001a: 16) notes:

> [c]oming to terms with these facts is one of the most important and difficult challenges for coloured people. Coloured, black and African ways of being do not have to be mutually exclusive. There are ways of being coloured that allow participation in a liberatory and anti-racist project. The task is to develop these.

Finally, she calls for a self-reflexive engagement with the variety of ways of inhabiting African and Black identities by unfixing the meanings attached to them. This is only achievable with the destabilisation of those positions within Blackness/Africanness which are seen to have assumed 'moral authenticity and political credibility' (Erasmus 2001a: 17). Asserting that a progressive coloured politics necessarily requires discomfort, she resists the position of identifying only as Black, seeing this as a safety net which 'denies the "better than black" element of coloured formation' (Erasmus 2001a: 25).

Erasmus's propositions have immense implications for thinking through specifically coloured but also more broadly Black cultural and identity formations in the post-apartheid moment. Because her first tenet stresses the need to historicise identity formation, its invitation is for an unpacking of how processes of hybridisation play themselves out in related identities. A reconceptualisation of colouredness cannot be an isolated project nor can it be locked in acontextual and simplistic declarations of its mixedness. It is positioned within the terrain of memory, and since memory is helix-shaped, à la Pennington, it shifts shape whilst constantly re-examining itself and its own process. Memory activity is relational, as are indeed all identity activities. Its reading requires a move beyond the mere fashionable declaration that all identity is hybrid to an interrogation of the consequences of this assertion for those identities which are labelled 'pure'. This project has direct bearing on the conceptualisation of the creolity of coloured identities and therefore demands that we imagine coloured subjects as human beings invested with agency who were not simply hybridised but participate(d) in creolisation. Viewed like this, they cannot be the objects of history but retain visibility as subjects.

Erasmus stresses the need to acknowledge the middle-of-the-hierarchy position occupied by coloured subjects under apartheid and colonialism. She returns to this as core to a progressive conceptualisation of this identity. In these classificatory systems, coloured people were oppressed and denied full subjecthood because they were Black whilst at the same time made complicit in processes which maintained the oppression of other Black people.

The imperatives identified above point to the specificity of coloured identities. They invite the continued fashioning of a politics and theory which is informed by history and the everyday. Whilst they chart a more vigilant engagement with the ways in which we participate in identity, they also point to their own theoretical limitations. Erasmus's final pillar relies heavily on and conflates the stability of the categories black and African in

South Africa. Erasmus, of course, knows that African identity is contested in South Africa in ways that make little sense to people who identify as African beyond its borders. In a country where 'Afrikaner' and 'Afrikaans' have been appropriated and reserved exclusively for white people of Dutch descent, it is not entirely accurate to refer to a stable category that is marked 'African'. This is especially so given that the two examples cited above demonstrate that there are pathways into identification with Africa which are always foreclosed to indigenous South Africans of any kind. There are certain expressions of 'African', for example 'Afrikaner', which are foreclosed to indigenous Africans, be they black or coloured. This remains the case even amidst assertions that there is such a category as 'bruin Afrikaners', whose very naming demonstrates the racism of what 'Afrikaner' means.

Furthermore, post-apartheid *public spherical* contestations over the meanings of 'African' have been precisely about the instability of the label. The widely publicised polemic between the late John Matshikiza, journalist Max du Preez and fellow journalists, Lizeka Mda, and academic Thobeka Mda from 17 June to the end of July 1999 in the pages of *The Star* and *Weekly Mail & Guardian* is one incarnation of an exchange characteristic of post-apartheid South Africa. Sparked in this instance by Max du Preez' article 'I am an African ... an Afrikaner' (*The Star* 17 June 1999), the debate asked questions about whether this assertion of 'white African' identity in South Africa was not without problems. Thobeka Mda's first challenge to du Preez was tellingly titled 'Can whites truly be called Africans?' (*The Star* 24 June 1999). While du Preez' claim to the identity foregrounded affiliation and geographical entitlement, the Mdas argued – differently – that white claims to African identity had a continuing history of displacement and non-recognition of Black South Africans. Even responses to Thabo Mbeki's 'I am an African' speech delivered on 8 May 1996 foregrounded how contested such identification remains.

Another visible manner in which African identity is not stable for Black South Africans inscribed with discourses that stress 'race purity', in other words, for black South Africans, is the adaptation of the signifier 'African' to mean 'born in Africa' more broadly than just 'Afrikaner'. Although b/Black subjects, in South Africa and beyond, heavily critique and resist this redefinition as appropriative and implicated in the history of colonisation and enslavement of African peoples, it nonetheless retains much currency in South Africa. Indeed, its precise contestation points to the weight of its circulation since those who resist it would expend their energies elsewhere were this not perceived as an urgent task. What societies revisit in heated public conversations is a measure of their importance.

The cheapening of the adjective 'African' to name commodities which range from recycled cans (Afri-cans) to the more elusive Diesel campaign about 'Afreaks' is part of the instability of what 'African' means.[2] These and numerous other positions on display in contemporary South Africa demonstrate that the identity African is contested and cannot generally be said to be invested with 'authenticity' in the manner that Erasmus argues. This is not to deny the presence of tendencies to essentialise and fix who can be African by excluding coloured subjects, but to postulate that coloured is the only Black position that this conservative impulse excludes is to invest the rather chaotic and reactionary project she critiques with excessive coherence. Having said that, it is ironic to note that in contemporary South Africa whites claim Africanness, blacks continue to embrace this identity, yet coloured claims to it are seen to be the most vocally contested.

I have linked reservations about the coherence with which Erasmus invests 'black' as a signifier, especially in relation to what she labels the 'moral authenticity or political credibility' (Erasmus 2001a: 17) bestowed upon the 'africanist lobby' (Erasmus & Pieterse 1999: 170). Her 'africanist lobby' includes those who police b/Blackness in terms of authenticity. So her use of 'africanist' here does not relate to the location of these authenticity police within an Africanist politics. For Erasmus, the most discernible manner in which Blackness is policed refers to the exclusion of coloured subjects from a Black and indigenous African identity by some black subjects. Here, she correctly critiques the conservative nature of this tendency, and points to the highly troubled and painful existence of such impulses, especially within what parades as the progressive ambit of national politics.

My point of departure stems from Erasmus's inference that reducing Blackness and African identity to the ambit of black people then invests the category 'black' with automatic security. The split and contestation is not between secure ways of being black/African versus insecure ones within colouredness. The same anti-coloured sentiment which Erasmus accuses of destabilising the Blackness/Africanness of non-coloured Black/African groups is credited with treating other ethnicities within black communities similarly. The reactionary political attacks from what Erasmus names the 'africanist lobby', when not targeted at suggested coloured racism, are aimed at 'uprooting' 'the Nguni conspiracy' or the 'Xhosa nostra', or demonising the 'Shangaan uncontrollability'.[3] These impulses can be gleaned in public culture, for example, in newspapers as apparently diversified in their politics as the *Mail & Guardian* and *The City Press*.

To discuss the silencing of coloured ways of being Black/African as though they are the object of a collective conspiracy by all other black/African groups is to ignore the successes of apartheid policies of divide and rule, as well as all evidence that they retain currency. It is to credit blacks with a unity of purpose which they obviously do not have in spite of all attempts by the Black Consciousness Movement. Thus, when Erasmus declares, 'If ever there is an unstable, restless, highly differentiated, hybrid place to be, it is the one I occupy' (Erasmus 2000: 199), her words ring true beyond coloured Black subjectivity. It is therefore not only a matter of barring access for coloured subjects into a safe Black collective. This emerges quite clearly when coloured subjects are seen as one of a range of Black subjectivities.

Indeed, contestations of Blackness through the bestowal of progressive subjectivities to specific Black ethnicities, and the Othering of other Black ethnicities through the projection of 'slave mentality' and/or 'collaborationist' lines, are typical of broader political contestations in post-apartheid South Africa. If we interpret coloured subjectivity as 'race' rather than as 'ethnicity', then it is possible to read coloured subjects as positioned in the unique position against which other Black people position themselves, as Erasmus and Pieterse (1999) argue. However, such a lens rests on the invisibilisation of similar political moves directed at different Black ethnic members at different political times.

Post-apartheid public discussions and controversies reveal that although there are groups of Blacks who can always be subsumed under that label, coherence does not mark the spot where these people reside. The certainty ends with being able to claim that name. What lies beyond that is silence about what *else* constitutes b/Black identity, and resistance to acknowledging the connections between this silence and the internal division within the ranks Erasmus (2000) and Erasmus and Pieterse (1999) use as examples. They justly critique the tendency to question coloured people's position within Blackness/Africanness at all and thus deny them unconditional entry into even this very small certainty.

My reservations about Erasmus's (and Erasmus and Pieterse's) reading of internal Black insecurities do not diminish the courageous and insightful ways in which she continues to theorise colouredness and its various entanglements in contemporary South Africa. Nor do they detract from the urgency of the project she charts, which forces a more nuanced engagement with national identities that are always differentially racialised, gendered and marked by class, among others. Her work continues to echo Amina Mama's reminder that:

> we are formed out of contradictions and yes we do have to live with them and with ambivalence and they need not necessarily be

41

resolved, although at some level you know extreme contradictions are uncomfortable. A sense of well-being is not about being not contradictory; it is about being able to live comfortably with one's contradictions and to be tolerant of ambivalence. (in Magubane 1997: 22)

In order to attain a state where it is possible to live comfortably with these tensions and 'be tolerant of ambivalence', wounds need to be reopened and attended to. The processes by which the sores are focused on require penetrating honesty and initiative. For Erasmus, they begin with an insistence on claiming coloured, African and Black identities *simultaneously* and participating in what those categories describe. In this manner she challenges other Blacks/Africans, and specifically blacks, to go to that dangerous place where it is no longer possible to, through self-censure, disown what *else* they are. There are parallel processes of difficulty in identifying along ethnic lines for all Black subjectivities. Apartheid legislation and violence have made it difficult to assert a progressive position within Blackness in ways that are not construed as 'tribalist/ethnicist', just like they made identifying as coloured complicated for those who reject that terminology. In opening up studies of coloured identities to progressive signification, she challenges other Blacks to reconceptualise the specific identities we dare not name except under heavily policed circumstances. This full project can be undertaken when we take Adhikari's warning of avoiding analyses predicated on coloured exceptionalism. Taking the dynamic agency within coloured identities seriously requires an accompanying attentiveness to the complementary complexity and contestations which characterise other Black subject positions.

Relationships to a history of classification as coloured vary. The path outlined by Erasmus above presents one alternative. A second alternative can be glimpsed through an analysis of the synthesis of Black and African identities by the !Hurikamma Cultural Movement (!HCM), whose membership identifies as Khoi and Brown. This self-identification is informed as much by the rejection of the label 'coloured' as it is by its proximity to other varieties of Blackness and African identities. It is also an engagement with a history of dispossession and enslavement. Section 1 of the Constitution of the !HCM (1993) defines its membership as only open to those:

> who are descended from the Khoi-Khoin (or Mens-Mens) and the slaves brought here from St Helena and Indian Ocean Islands, and who share a common history, culture and identity and pledge their alliance only to their Khoi ancestors, and who, because of their identity and history, have been deprived of their birthright, namely their right to their land, language, history, culture and freedom.

Central to the identification is the valuing of Khoi ancestry, itself a move that is in conversation with history in varied ways. This is particularly true given representations of Khoi/San peoples as backward and undesirable, or disappeared, which retain currency even today. In this respect, although the racial identification of the !HCM appears linked to that of the KWB, there is a marked difference. The valuing of Khoi and slave ancestry already participates in discursive terrain outside of, and partly subversive of, the colonial valuing of a hierarchy of races. By foregrounding the *choice* to identify with that part of their ancestry which has been most debased, the !HCM's engagement with history and memory is politically antithetical to that of the KWB. That both should appear so similar is only stressed by the commonality of B/brownness. At the same time, the exclusion of other African histories is telling and echoes some of the purity contained within the KWB's self-definitions.

The conceptualisation of b/Brownness gestures towards adverse political effects. Where the KWB, with its foregrounding of a 'pure brown' coloured race, echoes and allies with the right-wing AWB's insistence on racial purity as preferable and self-determination as necessary for these 'minorities' in light of the 'hostile black' government, the !HCM is clearly in conversation with other political traditions in South Africa. The !HCM chooses not to articulate a 'purity', and indeed demonstrates a lack of interest in this project. The mere foregrounding of slave and Khoi ancestry as a starting point demonstrates the !HCM's lack of interest in engaging with racist discourses of miscegenation by asserting purity. Rather, what is seen as central to the identity 'Brown' for the !HCM links to historically, socially and culturally constructed events and experience. The focus is on 'language, history, culture and freedom' as birthright in as much as this was disrupted through dispossession, genocide, slavery and apartheid.

Additionally, section 3.1 of the !HCM's Constitution states that one of the objectives is to 'restore in Brown people a pride in the culture of their forebears'. The intertextual political references here are multifold. First it is an engagement with the discourses which inscribe the relationships of those previously classified 'coloured' with shame when a relationship with their past is uncovered. In the place of the shame Wicomb observed, the !HCM intends to put 'pride'. It appears, then, that the !HCM recognises that the current relationship that people descended from the enslaved and Khoi people have with their past is characterised by shame. To choose to participate in a project which disarticulates this shame is to embark on a task of restoring pride and disavowing shame. This emphasis on pride resonates with the discussion of Wicomb's and Dabydeen's shame earlier. The !HCM's stress on pride links with other liberatory Black discourses in South Africa, such as the Black Consciousness Movement, and globally. The installation and reinscription of pride challenges the historic processes of humiliation. However, where other anti-racist Black movements foreground pride through inclusion, the !HCM's paradoxical exclusion gestures to other ambiguities about adjacent South African subjectivities.

The !HCM targets Khoi ancestry as its focus, not through an explicit negation of other foreparents who were also enshackled, but by prioritising the Khoi forebears in ways that implicitly deny the unnamed excluded others. It is an impulse which roots itself in African reality through accessing a stabilised indigeneity. In this respect, discursively, the processes of self-definition, backward- and forward-looking as they are like Pennington's helix, access the past through Pan-African liberation discourse. At the basic linguistic level this is echoed in the emphasis on the *combination* of descent and choice of loyalty to Africa. This echoes parts of Pan-Africanist ideology globally, but it also distances itself from these same ideologies.

The !HCM project is imaginative as much as it is recuperative. The Constitution sets out specific ways in which to use cultural and artistic production as grounds through which to participate in achieving the position of pride. This is because, according to the Preamble to the !HCM Constitution, 'culture is an integral part of our struggle to reclaim what is rightfully ours'.

These conversations with other liberation traditions which addressed themselves to the liberation of Black and African people globally permeate the remainder of the Constitution. That the connections are most markedly to Black Consciousness and Pan-African politics cannot be incidental given the prominence accorded to the cultural activities of the !HCM. Given the context set out in the founding document, it seems facile to assume that the mere use of the same word, brown/Brown, allies it to the KWB or other similar movements in straightforward ways. Attention to the use of language, which it to say the self-representation of the !HCM, suggests otherwise. It confirms Stuart Hall's (1997: 5) stance that:

[r]epresentation, here, is closely tied up with both identity and knowledge. Indeed, it is difficult to know what 'being English', or indeed French, German, South African or Japanese, *means* outside of all the ways in which our ideas and images of national cultures have been represented. Without these 'signifying' systems, we could

not take on such identities (or indeed reject them) and consequently could not build up or sustain that common 'life-world' which we call culture.

To extend Hall above then, 'being b/Brown', like 'being c/Coloured' can only mean in relation to how it is framed, and functions politically in the terrain of culture. Identifying as Khoi, African, Black and Brown simultaneously has several effects which serve to regulate the workings and meanings which ensue from self-representation in this manner. These meanings also participate in the necessary politics of interrogating colonialist and apartheid definitions of the descendants of slaves, whilst interrogating trajectories of self-representation. They are simultaneously grounded in and informed by Black Consciousness thinking and open up its silences and ambiguities for (re)interpretation. It is a narrow reading which reads the !HCM as wishing away history. The project is premised on the fact that members of this group, who claim all of the identities outlined above, are descended from slaves. Theirs is therefore not an ahistorical position since the chronological trajectory of this identity is foregrounded.

Rather, it is the meanings which ensue from this history which are contested. In other words, to the questions, 'What does it mean to be a descendent of slaves for your racial politics today?' and, 'Who does it make you?' the proponents of this view respond with a redefinition of how to inhabit Blackness in a post-apartheid South Africa: by identifying as b/Black, African, Brown and Khoi all at the same time. Thus, this legacy is interpreted in ways which are in accordance with the anti-racist projects of this location. They challenge not only racist labels but also conservative ideas about who can count as black (and within that, Khoi) and Black in contemporary South Africa. This space draws attention to the limitations of thinking about an anti-racism which influences the relationship people previously classified as 'coloured' have with not only a racist trajectory but also with liberation politics in South Africa.

Here the expressions of 'deformation, masking and inversion' in their application have the subversive *potential* to:

> demonstrate that forces of social authority and subversion or subalternity may emerge in displaced, even decentred strategies of signification. This does not prevent these positions from being effective in a political sense, although it does suggest that positions of authority may themselves be part of a process of ambivalent identification. Indeed the exercise of power may be both politically effective and psychically *affective* because the discursive liminality through which it is signified may provide greater scope for strategic manoeuvre and negotiation. (Bhabha 1994: 145)

First, identifying as Khoi in the context of the !HCM rejects the belonging to a third race marked 'coloured' in colonial and apartheid legislation. This is conscious anti-racist work that goes further than drawing attention to this appellation, as was necessary through the use of 'so-called coloured'. To engage with that history of naming is to participate in a particular kind of anti-racist practice which privileges colonial inscription. It entails a 'talking back to' as part of the larger initiative of contesting identity. The politics of dis-identification with 'colouredness' rejects a stance of talking back to and moves instead to a project of self-definition. It establishes a distance from such white supremacist forms of framing this identity and at the same time it *disses* and deconstructs them. This move to rename the self echoes earlier Black Consciousness rejections of 'non-white' for Black. For Black Consciousness activists in South Africa, 'non-white' represented a negation which had attendant materiality. Consequently, there were immeasurable gains to be made from moving from a positive definition. To identify as Khoi and Brown for the !HCS echoes this and stems, then, from the same political urgency. The postcolonial memory imperative cannot be about just addressing the problematics of historical location; it also needs to be mindful of what lies ahead.

In his inaugural lecture for the interdisciplinary Postcolonial Studies Graduiertenkolleg of the University of Munich on 25 January 2002, Homi K. Bhabha spoke eloquently of what he explores in his forthcoming book as 'political aspiration', which participates in ethical and textual interpretation as well as positionality vis-à-vis enactment and entitlement. For Bhabha, 'aspiration is not utopian, but imbued with the present imperfect and emerges from the desire to survive, not the ambition for mastery'. He goes further to discuss the meanings of the 'present imperfect' as mindful and informed by 'non-resolvable ambiguities'. Although I could find no published version of this address, Bhabha articulated similar sentiments in his interview with Kerry Chance (2001: 3), where he asserted: 'I think it is our intellectual responsibility to understand that the ground beneath our feet is a shifting, sliding ground, and to try to actually take account of that.' Mindfulness to the shifting grounds informs the kinds of critical vocabulary we develop so that the cultural sites we read inform our cultural texts, rather than being the space on which we apply pre-crystallised lenses.

I find Bhabha's theorisation of the aspirational particularly helpful to think about the activity of this space racially. In not being utopian the participants of this society are unwilling to frame their behaviour in terms of the binaries of utopia and its necessary other, dystopia; or the accompanying tropes of either racialised as 'pure white' or as 'pure African'. Centring survival is to emphasise and celebrate slave agency. It is to deny the violence of slavery and colonialism *complete* power over the body of the colonised and/or enslaved. In Patricia Williams's terms, to assert Khoi identity in the manner of the !HCM is to claim Black will. Rather than highlighting the position of the colonised and/or enslaved, it focuses on her/his *activity* – her/his survival – and celebrates this. It is to think about this ancestry as invested with agency, as humans living under constant physical and epistemological attack who survive genocidal attempts, and not as property. It is an invitation to rethink the position of people as slaves, a descriptive confinement, which is necessary for the fallacy of Black anti-will which is the 'description of master-slave relations as "total" ' (Williams 1991: 219).

To root a self-identification as Khoi, B/black, Brown and African in the face of previous classification as 'coloured' is to assert the presence of will in the lives of the ancestors who were objectified – dehumanised as property. This self-definition contests what it means to be descended from people who were property. Williams (1991: 217), in the essay 'On Being the Object of Property', declares:

> Reclaiming that from which one has been disinherited is a good thing. Self-possession in the full sense of that expression is the companion to self-knowledge. Yet claiming for myself a heritage the weft of whose genesis is my own disinheritance is a profoundly troubling paradox.

Self-representation as Khoi, African, Brown and B/black is a way of engaging this history of erasure and disinheritance. It is not the path of claiming a reshaped colouredness since the word is deemed irredeemably implicated in the aforementioned history of racial terror and genocide. It is to contest the narrative of the disappearance of the Khoi from the political, social and physical landscape of South Africa. It is anti-racist in privileging the excavation of the subaltern's voice not just in the present but also in the past. This is an example of postcolonial mnemonic work in practice. The enslaver's and coloniser's force does not need any help: it is the hegemonic power which silences the subaltern. The !HCM's self-construction does not deny the given: that those (previously) classified coloured feature in colonialist and apartheid discourse as the result of 'racial mixing' and constitute a 'third race' at once privileged (preferential treatment legislation) and 'inferior' due to 'lack' (without culture, 'barbaric', 'bush'). Nor is it informed by a refusal to mediate the dominant circulatory discourses on race which are responsible for the instances of their somatic reading as 'coloured' in accordance with the conservative meanings of that category.

Thus, foregrounding Khoi identity is not to pretend that these racist discourses do not exist, but to choose a particular self-positioning in relation to them. It is to contest the racist academic and popular discourses which declare that Khoi and San identities are vacated spaces. In Bhabha's terms, it is to exert/assert 'the right to narrate', to speak (not just talk) and be narrated, to draft a history, something to be interpreted. It also forces the remainder of the Black South African populace, regardless of which identity they prioritise or how they mediate their position within Blackness and in relation to Africa, to contend with what it means to celebrate identity. It forces the question of what it means politically to celebrate a history of survival. It is to assert, in the words of the old slave song, 'we are here because we are here' and to invite an interrogation of the untidy meanings we attach to survival.

In its political assertion, therefore, the !HCM does not deny history, but foregrounds it by contesting the meanings which ensue from it whilst underlining that historically its members are not invested with enough power to deny history in a way which would make any political sense, given that they must continue to live in a country and a world in which notions of 'racial hybridity' retain currency. So that even as the members self-identify as Khoi, Black and African, and as Brown instead of coloured, the possibility remains to be read and interpreted, through the signs mythologised as evidence of classification, as 'coloured', 'mixed-race' and so forth. The political imperative adopted by the members of this society does not gesticulate towards a mystical wholeness, but contests dominant discourses about the constitution of all South African racial identities. Such identification also draws attention to shifting meanings in ways akin to those of other western Cape Black anti-racists, examined in Chapter 4, who claim post-apartheid the very diasporic identity they disavowed as anti-apartheid activists.

The !HCM's self-definition is to assert agency in the face of this changing political landscape, to insist on a self-representation which is more than somatic, but one which revolutionarily claims will and psychic presence. It shifts the terms of the debate and the terrain of race and self-representation in a democratic South Africa where, because the country cannot be an island cut off from the rest of the world or from its own past, there are always colonial discourses circulating.

It recognises the fact of multiple histories, diverse ancestry and therefore creolity even as it chooses to stress specific African ancestry. The choice of which ancestor to foreground is neither arbitrary nor unique. Most people with a known varied ancestry prioritise one with whose name to identify themselves. Whilst it has become almost mandatory in cultural studies to lay claim to the always already hybrid forms of all cultural production and identity formation processes, the case of the !HCM poses challenges for the meanings attached to this declaration. Dutch and British slaves forced to work in the Cape were captured from a variety of locations in South (East) Asia, East Africa, as well the South African interior. Those from the interior were mainly Khoi and/or San.

The !HCM insists on claiming and prioritising its Khoi legacy, rooting itself within an African history not just because of physical location. It can participate in other histories of Africa located elsewhere and also informed by slavery, but the premise must be different because it is not diasporic but continental. Identifying as Khoi declares !HCM entry into a specific African identity through means other than geography and sociology, although these are not completely eliminated either. It is thus not only a political assertion but a shifting of the terrain and a signalled rejection of the terms of participation in African identity spelled out by white South Africa – that is, birthright – because Khoi suggests links with the African

51

world and other indigenous people as another kind of claim to African identity. It is to acknowledge that claiming an African identity for people of African descent in South Africa is *always* a process accompanied by contestation and denial, that it is a declaration of will in choosing an association with this particular continent.

The decision to identify as Khoi challenges the narrowness of conservative definitions of who can people the space labelled 'African'. Brown identity within !HCM parlance and its relationship to emancipatory language, among other things, marks it as different from Afrikaners who pretended to be 'racially pure' and premised their identity on the suppression of African foreparents. It is not premised on 'racial purity'.

Further, it does not claim a position of privilege as its entitlement because of where it is. It broaches the difficult terrain, like Erasmus's theorisation of colouredness, of identifying what *else* these subjects are in addition to and in proximity with always being Black and African. In other words, it is 'aspirational and does not aspire to mastery or sovereignty', in Bhabha's (2002; see also Chance 2001) terms. It remains subversive because it is empowering to the concrete historical subjects who assert this identity without alienating others who are less powerful. It is also an anti-essentialist position because it destabilises all the categories it is in conversation with and draws attention to the processes of racial identity formation. By claiming this allegedly vacated space, it does not displace anybody else, even as it questions how indigeneity is constructed, and in this very action contests the vacancy of the identity 'Khoi'. It challenges the lie of successful Khoi and San extermination by posing the question, 'How can there be at once no Khoi people alive and there be thousands alive who identify as such?' It works also as an alternative to 'coloured' because it chooses an indigenous African trajectory of naming over a colonially imposed one. It chooses to be Khoi instead of '*mixed*'. It therefore does not negate that others may inhabit colouredness differently and reclaim it, but this is not its political imperative.

Resistance to articulations of Khoi and San identities in contemporary South Africa is problematic. It tends to lump all these very different articulations together. In this manner those who question the ability of Khoi people to identify as such avoid addressing the specificities of each and betray contemporary (internalised) racist notions of what we expect a Khoi or San person to 'look' like. Much of the anxiety over the choice of 'Khoi' over 'coloured' stems from a hypocritical relationship that many South Africans have with Khoi identities. Thus, in spite of the assertion of all cultures' dynamism, predominant concepts of the Khoi are as timeless people trapped in space. To be Khoi is to appear as 'Bushmen' in some tourist brochures, or as naked 'Hottentots' running around in the desert. The problem posed by progressive articulations of Khoi and San presence and identities is that they unsettle the belief that the somatic holds the key to meaning-making. This lie has been central to South African society in relation to race for over three centuries.

CONCLUSION: THE KHOI–COLOURED CONTINUUM IMAGINATIVELY RENDERED

> The capacity to live with difference is, in my view, the coming question of the twenty-first century. (Hall 1999: 42)

> I speak appropriating all the knowledge that interests me, that is accessible to me, and that can help me and my territory to deal with new emergent realities, since I am also a new and emergent reality. (de Torro 2002: 117)

The above demonstrate the complexity in contesting meanings which attach to identities that apparently cannot be inhabited progressively. There are charges that in a post-apartheid South Africa, given the rejection and problematisation of the label 'coloured' during the liberation struggle, it can only be racist to reclaim it (now). Similarly, it is argued that laying claim to Khoi identity is a denial of history of 'mixing' and an aspiration towards 'purity' and authenticity. Therefore, in crude terms the first is denounced for apparently 'not being Black enough', while the latter is seen to aspire to a Blackness that is 'too authentic'. These readings are equally problematic for they read these subjectivities within the confines of the very discursive binaries that are rejected by those who claim 'coloured' or 'Khoi' identities, in the manner analysed above. Indeed, an attentive examination of the two articulations discussed above reveals that '[r]ather than expanding the category of "real" blackness, they suggest that if all identities are discursively produced and under negotiation, then all identities are inauthentic' (Smith 1998: 67).

The challenges of fashioning new identities in a democratic South Africa include being able to move away from the few 'safe' spaces of racial identification that Black South Africans could inhabit under apartheid. Given the recent demise of the systems of violent state-sponsored racist terror which ended with apartheid, it is not difficult to see why exploring racial identity anew is a daunting task for South Africans. Black Consciousness gave us a Black skin to be proud of and one through which to contest the shame associated with everything Black.

Receiving and adorning this pride and comfort, and thus resisting shame, meant that political gains could be achieved through collective assertions of identity across Blackness and Africanness. It meant that the terrain of dividing us up in racist fashion according to whether we were amaXhosa, baTswana, coloured, and so forth, was left to the state. The Black Consciousness stress on unity was a counter-narrative to apartheid's policy of divide and rule. It also relied on homogenising expressions of Blackness which, although functional during apartheid, are untenable in a democracy.

Freedom presents new challenges and the unreflexive discourses which bandy 'race neutrality' feed off the anxieties of owning differential racialisation and ethnic marking by Black South Africans. The progressive reclamation of coloured identity and/or Khoi subjectivity foregrounds the already always hybrid nature of all other Black identities. !HCM assertions of Black, Khoi, Brown and African identities at the same time, along with acknowledging forebears who were enslaved, problematise the ability of black South Africans to adhere to the simplicity of identity formation. It suggests the necessity of identifying that, for example, Xhosa or Tswana identity is already always invested with Khoi ancestry even as this is not included in the ethnic *naming* of this identity. Khoi ancestry is explicitly acknowledged in many other forms of identifications within these 'ethnic' groups, such as in *iziduko* among the Xhosa. The extent to which ambiguity remains when the labels 'coloured' and 'b/Brown' are inhabited and asserted as identities, also points to the continued complication of racial identities in South Africa. This is especially the case with Black identities countrywide. In this regard, creative infusions of coloured and Brown contain 'thresholds of meaning that must be crossed, erased, and translated in the process of cultural production' (Bhabha 1990: 4).

I have suggested that moving beyond assertions of Black/African heterogeneity, whilst resisting and fighting the continued racist practices of erasure of historically inscribed Black subjectivities in the larger South African society, is a necessary project. It is one which can no longer be postponed and to the extent that coloured identities and their various articulations are a reminder of this urgency, they destabilise the myth that nation-building can be a safe project or that it has been completed. Helix-like, they are a reminder of the processual dimension of identity that Stuart Hall's (1990) work reminds us of. The anxiety-laden and contradictory responses to coloured and Khoi cultural practices demonstrate the inability of the category 'coloured' to function as a buffer zone for other processes of racialisation in contemporary South Africa. A meaningful engagement with articulations of, and responses to, previous classification as 'coloured' results in entertaining fertile new ways of exploring what it means to be

Black/African in relation to others marked in the same way *and more*. It requires the *a priori* recognition that all who identify as Black/African are always also, in the helix, *and more*. Rather than being a taken-for-granted reality, this is an invitation to work and reconceptualise ways of giving meaning to Blackness/Africanness and South African identity.

Responses to coloured identities reveal the insecurities of the new South Africans. They are evidence that not only is the *uhuru* (freedom) project unfinished in relation to the continued racism and predominant economic powerlessness experienced by Black South Africans, but also that more work needs to be done within and this is a necessary step in memorialising and remembering the past.

The texts examined in this chapter traverse the terrain of memory and its multiple relationships to written representation and identity formation. They require imaginative agency as the expression of will in their exploration of relationships to memory and history. The 'messing up' of timelines is a necessary condition in re-imagining identity and participating in the process of its constant construction in Hall's formulation.

Public, political and academic processing of identities in relation to Khoi and coloured subject positions is part of this process of developing emergent frameworks to participate in the projects of memory in exciting ways. The refusal to confine oneself to timelines is evident in Erasmus's re-evaluation of what it means to self-identify as coloured in a democratic South Africa. Her conceptual framework muddies the waters, suggesting that there are multiple paths to an identification as coloured. It is not a mere celebration of apartheid labels. In keeping with Pennington's formulation of the helix-like structure of memory and its influence on identity, Erasmus suggests that identifying as coloured gives rise to several meanings at different times. The same is true of all other Black and white subjectivities. Thus, for those who problematised the identity 'coloured' during apartheid, but now choose to use it as self-descriptive in a democratic South Africa, the meanings have changed. It is too simplistic to equate its use now with its earlier meanings for the apartheid state. Similarly, at different points in the helix, even at the same time, the impulse to self-identify as coloured can be progressive or conservative.

The helix structure works well to illuminate the performance of memory in relation to the !HCM. It simultaneously works to challenge two divergent discourses on the constitution of Khoi subjectivities. Whereas the dominant discourses have, until recently, declared the complete genocidal extermination of all Khoi communities, !HCM claims to Khoi subjectivities challenge this mythologisation of 'Bushmen' and 'Hottentots' who survive only in the form of the body casts on display in museums. Along with various other Khoi and San formations, the !HCM challenges the discursive erasure of these identities, bearing testimony to Khoi and San survival in spite of several explicitly genocidal endeavours aimed directly at these communities. It problematises the linear narrative of traditional historiography since, although academics and politicians have previously declared that no Khoi survive in the country, there is a visible Khoi presence in contemporary South Africa. This suggests that there had been 'no remaining Khoi' people and thousands at least surviving throughout apartheid South Africa at the same time. The existence of two mutually deconstructive possibilities at the same time is in keeping with the helix-like form of historical consciousness, as well as with Prins's conceptualisation of multiple branches on a tree analysed in the previous chapter.

In addition to unseating dominant declarations of Khoi extermination, formations like the !HCM further challenge other claims to indigeneity through their deconstruction of notions of racial purity. As subjects previously classified 'coloured', they are inscribed with white supremacist hierarchies of 'miscegenation'. Given that indigeneity is inscribed through ideas of 'pure' African parentage, the !HCM challenges the terrain of identity performance by resisting being implicated in declarations of 'race purity'. The Movement thus challenges both attempts to erase

Khoi subjectivities and those which police entry into African identity by restricting its entry to those considered 'pure blacks'. Further, in claiming a slave parentage but choosing to highlight a particular aspect of that identity, the !HCM Constitution demonstrates the manner in which self-identification and naming is always about choosing between various available multiple identities.

CHAPTER 2

(NOT) REPRESENTING SARAH BARTMANN

Steatopygous sky
Steatopygous sea
Steatopygous waves
Steatopygous me

Oh how I long to place my foot
on the head of anthropology.
(Nichols 1984: 15)

All the world could come to see her during her 18 month period in
our capital, and witness the huge protuberance of her buttocks and
beastly look on her face. (Cuvier 1817: 263)

As the casket left the embassy, I wondered if Sarah Baartman was
looking down from heaven and having a chuckle. The empire had
indeed struck back, her people had come to claim her, and the
'savages' were running the show. (Smith 2002: 4)[1]

Sarah Bartmann was an enslaved Khoi woman, transported to Europe
by a Dutchman, Hendrik Cezar, and displayed, to great controversy,
in Picadilly Circus in London and later in Paris. The simplicity of
the above sentence belies the convoluted manner in which she was
exhibited, became known pejoratively as 'the Hottentot Venus', died
under mysterious circumstances – owned, at that stage, by an animal
trainer – and had volumes of scientific and anthropological works
written 'about her'. It leaves out the fact that Cezar was forced to sell

her to an unnamed 'Englishman' because, as the former would write in the *Morning Chronicle* of 23 October 1810, the controversy in England over Bartmann as slave, and the subsequent decision by The African Association for Promoting the Discovery of the Interior of Africa to sue Cezar on behalf of Bartmann, made it untenable for him to keep her in his ownership (Y. Abrahams 2000; Magubane 2001; Walvin 1982). The deceptive straightforwardness of the outline above also occludes the fact that George Cuvier, fêted anatomist and one of the pre-eminent European scientists of all time, had her genitalia and brain pickled in formaldehyde and kept at a museum in Paris. It speaks nothing of the self-satisfaction which saw him write, 'I had the honour of presenting to the Academy, the genitals of this woman, prepared in such a way, that leaves no doubt on the nature of her "apron" ' (Cuvier 1817: 266).

While any academic labelling of Sarah Bartmann as slave inevitably meets with some resistance and claims that she was a willing agent in her transportation to Europe, her display and ultimately her 'prostitution' and 'alcoholism' (Crais & Scully 2008; Holmes 2007), Bartmann's status as slave is made clear in much scholarship, including Yvette Abrahams's (2000) painstaking research, as well as the specific way in which responses to her in Britain saw her as a slave (Magubane 2001; Walvin 1982). This is the source of the controversy around her display: she was treated like a slave in all respects by Cezar and those who objected to her exhibition.

Much research into Black presence in Britain also suggests that Bartmann slotted into existing representational idioms and debates about the nature and manifestations of slavery within the British Isles (Gerzina 1999; Walvin 1982). Her renaming as 'Hottentot Venus' was in line with a slavocratic 'humorous' tradition, traced by Dabydeen (1987a, 1987b) back to the late seventeenth century, which saw African house 'servants' (slaves) given classical Roman names, and sometimes dressed up ornately for posing in their owners' portraits as decorative figurines or to walk behind their mistresses carrying accessories and smelling salts (Gerzina

1999: 21). Venus was the Roman goddess of love, fertility and romance. Humour here was derived from the juxtaposition of slave (Hottentot) with goddess (Venus). Writing of the eighteenth century, Dabydeen notes that there were developing ways to think and speak about the Black presence in Britain, most notably in its cities, such as London, where Bartmann was placed on display. He notes that '[a] city like London then, if not actually "swamped" ... by flesh-and-blood-alien blacks, was "swamped" by *images* of blacks. London in the eighteenth century was *visually* black in this respect' (Dabydeen 1987a: 18). Within this idiom, a century before Bartmann's display in London, Africans and animals were often the subject of similar characterisation in art, literature and public discourse. By the time she was displayed as a curiosity in London, such idioms were commonplace. This is part of the context of reading Bartmann's passage and her renaming in the condescending idioms of the Cape – as Saartjie, although her baptismal certificate spells her name 'Sarah' – and Britain, as Hottentot Venus in established slavocratic humorous idiom.

Bartmann's remains were kept in Paris, and a cast made from her body and skeleton was on display at the Musée de l'Homme until 1974. Bartmann's body could not be returned for burial until May 2002 because an official from the Musée de l'Homme alleged that her remains had been lost. She was buried in her birthplace, Hankey, in the Eastern Cape on the ninth of August, the day on which she was born in 1789, ironically the inaugural year of the French Revolution.

The South African Broadcasting Corporation quoted the Khoi-San leader Cecil Le Fleur, on the fourth of August, as noting that the return of Bartmann and her funeral on the day of her birth was important. 'It also symbolises the rights of women worldwide,' he is reported to have said.[2] The traditional Khoi enrobing ceremony performed by elders at the Cape Town civic centre six days before her burial, as part of the preparation of the body, took on an added significance for the woman who had been exhibited naked so that those interested could gawk at her.

Her return, preparation for burial, and interment ceremony were also framed explicitly as participation in a memory project. Thus, while pre-funeral rites are customarily referred to as activities performed in memory of the departed, the use of memory evoked, in this instance, an additional set of associations and was linked to other memory activities in the democratic era. The deputy minister of Arts, Culture and Technology, Bridget Mabandla, suggested these connections in the following way:

> [t]here have been many misconceptions about Saartje Bartmann, one being that she was a prostitute. Sarah was a slave and victim of an extreme form of prejudice. It is proper to see her as a symbol for human rights and nation building, because she was one of us. The ceremony is to celebrate her memory through poetry, song and dance by providing a platform for all South Africans to express solidarity in her memory.[3]

The speech by the president at Bartmann's funeral echoed this position of Sarah Bartmann's reclamation and return as linked to brutal histories of enslavement and oppression, and its role as part of the larger coming to terms with the past. This marks her return, therefore, as participation in the terrain of public memory. Participation in this memory involves a negotiation of anger and celebration. Indeed, as Mbeki pointed out:

> there are many in our country who would urge constantly that we should not speak of the past. They pour scorn on those who speak about who we are and where we come from and why we are where we are today. They make bold to say the past is no longer, and all that remains is a future that will be. But, today, the gods would be angry with us if we did not, on the banks of the Gamtoos River, at the grave of Sarah Bartmann, call out for the restoration of the dignity of Sarah Bartmann, of the Khoi-San, of the millions of

Africans who have known centuries of wretchedness.

Sarah Bartmann should never have been transported to Europe.[4]

In the remainder of the speech, President Mbeki proceeded to make connections between Bartmann's individual story and the larger dispossession and racist project which influenced slavery, colonialism and remaining systems of white supremacy in the contemporary world. This project is linked to discourses which frame Africans as those without a past but, more immediately within the context of the South African dispensation, it should link with efforts to 'restore the dignity and identity of the Khoi and San people as a valued part of our diverse nation'. Bartmann's burial place was declared a national heritage site, with additional plans to create a memorial in Cape Town.

The marked celebration that met Bartmann's return also motivated various artistic representations of Bartmann, with varied effects. When Willie Bester's sculpture of Sarah Bartmann was placed near the science and engineering library of the University of Cape Town, it was met with ambivalence. At a panel on 30 April 2001 – including the artist, historian Yvette Abrahams, representatives from the African Gender Institute, the Womyn's Movement at the Centre for African Studies – speakers challenged the lack of context given by the Work of Art Committee's (WOAC) of its decision on where to position the sculpture. While the WOAC's choice of location, as well as the specific choice of Bester's sculpture, was meant to destabilise precisely the history of Bartmann's exhibition in the name of science, Memory Biwa of the Womyn's Movement argued against the absence of any contextualisation at the site of the sculpture's exhibition. Abrahams noted the absence of any other art by indigenous artists in public spaces at the institution which then aggravated the fact that people were forced to look at the sculpture at the entrance of the library. She thus problematised the manner in which this unmediated gaze, coupled with the statue's exceptionality on the campus, inscribed the piece in ways dangerously close to the politics of Bartmann's exhibition.

Her baptismal certificate spells her name 'Sarah Bartmann', but much writing also uses Sara, Saartje and Saartjie; and her surname Bartman, Baartman, Baartmann and Bartmann is linked to the lack of clarity on how she spelled her own name. Nor is there conclusive evidence of what her birth name was. She is referred to most commonly as Saartjie, sometimes spelled the Dutch way, 'Saartje', little Sara(h). I have chosen to use 'Sarah' here because that is the name and spelling used in her baptismal certificate, and in recognition of the history of a slavocratic, colonial and apartheid trajectory which infantilised adult Black men and women in the service of white supremacist patriarchy. 'Little' or '-tjie' is also often added to show close personal proximity to an individual.[5] The diminutive put Black people into the much theorised position of always being assumed to be intimately available to white South Africans. To the extent that I do not have intimate access to Sarah Bartmann as a contemporary or close associate, there is no justification for using 'Saartjie' without being complicit in this history of naming and objectifying African subjects.

The quotation at the beginning of this chapter is from a poem by the celebrated Guyanese/Black British poet, Grace Nichols, from that part of her poetic *oeuvre*[6] which challenges the stereotypes of African women in the world throughout history. It is an endeavour to imagine a world with a sky, a sea and waves which reflect African woman's body as norm rather than pathology. If everything in the world Nichols's persona imagines reflects her form, then the world cannot at the same time cast her as a freak; it is a world within which she is comfortable and normal. The stress in Nichols's poem is on the 'fat black woman' thinking, imagining and feeling anger; in other words, expressing her will and interiority. Her anger is directed at various epistemic projects responsible for constructing Black women as excessively corporeal, housed in the disciplines of anthropology, history, theology as well as contemporary patriarchal capitalist industries which capitalise on this racist violence. Such sites are part of the logic that placed Sarah Bartmann in slavery, on display and in specimen jars as evidence of 'steatopygia'. Nichols's use and recognisability of the medico-scientific term 'steatopygia' echoes Bartmann's display and dissection.

To the extent that most traditions, either racist or patriarchal or a combination, do not represent *thinking* African women subjects, Nichols's 'fat black woman' fantasising about a better world while lying in the bath is powerful and necessary. Its importance is not so much because it charts a counter-narrative, but rather because it significantly alters the terms of the debate altogether where Bartmann is concerned.

The second extract is from the respected nineteenth-century French scientist Georges Cuvier, about whom Gail Smith – feminist essayist who wrote the scripts for both Zola Maseko's documentaries on Sarah Bartmann, *Hottentot Venus: The Life and Times of Sara Baartman* (1998) and *The Return of Sara Baartman* (2003) – has mused 'one thing that has always puzzled me, if Cuvier was such a brilliant scientist, why was Sarah Baartman's official cause of death never known?'[7] The quotation refers to how Cuvier saw and spoke of Sarah Bartmann. It speaks volumes for what he considers as 'All the world', and the implausibility that one day Blackwomen subjects would assume positions as makers of academic knowledge. Cuvier's immediate audience is the scientific community in nineteenth-century Europe. They are the possible viewers and intended readers of his text, not those who for him fell into the bracket of 'Negro women, Bushmen women and female monkeys' (Cuvier 1817: 269).[8] It is the tradition against which Nichols writes. It is Bartmann's body of which he speaks as a 'huge protuberance', and whose face is 'beastly' in his eyes. He assumes that this is a discovery which advances science, as do his peers. It is testimony to the extent that his peers, and those who came after him, valued this as important scientific knowledge that Sarah Bartmann's remains could not be returned for burial until May 2002. It is confirmation of the resilience of resistance that the 'savages' are able to run the show and claim her back, even if it is several centuries later in Gail Smith's citation which follows Cuvier's at the beginning of this chapter.

The story of Sarah Bartmann has been one of the fascinations of academic writing on 'race', feminism and post-structuralism in the late twentieth and early twenty-first centuries. An enslaved Khoi woman, she was transported to Europe where she was displayed for the amusement, and later scientific inquisitiveness, of various public and private collectives in London and Paris. Yvette Abrahams (1997, 2000, 2004; Abrahams & Clayton 2004), Jean Young (1997) and Zine Magubane (2001, 2004) have written on the contradictions that characterise her story. Bartmann's paradoxical hypervisibility has meant that although volumes have been written about her, very little is recoverable from these records about her subjectivity. This is because for the bulk of her writers over the centuries, she has been the body of evidence. Magubane has noted that in the eighteenth and nineteenth centuries the black body offered for much colonial thought 'the meeting of two contrary impulses – of a suffering that could not be denied but that nonetheless had an incredibly fungible character' (2004: 103).

This chapter begins with these quotations because it seeks to explore the possibility of writing about Sarah Bartmann in ways unlike those traditions of knowledge-making that dubbed her 'the Hottentot Venus', and were therefore complicit in her slavery. It reads a variety of texts which position themselves in relation to her, as a means of arriving at a Black feminist/ womanist[9] engagement with the histories which fix representations of Blackwomen in colonialist epistemes. The entry of Sarah Bartmann, and Khoi people generally, into historiography was through their corporeality (Abrahams 1997). This has also become acceptable supposition in much academic and creative literature concerned with the enslavement of African people, and their forced transportations to the Americas and Europe. Corporeality, then, becomes one of the dominant ways in which, within colonialist epistemes, African people enter public discourse. More specific to Khoi people, it is through 'observations' about the variety of ways in which their genitalia are 'deformed', whether naturally or through some extensive manipulation, that the reader is led to 'one testicle' for Khoi men or the 'Hottentot apron' for women (Abrahams 1997).

Representing Black women, or colonised women of colour more generally, offers challenges for feminist writers. In Chapter 1, Carli Coetzee (1998) suggested one of the murky areas in this regard. She has written on the tendency of white feminists to use colonised women as symbols, and references the work of several women of colour globally who critique this tradition. The difficulties of representation are aggravated when the colonised woman is a famous one, Sarah Bartmann, who has so extensively been mythologised. bell hooks (1996) has noted the manner in which this hardship is exacerbated when Blackwomen's subjectivities feature in certain versions of anti-racist thought. hooks observes that in Frantz Fanon's *Black Skin, White Masks* (1967), 'not only is the female body, black or white, always a sexualized body, not the body that "thinks," but it also appears to be a body that never longs for freedom' (1996: 84).

How have African feminist literary projects approached Bartmann's absent presence as mnemonic activity? If the general hegemonic status of Black bodies has been as spectacle, 'made to function less as flesh and blood entities than as fertile discursive sites to be mined for images and metaphors' (Magubane 2004: 106), what happens when the most famously embodied Black subject is imagined creatively in ways that do not foreground her corporeality? This is one of the most striking similarities in how feminists of the African world[10] have chosen to engage with Sarah Bartmann's legacy as the 'Hottentot Venus'. This legacy, and the power of its accompanying scientific knowledge, is such that several centuries later, in the twentieth century, feminists would continue to write against the *felt* effects of the gaze which fixes them/us as oversexed, deviant object.

Faced with the slew of creative writing on Sarah Bartmann by feminists in the African diaspora and beyond (Gordon-Chipembere 2006), I remain uninterested in charting, reviewing and analysing the varied ways in which she has been characterised in literature. My concern here is with the emergence of a very specific idiom which arises in literature of the African feminist world, and which, as I will show, offers radical departures from conventional representations of her as only embodied (object), pathologised (deviant), evidence (knowable) and/or singular ('freak', myth).

I draw from the insights gleaned from African feminist work in non-literary genres, and recognise this scholarship as invaluable. Still, the three central creative texts which will be used in addition to Nichols's are Zoë Wicomb's *David's Story* (2000); Ferrus's poem 'I Have Come to Take You Home' (2002), previously listed and performed as 'A Tribute to Sarah Bartmann'; and Gail Smith's 'Fetching Saartje' (*Mail & Guardian* 12 May 2002). These texts offer refreshing narrative possibilities which are more imaginative than 'the science, literature and art [which have] collectively worked to produce Baartmann as an example of sexual and racial difference [which also] offered exemplary proof that racial and sexual alterity are social construction rather than biological essences' (Magubane 2001: 817). As Zine Magubane demonstrates, these traditions are informed by a variety of ideologies on race, gender and class positions, but have nonetheless been strengthened in their ahistorical usage to explain how Sarah Bartmann became the icon for sexual alterity in theory.

'Molara Ogundipe's invitation to African feminists is that '[w]e should think from our epicentres of agency, looking for what is meaningful, progressive and useful to us as Africans, as we enrich ourselves with ideas from all over the world' (quoted in Lewis & Ogundipe 2002). The texts analysed here embark on and approach the topic at hand from various angles, but will be read, nonetheless, as participating in the same larger African feminist project. While the specific structures of the narratives differ, these texts exist along the same continuum. All grapple with the (im)possibility of representing Sarah Bartmann, and in turn probe how history's silences are more interesting than the overwritten volumes about Bartmann during her lifetime, or since.

70

My motivation is informed, firstly, by my conviction that creative texts offer an ability to theorise and imagine spaces of freedom in ways unavailable to genres more preoccupied with linearity and exactness. I have become increasingly intrigued (Gqola 2001a, 2005) by the creative theorisation in the arena of African feminist imagination. By 'creative theorisation' I intend the series and forms of conjecture opened up in literary and other creative genres. Theoretical/philosophical epistemological projects do not only happen in those sites officially designated as such, but also emerge from creatively textured sites outside of these.

Secondly, read against the texts I will discuss, I find Nthabiseng Motsemme's thinking on silences and African women's subjectivities compelling. Motsemme asserts that 'the mute always speaks'. Like her:

> My aim is not to romanticise silence and thus undermine the power of giving voice and exposing oppression. It is rather to remind us that under conditions of scarcity and imposed limits, those who are oppressed often generate new meanings for themselves around silences. Instead of being absent and voiceless, silences in circumstances of violence assume presence and speak volumes. (Motsemme 2004: 5)

CRAFTING EPICENTRES OF AGENCY

Zoë Wicomb's novel *David's Story* (2000) directly confronts the dilemma of historicising. Her novel is the fictional biography of David, an activist who decides to narrate his life story during the transition from late apartheid to democracy. David's sense of how lives are told and rooted in past lives' trajectories differs substantially from his fictional amanuensis' preferred working style. The novel is both David's story and not. He takes no joy in the private ownership of it that the biographer imagines should determine his relationship to the story. He chooses not to claim it in a tidy sense, although the presence of an amanuensis suggests that he has taken some initiative in recording his story, thereby deeming it worthy of capture. In her communication with his scribe, he insists that his story is one that starts with the Khoi women Sarah Bartmann and Krotoä, the latter of whom is also known as Eva. Both these women are positioned as 'firsts' or symbolic beginnings in some ways: Krotoä, as the first indigenous translator between the Khoi and the Dutch, and Bartmann as the beginning of many narratives of belonging.

However, Wicomb writes David so that he does not simply position them as his foreparents. He repeatedly refuses the psychic safety that would flow from simply claiming and embracing them. They are part of a difficult and necessary identitiary project aligned to both memory and the imagination, a venture he cannot completely preside over. For David, then, these women do not point at clear meaning, but they are significant nonetheless. This marks his claim over them as quite different from the one critiqued by Carli Coetzee in Chapter 1.

Symbolically, then, David's story as an activist who dedicated his life to the end of apartheid begins with those who sought to mediate between cultures of the colonised and colonisers. Secondly, coloured and Khoi subjectivities attach to a *continuum* of personal identification in the novel. The above positions of colouredness and Khoiness, represented as internally uncohesive, are engaged in a fluid exchange which at different times takes on competitive, supplementary and elusive edges. He will not participate in a project of 'denying history and fabricating a totalizing colouredness' (Wicomb 1998: 105) because he realises the impossibility of closure. Instead, he appears to embrace the possibility of 'multiple belongings' which offer:

> an alternative way of viewing a culture where participation in a number of coloured micro-communities whose interests conflict and overlap could become a rehearsal of cultural life in the larger South African community where we learn to perform the same kind of

negotiations in terms of identity within a lived culture characterized by difference. (Wicomb 1998: 105)

The foremost anxiety with which he grapples even as he recognises his powerlessness over it, is the meeting point of history, memory and the imagination. It is these interconnections that Wicomb's novel negotiates.

Interestingly, his amanuensis, acting more like a biographer than mere scribe, is at pains to steer him in the direction of stability. For David, who does not imagine himself participating in an individual project, the disquiet centres around what is missing from his narrative and what is elusive. David's story as an Umkhonto we Sizwe combatant is told through recourse to stories of other activists as well as these jarring beginnings represented by Bartmann, enslaved woman, and Eva, the first mediator between the cultures of the colonisers and colonised. His resistance to narrative precision leads his fictional biographer to muse that 'promiscuous memory, spiralling into the past, mates with new disclosures to produce further moments of terrible surprise' (Wicomb 2000: 194–195). This is because she has long noticed how:

[h]is fragments betray the desire to distance himself from his own story; the many beginnings, invariably flights into history, although he is no historian, show uncertainty about whether to begin at all. He has made some basic errors with dates, miscalculating more than a hundred years, which no doubt is due to the confusing system of naming centuries; but then, as I delighted in the anachronism, he was happy to keep it. (Wicomb 2000: 1)

This anachronism is deliberate on Wicomb's part and points to the relationship between different modes of telling stories, ways more nuanced than timelines. It also attaches to the challenges of historicising experiences when there is no dependable narrative, only the colonisers' in written form, plotted along a date line which is not in itself logical, even as it is paraded as neutral. David's interest in history suggests that he has reshuffled the events to highlight the desired associations with other herstories, to display more clearly, in Deirdre Prins's (2000: l. 18–25) words:

> Because even though I do not know when my ancestors lived
> I know that each one of their lives
> Left a mark on my life
> …
> Even though I do not know

Such a desire is highlighted in his insistence, for example, on the anchoring of his story through Krotoä and Sarah Bartmann even though he makes little attempt to mythologise them. He is at pains to avoid their erasure, as well as making them icons. His response, '[o]ne cannot write nowadays … without a little monograph on Bartmann; it would be like excluding history itself', can mean this (Wicomb 2000: 1). As his amanuensis suggests, 'the many beginnings, invariably flights into history, although he is no historian, show uncertainty about whether to begin at all' (Wicomb 2000: 1). Wicomb's David is convinced of their importance to his narrative, but need not dwell on the precise manner in which their narratives intersect with his, a detail which proves increasingly frustrating to his amanuensis. Rather than wanting to control the narrative, David is content to testify to a collective history which self-consciously points to its constructedness. Succeeding in this venture makes it clear that his narrative does not contain everything. For Wicomb's purposes, the project of writing history requires that the imagination perform differently, chaotically, in a manner that messes up centuries. Irritated by his logic, his amanuensis asks him, 'what on earth has Baartman to do with your history?' To this, he replies:

But it's not a personal history as such that I am after, not biography or autobiography. I know we're supposed to write that kind of thing, but I have no desire to cast myself as hero, he sneers. Nothing wrong with including a historical figure. (Wicomb 2000: 135)

When in further response to her, 'She may not even have been a Griqua,' David says 'Baartman belongs to all of us' (Wicomb 2000: 135), this is particularly telling. His claim to her is not because they both may have Griqua ancestry. Rather, David's recognition of Sarah Bartmann as important is neither about the 'recovery' of indigeneity nor the celebration of 'colouredness'. It is akin to Diana Ferrus's acknowledgment in her poem 'A Tribute to Sarah Bartmann' (1998). David and his biographer both note the extent of his outrage at the mere mention of Cuvier's name. This indignation finds accompaniment in Ferrus's persona's emotions, expressed in the second stanza:

I have come to wrench you away –
away from the poking eyes of the man-made monster
who lives in the dark with his racist clutches of imperialism,
who dissects your body bit by bit,
who likens your soul to that of satan
and declares himself the ultimate God! (ll. 10–15)

Ferrus's poem, written in Holland in June 1998, would eventually be reported as responsible for the release of Sarah Bartmann's remains by the French government, facilitating her return for burial in South Africa. The real story of the return is more complex, and less romantic, involving as it does protracted legal wrangling between the French and the first democratically elected South African government. While historian Yvette Abrahams wrote the first full-length study on Sarah Bartmann after noting the absence of academic material which sought to make sense of the historic figure as individual rather than symbol, Wicomb and Ferrus provide two imaginative texts that humanise her.

Through varied mediums, the acts of self-definition for both narrating subjects in Wicomb's and Ferrus's projects are thoroughly historicised, and acutely mindful of the interaction between the present and various possible pasts. For David, then, historicising his experience is necessary but difficult. His recognition of such complications facilitates his surrender of the narrative once it is written down.

A similar impulse hides in the narrative uncertainties that are left unresolved by Ferrus in her poem. These find expression in the speaker's desire to use peace as the emotional currency that clears space for her conversation with Bartmann. The persona claims Bartmann as one of her own, bringing her peace through Bartmann's return home. Yet, it is unclear how Bartmann has managed already to bring the speaker peace. Lines 21–22 and 29–30, respectively, read:

> and I will sing for you
> for I have come to bring you peace.

> and

> where I will sing for you,
> for you have brought me peace.

Within the context of the poem, where the reader is positioned as listening in on a private conversation between two 'people' joined by a relationship s/he is excluded from, there is no room for explanation of what may already be understandable to the two conversing women. This seems a deliberate absence from a poem which, in its written form, is always accompanied by a glossary. Ferrus's choice suggests privacy and the listener's exclusion from how knowledge is exchanged between the two insiders. It is therefore not a failure, any more than David's bungling narrative is a fault. Although both Wicomb and Ferrus use distancing techniques in their representations of a slippery Bartmann, the two writers craft varied effects. Ferrus forces her reader into the position of onlooker, excluded from the intimate space between Bartmann and her speaker. Consequently, Bartmann is made more elusive, not because she is mythic, but because human beings are entitled to some choice over whom to include and whom not. This is an important distinction because Bartmann is historically denied a private intimate space through readers' access to her naked body (parts).

Wicomb's text is rife with distancing strategies. Writing on representations of Krotoä and Sarah Bartmann, Kai Easton (2002) has commented that the two are 'very allusive and elusive characters who figure in [*David's Story*], only to slip out of the story'. Further, Easton continues, '[d]espite their fleeting presence in Wicomb's novel, both of these women, I would argue, are integral to a book that refuses to engage them wholeheartedly in its plot' (2002: 237). While I agree with Easton about these characters being integral to Wicomb's novel, my reading of the novel suggests an oblique engagement of the characters rather than a limitation. This 'refusal' is part of the plot's construction and Wicomb's hint at the failure of representation, rather than an unresolved anxiety. Although Bartmann must be written, she is evoked without the unwavering certainty in older colonial scripting – or even more recent celebration and biographies – of her.

In the same issue of *Kunapipi* as Easton, Margaret Daymond (2002) argues that *David's Story* confronts the politics of coloured identity within the larger texts of a nation in formation. For Daymond, the novel participates in a larger creative project which asks questions through coloured protagonists about belonging and self-identification. It is therefore an exploratory exercise into the terrain of belonging and location, especially for coloured subjectivities in an era where certainties have vanished. It is also a questioning of whether this secure self-location is at all possible if the narratives of history, and race, and shame are ever-shifting.

That Sarah Bartmann and Krotoä are not portrayed in any detail save for their importance in understanding David's story testifies to the validity of Easton's argument. However, to the extent that Wicomb's reader is not allowed to forget their presence, through the various narrative techniques discussed below, it is inaccurate to characterise the novel as 'a book that refuses to engage them wholeheartedly in its plot'. Rather than a character, Bartmann assumes a ghostlike status in Wicomb's novel, in a move that has the novel folding in on itself as Wicomb's reader negotiates the intangible presence of Bartmann in the narrative. This is also part of the larger exercise of disaffection and subversion devices throughout the novel, such as the intrusive amanuensis, the messy periodisation, the irregular naming and the deferral of closure.

Although the novel is located in 1991, its relationship to key moments and subjects of earlier colonialism is explicit. It makes connections between past and current uncertainties in the terrain of identity. The 'as told to' structure of the novel echoes eighteenth- and nineteenth-century slave narratives from the Americas, and the references to Krotoä and Sarah Bartmann reinforce this connection. Yet, David is on the verge of the freedom he has dedicated his life to. Some of David's beginnings, he thus seems to insist, lie in slavery and colonialism. These origins also linger in multiple discursive and linguistic registers, and require meticulous and constant translation. It is not coincidental that Krotoä was a translator who spoke English and Dutch in addition to her mother tongue; or that Bartmann spoke English and Dutch, and had learnt some French by the time she died at the age of 28. The reader is invited to constantly translate first between the biographer and the protagonist and then also between tangible presences and implied ones. Nor is it accidental that both women are rendered homeless: one transported to another continent, and the other banished to an island off the coast of her homeland. They are both exiled, and therefore separated from any sense of 'authentic' rooting through various tropes. A tale that begins with them, therefore, cannot be one with narrative certainty since this requires the very stability undermined by their inauthenticity and homelessness. What is required of the reader is constant mediation between the various worlds of meaning uncovered and re-covered in the pages of Wicomb's novel. Here, then, Wicomb's reader is invited to participate in the contact zone as theorised by Susan Bassnett and Harish Trivedi (1999). This contact zone is 'a place where cultures met on unequal terms, the contact zone is now a space that is redefining itself, a space of multiplicity, exchange, renegotiation and discontinuities' (Bassnett & Trivedi 1999: 14). This space foregrounds the reality that 'languages articulate reality in different ways' (*The Guardian Education Pages* 12 March 2002: 13).[11]

Inattentive to this, David's amanuensis is plagued by a divergent set of practical concerns. Given that there are numerous written texts on Bartmann, would it not make more sense to use a short cut and simply quote these here, she asks. What she cannot understand, an aspect Wicomb's reader may not miss, is that rooting his narrative with Bartmann has little to do with a linear historical chronology which she criticises him for 'bungling up'. Wicomb both suggests and subverts the importance of using Bartmann as historical referent to 'root' David's story as fictional narrative. Given how little certainty there is about Bartmann's life, she cannot provide firm anchorage in the past.

Having established Sarah Bartmann as starting point, although Wicomb proposes that Bartmann cannot anchor, there are a few more references to her in the text. All of these entail writings by David, or sketches, or a combination. Each time the amanuensis is stunned by their significance. They illustrate nothing for her, except the impossibility of excavating their relevance. D/*David's Story* does not mention Sarah Bartmann again, apart from brief references to her on pages 33, and then again 134–135, or in any explicit manner. D/*David's Story* is both the fictional narrative that the character relates, and the larger novel that Wicomb writes. There is no new material except the constant assertion that she will not be inserted into this narrative in the usual way. Wicomb does not allow us to forget Bartmann, thereby choosing to engage in mnemonic script. At the same time she will not write (about) her in ways that mythologise or fix her. The challenges for a reader of this novel, perhaps in search of Sarah Bartmann but who doubtlessly has also read about this woman at great length, are to make sense of the ways in which Wicomb opts to engage with Bartmann's legacy and to represent her physical absence from the text. Clearly, to speak her name is to invoke more than associations with the concrete historical subject that Sarah Bartmann was; it is also to awaken a litany of images and narratives seen to be easily associated with her. As David reminds his biographer, '[t]here've always been other worlds; there always will be many, all struggling for survival' (Wicomb 2000: 197). The reader is to participate in the contact zone, 'for to interpret is no less than to act' (Wicomb 2000: 89).

When Wicomb writes a novel that begins with Sarah Bartmann but does not participate in the project through which she has been the subject and object of myth, the writer is in conversation with the literary and theoretical lives of Sarah Bartmann. Bartmann's treatment is not isolated, however, so Wicomb scripts a fictional world peopled with elusive Blackwomen characters who 'appear' subservient only to turn out as revolutionaries. Because Sarah Bartmann's specific resistance cannot be pigeonholed, it can be rendered imaginatively as the participation of various young women, Griqua and coloured, who are the backbone of the armed struggle in Wicomb's text. These coloured characters, who are linked to earlier Griqua women, are placed along a continuum with names that begin with Saartje, proceed to Sarah and end with Sally. At other times, they return to Saartje. They appear docile as they sit in the sun with their *swirlkouse*[12] but through Wicomb's pen they are invested with revolutionary subjectivity. Thus, what is often rebutted as signalling aspirations towards whiteness is charged with the ability to function as mask, or disguise, for many of the coloured women characters in Wicomb's text. Thus, we are confronted with descriptions such as '[t]heir tilted, stockinged heads were those of guerrillas deliberating over an operation' (Wicomb 2000: 17). The preponderance of names like Saartje, Sarah and Sally as a continuum where the same character moves back and forth, again locate the most famous Saartje or Sarah within a context that normalises her, like Nichols's poem where the world reflects and centres 'the fat black woman'. The insertion, but not definitive description of these Saartje/Sally/Sarah figures' interiority, signals that their histories begin with and link indefinitely with Sarah Bartmann's and Krotoä's in as much as David's does. It prevents the location of the two Khoi women in a position where they simply illuminate another male narrative of insecurity.

Similarly, the activist Dulcie, whose name peppers the narrative because of her association with David's own activism, proves as elusive as Sarah Bartmann or Krotoä. Although her name finds its way into the various explanations and self-narrations offered by David, little is known about her at the end of the story. The amanuensis goes to great pains to extract specific details about her, but in the end she fails. Dulcie often appears shortly after the mention of Sarah Bartmann, or rather, after David's attempt to speak his anxiety more coherently about these women. This becomes quite important in light of the connections between Bartmann and Dulcie (September), both elusive women, one from the nineteenth century and the other from the twentieth.

Their separate and joint elusiveness, as well as their immersion in various narratives of masking and unmasking, and of narratives by Blackwomen, are significant pointers to multiple perspectives. Bartmann's resistance, like Dulcie's and that of the numerous coloured women who are guerrillas, points to the activity of alternate storying, and suggests the ever-presence of sublimated histories of struggle which reside in spaces that do not easily give up meaning. Wicomb's project makes the imagining of these sites possible. Dulcie is central to David's life, yet few details about her are provided.

In Gail Smith's essay 'Fetching Sarah' (*Mail & Guardian* 12 May 2002), the author notes a rare moment of relaxation for those South African officials responsible for the particulars of Bartmann's repatriation. After Bartmann's coffin has been loaded onto a plane headed for South Africa, the deputy minister of Arts and Culture, Bridget Mabandla, reminisced about 'exile travel stories, and a rare moment of poignant remembering of Dulcie September, another great South African woman who had died a horrible death in Paris'. Dulcie September was assassinated by agents of the South African apartheid state on 29 March 1988, as she was opening the ANC office in Paris after collecting mail from the post office. A highly visible, if convoluted, gathering of information on possible assassins notwithstanding, nobody has ever been charged with her murder. Her death remains an object of speculation even with so much information at the French's disposal.

To the extent that Dulcie September's name is well known, it is she who is hinted at when the trajectory of varieties of Blackwomen, specifically coloured or Khoi, are unearthed in Wicomb's novel. Dulcie, the character, then suggests September, or others whose names are less known, to chart along with the numerous Sallys, Saartjies and Sarahs in Wicomb's narrative, varieties of participation in anti-colonial struggle. Wicomb's text charts a pattern of Blackwomen's participation, not the exceptional one that is registered in nationalist struggles.

It pays 'broad attention to voice, communication and agency [in ways that] enlarge conventional understandings of women's agency and transcend the "resistance" models that have often constrained understandings of women's roles as political and historical actors' (Lewis 2002: 1). It also charts continuities of agency, recognition, languaging, and blurring from slavery to now. In response to the challenge of how to develop a representational idiom that homes varied Blackwomen, Wicomb and Smith respond differently, even if their preferred historical figures are similar.

D/*David's Story* invites us to question to what and whose ends stories work and, more specifically, to ask these questions in relation to the various discursive constructions of Sarah Bartmann. More importantly, Wicomb's novel bravely defies and resists closure. Unlike much of the writing on Bartmann, it at once acknowledges that she is more than object and/or icon, and refuses to make her a clear subject of the imagination. It is important that we remember her, but it is not necessary for us to have specific details projected or historically verified in order for this memory to work. Writing on her which does not recast her as a 'freak', reading her in ways that parade her as the ultimate icon of alterity, can only draw attention to the reality that we know nothing about her. Yet her presence continues to haunt us in Wicomb's text, as Zola Maseko says of Bartmann generally. He remarks that after finishing making his first film about her, the award-winning *The Life and Times of Sarah Baartman* (1998),[13] 'I knew even then that this was not the end of the story ... Sarah's spirit and her soul continued to haunt us, to follow us, inspire us – she shouted for justice, and would not be ignored' (quoted in Setshwaelo 2002: n.p.).

REMEMBERING HOME

I have lived in so many places, I think I have forced myself to find home in smaller things.[14]

Making a home has become a critical instinct in all living creatures, and for humans who claim that they are above all other creatures in terms of intelligence and the ability to survive, home is the true marker of having arrived, of being there and having lived. (McFadden 1999: n.p.)

The above quotations seem to speak to two antagonistic impulses in the naming and definition of home spaces. In the longer citation, Patricia McFadden points to the sociability of home. It is that space which, although usually physical, bears the mark of relationship to human selfhood. This relationship to self is always marked in relation to other creatures, and is a stamp of humans' superiority over other living beings by the level of sophistication human abodes represent. Human homes are evidence of people's existence, and as such are of enormous importance. For Jessica Horn, home is mobile and more conducive to carrying within. It is not so much proof of having been here, or there, but a condition which responds to obligation or necessity. Like McFadden's, it is a relationship to the human self.

Both highlight the negotiated element of home, its choices, its locations and its necessity. Horn makes it smaller, but still needs to 'find home'; McFadden defines it as a 'critical instinct' at the same time as she underscores its social value. In both cases home is necessary.

Sitting in Holland in June 1998, Diana Ferrus wrote one of the most famous pieces on Sarah Bartmann. It might be more appropriate to describe it as a poem *to* her. In its very title, 'A Tribute to Sarah Bartmann', the poem unsettles expectation and marks itself as participating in an undertaking markedly different from many of those who have scripted Bartmann. A tribute is an acknowledgement, a mark of respect. It is the opposite of the degradation Sarah Bartmann endured in the last years of her life. However, the relationship Ferrus's persona details with Bartmann need not be mediated through colonialist and other related mythologisations of Bartmann. The poem is not a celebration of Sarah Bartmann. Instead, the persona is concerned with the comfort of Bartmann's inner workings, her emotional and psychic health. Bartmann is being taken home.

In an interview, Ferrus has noted how she came to write the poem, from a place of empathy:

I was doing a course that included a segment on sexuality in the colonies, so my mind went to Sarah Bartmann and how she was exploited ... But more than that, the really big thing was how acutely homesick I was. ... My heart went out to Sarah, and I thought, 'Oh, God, she died of heartbreak. She longed for her country. What did she feel?' That's why the first line of the poem was I've come to take you home. (in Setshwaelo 2002)

Further, Ferrus's refrain 'I have come to take you home' (l. 1, rpt. as 24 and 29), and the title under which she was to later publish the poem, addresses Bartmann directly as one who has a home. Taking her home is a gesture of intense emotional saliency. The meanings which attach to home challenge the status of Sarah Bartmann as object, positioning her instead as a loved one. Home is a place of particular importance for the exiled and enslaved. It is a space which provides the possibilities of belonging, of acceptance and special significance. The love suggested in the act is further intensified given the specific meanings which attach to the act of taking her home. Taking somebody home is always an intimate act of rescue given that only specific people can participate. Ferrus's interview underscores this when she speaks of the possibility of dying from heartbreak when the possibility of going home is taken away.

The late Edward W. Said (2000), who has written movingly about exile and the condition of homelessness in great detail, called it the feeling of being 'out of place', the title of his memoir. When Ferrus's persona offers to take Sarah Bartmann home, it is a declaration of immense affection and connection.

I have come to take you home –
Home! Remember the veld?
The lush green grass beneath the big oak trees?
I have made your bed at the foot of the hill,

your blankets are covered in buchu and mint,
the proteas stand in yellow and white
and the water in the stream chuckles sing-songs
as it hobbles over little stones. (ll. 1–9)

The tone of the poem, which stresses relationship, intensifies the link between the speaker and the addressee. The memory of home is one that is shared, gesturing to a common past. Ferrus's character is a historic projection who has ensured that upon her return home, Sarah Bartmann will be comfortable. Home is more than the physical dwelling inside which people live here. It represents the familiar which brings peace. The evocation of proteas, mint and buchu, along with the use of 'veld', clarifies where this home is located geographically. However, it also captures the presence of smells, tastes and other feelings which do not correspond to how Bartmann feels in exile. These familiar things are also put in the position of being desired because they represent, and are from, home. The memory that is evoked and stressed is one of familiarity through which Bartmann knows how to shelter herself from the elements. It is one that entails Bartmann's freedom to roam about in the veld, unlike her enslaved position in Europe. Home offers pleasures by way of beautiful proteas to behold, and musical water flowing over little stones. Home is a site of pleasure and ease.

Further, the speaker is also committed to the project of restoring Bartmann to herself, which is to say, bringing her home. Because home is a place that one voluntarily goes to, the fetching marks the event as somewhat urgent, bearing as it does strong overtones of rescue. The emotional prominence of home is further complicated as the persona imbues it with additional layers of meaning.

Home is signalled here by everything that the addressee's current location is not. Home has buchu to soothe the effects of the humiliation from being displayed, to counteract her objectification as slave, freak, specimen and her dissection for further examination after her death. Home in Ferrus's poem has open spaces ('veld') and protection ('shade'), which are a contrast to the confinement of Bartmann in Europe. She is not peered and poked at there. The proteas, too, which are missing from the Europe she remained enslaved in, represent something particular to home. The speaker appeals to an emotional memory as well as a memory of the senses. Home is cool, and she can lie in the shade unexposed. She can see the breadth of the veld, and the colours of the proteas. It is her eyes, and the eyes of the persona from her home, that are privileged here. The smell of buchu and mint, as well as their healing possibilities, are also foregrounded. To complete the image of home, Ferrus offers the playful sounds of water flowing freely and singing.

In the writings of late eighteenth-century Europe, in various public debates and court cases, it became clear that colonialism was being explained in a variety of intertwined ways. First, the colonised space 'tempted' the coloniser to subordinate it, and the very difference offered and embodied by the territory and peoples invaded 'propelled' the colonising mission into a justification of an increasing spiral of violence in an effort to make it knowable, and thereby controllable (Kitson 1998). Within this violent regime of knowing, or making knowable, was the body of the slave or colonised. Clearly, then, this was a quest which had no illusions about the coupling of material and epistemic violence. To be known, the colonised and enslaved had to be brutalised, and their home fundamentally altered. Further, this violation of the subjected was an integral part of the coloniser's own self-definition and constitution as ultimate power, and exclusively authoritative (Kitson 1998). This pattern inevitably affects the ways in which (previously) colonised subjects then interact with each other, which is not to argue that the colonised/enslaved is defined wholly by the experience of having being brutalised.

It is important that Ferrus offers descriptions of the landscape as part of her reminder to Bartmann's imagined self, since part of the alienation of colonialism is the separation of the 'native' from her land. In Bartmann's case, as well as that of many other slaves, it is displacement from this home. It was important, as the Dutch became Afrikaners, that the same land(scape) be emptied of its indigenous occupants. One of the consequences of this pertains, more recently, to the paucity of landscape in Black South African literature written in English, as opposed to its centrality in the Afrikaner novel, especially the *plaasroman* (farm novel) (see Coetzee 1988). For the speaker who intends to take Bartmann home, to position herself as having access to this land in order to be able to prepare it for Bartmann's return charts a different location to land in the literary imagination. Part of her return, part of the mutual exchange of peace, has to do with being at home and having part of one's humanity restored.

Wicomb leaves her reader with an elusive Sarah Bartmann, who will not be represented fully by either the amanuensis of David's story or the author of *David's Story*. For Wicomb, Bartmann is an important memory but she may not be a character. Ferrus allows her persona anger and gentleness depending on who is being addressed. Bartmann is the rescued beloved, verbally soothed and physically transported. Because of how she is addressed, we assume commonplace feelings and experiences for the addressed Bartmann. The simplicity of this move serves to highlight the utter brutality of the systems that put Bartmann on display.

When Wicomb resists showing Bartmann as knowable, and Ferrus speaks to a Sarah Bartmann whose interiority is privileged, this stems from a refusal by both writers to describe Bartmann, to offer her as a known and knowable subject. It is enough that she is human, and to explore the obvious things that accompany that recognition.

For Ferrus, this means that she must have experienced emotions, felt sensations, and recognised the humiliation she was subjected to. It also is obvious that she must have resisted it. Wicomb casts her as impossible to know, a condition of full humanity. Both texts participate in a new politics of representation, crafting new languages through which to speak to the creative imagination at hand. This is based on the recognition that:

> [o]ne difficulty with the assumption that language can be overturned in favour of an entirely new lexicon and world outlook is the problematic assumption that words and their meanings can be neatly separated from a globalised cultural repertoire pervasively underwritten by centuries of western discursive dominance. (Lewis 2002: 3)

Ferrus's third stanza further challenges conventional representations of Sarah Bartmann by showing her as one who is loveable, desirable and aesthetically pleasing. Line 20's 'I will feast my eyes on the beauty of you' highlights a different way of looking at Bartmann than fills the volumes penned about her in the last 200 years. Here again Ferrus's project intersects with Wicomb's who, without specific reference to Bartmann each time, nonetheless installs the image of steatopygia as normal for all the women in her novel, and later points to its valuation in another context as beautiful. It is also a location which welcomes her, like the world of Nichols's poem. It is a worldview which is not hostile to Bartmann; a home. All four feminist writers examined here choose not to reinscribe Sarah Bartmann's discursive hyper-corporeality; at the same time, they do not pretend that she is without a body. She is not invisible physically or metaphorically; but in the imagination of feminists of the African world, her body is like many others: recognisable, and therefore not the focus of their attention.

The saliency of 'fetching' her finds further emphasis in Gail Smith's account of participating in the ceremonies in France and South Africa leading up to Sarah Bartmann's burial. A member of the team responsible for repatriating Sarah Bartmann's remains for burial, and the scriptwriter on a second Sarah Bartmann collaboration with Zola Maseko, Smith's speaker also echoes Ferrus's more figurative home-bringing. The act of 'fetching' signifies more than mere collection. One fetches things and people one claims ownership of. Additionally, to fetch somebody suggests that you will ultimately return home with that person. This is why for Smith's narrating voice the act of fetching is linked so closely to the ability to claim Bartmann back.

Like Ferrus's speaker's tone in the second stanza, 'I have come to wrench you away' (1.10), there is indignation in Smith's piece at the degradation Bartmann had to suffer. Smith acidly lashes at the celebrated anatomists who took pleasure in such depravity. However, she is unsurprised by the rise of right-wing sentiment in present-day France because events in history are linked. Thus, her troubled stance as she recognises the pattern is exacerbated by the surprise she finds expressed in the French media. There are no shocks for her in the politics of contemporary France, with the threat of Le Pen taking leadership as she writes.[15] Historical narrative is portrayed as a series of links rather than sporadic moments. All pasts are linked, whether the commentary is on South Africa then and now, or the various events in France.

In respect to Smith's continuum and her critique of forgetfulness that is at the heart of both Bartmann's twentieth-century treatment as well as the 'surprise' of Le Pen's rise, it is as Barnor Hesse (2002: 165) argues:

> In postcolonial memory it is the memory of present predicaments that recalls the dislocation of the past. In the ethics of postcolonial memory, remembering slavery can no more be experienced than generations of racism can be experienced. It is less a structure of feeling than a passionate intervention. The *oughtness* of Atlantic slavery's memory and the justness of its excavation reside in refusing to efface through forgetfulness and historical complicity and contemporary failures of Western liberal democracies. It is this which foregrounds the passage from ethics to politics, rather than the reverse.

Such links are not just important at a temporal level, since there are clear connections between Smith's speaker, Sarah Bartmann's spirit, Dulcie September and Bridget Mabandla. Consequently, Le Pen, the exhibition of Bartmann and the lies which aimed to keep her remains in the Musée de l'Homme are not unconnected. They occupy moments apart in time, but are all part of the same logic.

Thus, while Ferrus and Smith are in different turns angered and softened by the same historic characters, their approaches are poles apart. Smith crafts a dual persona: pacey, intellectual and assertive on the one hand, and emotionally wrought, spiritual and gentle on the other. Where Ferrus's speaker offers passing insult to Cuvier *et al.*, Smith's persona offers intelligent critique that argues, like Patricia Williams, that history is a hovering presence that shapes current experiences of selfhood. Smith focuses on Bartmann by dedicating the bulk of her narrative on reflections on just how Bartmann retains significance.

Clearly comfortable in intellectual terrain, her 'earth self' persona turns the tables on Cuvier, the French and other Europeans, according shame to them as they become the subjects of her scorn and mockery. It is inconceivable to her split personality that a celebrated scientific pioneer left such gaps in his investigations, so Cuvier is seen as sloppy in addition to whatever else he was.

Gail Smith's essay, unlike Wicomb's and Ferrus's texts, was written after Bartmann's return, reflecting on the process of fetching her from Paris. Wicomb's novel was finished long before and published prior to Bartmann's return. Although Ferrus's poem would eventually 'bring about' the return of Bartmann, to do this it had to be written long before the actual event. Ferrus's tribute, then, is in some respects prophetic.

Smith eschews the distance prized by conventional malestream academia between the knowledge-maker and the subject, or 'object', of her text. As feminist academic turned journalist, Smith's speaker is unapologetic about her evaluation of historic projects that seem obviously connected to her. She is equally confident in not only combining the ostensibly separate realms of the intellectual and spiritual, but also fuses journalistic and fictional aspects in the presentation of her narrating voice.

Named as split personality, but at home in various realms, and confident enough in the knowledge sphere to deliver judgement on both spiritual/moral (Cuvier's and lying director's shame) grounds and on an intellectual basis, Smith's narrator points to Cuvier's sloppy investigation and the French's failure to see obvious connections.

Fetching is an emotional act of bringing back, clear enough when Smith's narrator comments, 'My spirit self was reclaiming an ancestor', making Bartmann part of her past, and herself (like David in Wicomb's novel) part of Bartmann's future. The narrator positions herself in relation to Sarah Bartmann as more than object, as someone whose relationship to her is circumscribed by a subjective history. No pretence at objectivity is made by either speaking personality. Such feminist self-positioning is poles apart from the allegedly objective, unemotional treatment which saw Bartmann treated so violently and degradingly. Smith's speaker does not shy away from the contradictions that this poses but rather acknowledges the split between the self who is claiming an ancestor and the other one, the 'earth self', making a film about the return of Sarah Bartmann. There is no need to mask such a conflict, and Smith's narrating voice makes no attempt at this. This is not a tale that this African feminist chooses to tell from a distance, coldly. Bartmann's life and hers are influenced by similar discourses, even if not to the same extent.

Reading Smith against Helen Thomas's (2000) theorisation of African metaphysics often evoked in slave literature adds another layer to Smith's choice of splitting voice, as well as its links to an ancestral spirit in the guise of Bartmann. Thomas (2000: 12) notes:

[w]hereas Western subjectivism posits the subject as a self-sufficient, relatively 'free' egocentric agent, African metaphysics and philosophy

offer a communicentric view of the subject, whose status is affirmed via the cultivation of contacts and exchanges with others. Within such an existential framework, therefore, 'death' does not destroy the tissue of human possibilities and aspirations but rather confers personal immortality and continued existence via generations of descendants and ancestors, the guardians of the community. Differences such as these can perhaps serve to register the counter-discourses to Western subjectivism, colonial expansionism and imperial historical frameworks.

Against this backdrop, Smith's stylistic choices at the same time invoke a different meaning-making system from that which objectified and killed Bartmann. Further emphasising the networks of meaning, Sylvia Tamale has underlined that 'no African woman can shield herself from the broad negative and gendered legacies left behind by forces such as colonialism, imperialism and globalisation' (2002: 7). Given this recognition, it is possible to see contemporary lives as being shaped by the histories which so demonised Bartmann, to the same extent that the French cannot be free of histories of men like Cuvier. This is how Smith's concept of shame works: it is the brutalisers, in the legacy of Cuvier and the other curators at the Musée de l'Homme, who lied about having lost Bartmann's skeleton, genitalia and brains, who should be ashamed. More importantly, Smith can place such shame on the doorstep on which it belongs.

The angry self who can allocate the shame to those who displayed Bartmann, rather than to Bartmann herself, has a different kind of engagement with the ancestor she fetches from Paris. The observer is introduced as one who is split from the onset, one who is divided, torn by the project she has in front of her. Her ambivalence underlines the intimacy and connection between her two selves. The split-spirit persona that Smith constructs disavows the objective distance that is valued by science and, later in her piece, she points to some of the reasons why this is both important and possible. Her stance is different from that of Cuvier, who felt greatly honoured to present Sarah Bartmann's corpse after he had dissected her. Expressing his pleasure, Cuvier could write 'I had the honor of presenting to the Academy, the genital organs of this woman, prepared in such a way, that leaves no doubt on the nature of her apron' (1817: 266).

Encountered with Bartmann's separate body parts, her skeleton and her bottled remains, Smith (2002: 1) comments:

> [s]even years of research, discussion and fascination with Sarah Baartman did not prepare me for the face-to-face meeting with her. Or rather the disembodied bits and pieces deemed crucial for scientific research by the scientists who were 'auspiciously' entrusted with her remains just hours after her death, and who wasted no time getting to the heart of the matter: making a cast of her body, dissecting it, and preserving her brain and genitals.

While she has been fascinated with Bartmann, this means something quite different from Cuvier's absorption. Smith later recounts how 'unremarkable' the bottles containing Bartmann's body parts are to her, and wonders about 'what treasures of scientific discovery they could possibly have yielded': her eyes are unlike Cuvier's because perspective and location are everything. Unlike Cuvier *et al.*, she reflects on the implications on trying to ascertain something spectacular in the parts of Bartmann's body that lie pickled in the jars. Repulsed by responding in a manner that may be seen to mirror Cuvier's, she remarks that she stopped trying to ascertain what was so remarkable about Bartmann's brain and genitals.

It is not only Smith's self-positioning in relation to Sarah Bartmann that is remarkable, however. The essayist is equally struck by the contexts within which she was kept at the Musée de l'Homme. Walking through the Musée de l'Homme, Smith is struck by the many bodies meticulously catalogued in the name of science. The neatness of the cataloguing system leaves her 'horrified', 'appalled' and 'disgusted' by the rows of cupboards, each with a page that 'listed the contents ... skeletons, skulls and other bits of indigenous people from every corner of the earth, but mostly Africa, North & South America' (Smith 2002: 2).

The catalogued bodies are 'France's colonial shame' (Smith 2002: 2) and Smith speculates about the 'shame-faced' officials who were caught in a lie about the whereabouts of Sarah Bartmann's remains. In addition, she muses, 'the French are both proud and ashamed to be in possession of what is the biggest collection of human remains in the world' (Smith 2002: 2). The shame is larger than that, however, as she now turns her ire on Cuvier as indictment of the kind of society and epistemic violence that he was part of:

> Georges Cuvier was not just any old scientist. He was the best of the best, a respected surgeon who counted Napoleon amongst his patients, and a man obsessed with human anatomy and the secrets it held about different races. He apparently did not believe in evolution, and was more of a liberal racist who believed in the abolition of slaves. He also wasn't too interested in actually going to far-flung lands inhabited by fascinating fauna, flora and savages. He preferred to stay at the Jardin de Plante and have the specimens come to him. (Smith 2002: 3)

The science of Cuvier that legitimates a feeling of honour at the display and dissection of human beings and animals contrasts with the spirit Smith speaks about: both her own that comes to claim an ancestor and make a film about the return, as well as Sarah Bartmann's own which must have 'cried out again and again to be taken home, and her cries have reverberated through the centuries, and her name has lived on' (2002: 3). In Ferrus's poem, 'the ancient mountains shout [Bartmann's] name'.

Although the cries are in anguish in both texts, they point in different directions. Ferrus's poem has a landscape calling out to one of its own. Smith's Bartmann has an unbroken spirit that would not be silenced until she was put back in her place.

Cuvier is honoured with an avenue named after him next to the Jardin des Plantes. What is more, the contrast in which the two people's lives were cast when alive was only to come to an end when Sarah Bartmann was taken home. Until then, as Smith (2002: 4) says:

> Cuvier is buried in the famous Parisian cemetery, Père Lechaise, as is Jim Morrison, Sarah Bernhardt, Colette and other historic figures. Sarah Baartman's remains lived in case #33 in the Musée, and later in the parts of the museum still dedicated to anthropology and research and which the millions who cross its doors never see.

This process also illuminates the lies which the director of the museum, Andre Langenay, had manufactured, and which are recorded in the earlier film by the same Smith and Maseko team, about how Sarah Bartmann's remains had been destroyed in a fire long before he was employed by the institution. About this incident, Smith (2002: 2) remarks mockingly in retrospect:

> Sarah Baartman was not simply a powerful symbol of scientific racism, but she clearly has magical powers. She could bring her own genitals and force the modern day representatives of the men who dissected her into a shame-faced apology at being caught out in a very public lie.

Linked to those who ensured Bartmann's ongoing degradation, Langenay is now the shamed one, exposed on camera by one of Bartmann's own, in a reversal of fortunes. The spirit Smith invokes as part of her essay is diametrically opposed to the hierarchies in European science of the nineteenth century. It also offers a reading of the contradictions of Europe at the time. One of the centres of contention which made slavery impossible to justify for the abolitionists related to the spiritual ability of Africans (Thomas 2000). While enslavers classified Africans in their capture as property, thereby objectifying them, Smith stresses how powerful Bartmann's spirit must have been to survive resolute for two centuries.

Smith's speaker makes connections between the logic of lies at the French scientists', curators' and directors' words. She deconstructs their privileged claims to knowledge, setting these up against the more complex creative and spiritual histories. She and Bartmann have spirits that find expression in ways that need no forced or linear narrative of lies. Interestingly, in her choice of language, Smith rejects the Eurandrocentric violent heritage of lies, taking risks instead with complexity that cannot be flattened out as her own voice splits and Sarah Bartmann works her magic from beyond the grave.

TURNING THE CIRCLE

Representations of Sarah Bartmann have incensed feminists of colour the world over due to the manner in which she has been instrumentalised as part of inscribing Blackwomen's bodies in white supremacist colonial culture as oversexualised, deviant and spectacular. In her 'Thoughts Drifting through the Fat Black Woman's Head while Having a Full Bubble Bath', an extract from which opened this chapter, Grace Nichols reclaims and subverts dominant representations of African women's bodies. Her speaking subject lies in her bath, thinking about a world that reflects her interestingly rather than oppressively. It is with anger that the bathing 'fat black woman' responds both to the multiple sites of this inscription, and to the combined authority they continue to exert. Lying in the bath, she allows for the possibility of enjoying her own body, her own mind, of being more than she is to the white supremacist capitalist epistemic systems that

97

she must continue to endure. These epistemic systems continue to exert power over her. Importantly, she links her positioning as a contemporary Blackwoman to the historical constructions of that subject category, whether these take the form of anthropological discourse, historiography, theology or the diet industry.

Nichols's narrator locates her reality in tandem with the violence with which Sarah Bartmann was inscribed. Like Smith, Nichols refuses to pretend that the volumes penned to make sense of Blackwomen's bodies are removed from her own persona's lived experience. The vision her speaker immerses herself in, like the full bubble bath, is a fantasy that she needs to create for herself, where steatopygia is the norm and where the world reflects her. It is not a distant reality, but one which intersects in a variety of ways with her lived experience.

Wicomb's text asserts the necessity of historicising Bartmann and Krotoä, which is to say, the need to make them human, and at the same time demonstrates that this project of representation and historicisation is not one which offers wholeness or closure. Indeed, Wicomb's text both structurally and metaphorically resists offering definitive answers, or seeking refuge in explanatory narrative. Yvette Abrahams (1997: 45) points out that:

> *Dismembered, isolated, decontextualised* – the body in the glass case epitomises the way white men were trying to see Khoisan women at the time, as unresisting objects open to exploitation. ... After reams of measurements and autopsy notes, we do not know the simplest thing about Sarah Bartman. We do not know how she laughed, her favourite flowers or even whom she prayed to. We cannot even know with certainty how she looked.

Later, Gail Smith (2002: 3) would write:

Very little is known of Baartman's experience in Paris. No one can say for sure where she lived, if she had friends, what she took for menstrual cramps, what she thought of French food, or the cold.

Given the many years both writers spent researching the history of Sarah Bartmann, combing the archives for any information about her, the manner in which their declarations rhyme in this respect is staggering. This shared frustration points to how Sarah Bartmann remains an icon put to the use of various systems of logic. Given the near total absence of information about her person, (how then) is she representable? And what available tropes are there for this representation in ways unlike those systems that mythologise her? Wicomb chooses to weave traces of Bartmann's ghost into her novel, never allowing her to be a (knowable) character. In this way she ensures that Bartmann is seen as relevant to the larger picture in a myriad of ways. Similarly, that Bartmann is found in echoes throughout Wicomb's text highlights the difficulty of representing her in refreshing ways. Wicomb's novel, like Smith's essay and Nichols's and Ferrus's remarkable poems, partakes in the larger ideological project of *remembering, connecting, contextualising* Bartmann and Krotoä. Aesthetically, this is achieved very differently by the four writers. For Smith, Sarah Bartmann's history is linked to her own, and it is not one from which the writer feigns emotional distance. It is linked to Dulcie September's. Equally, it intersects with the struggles over identity and self-positioning which accompany the readings of Blackwomen's bodies in ways that trap them/us in discourses of hypersexualisation. Smith's connection and contextualisation brazenly deconstructs the circulation of 'white supremacist, Eurocentric beliefs about knowledge and its production' which perpetuates 'practices that invisibilise black women' (Matlanyane Sexwale 1994: 65).

The writers here examined suggest that there is necessarily a variety of lenses brought to bear on representing Blackwoman subjectivities, and also that these are linked to Bartmann as one of the women most conspicuously subjected to the violence of this gaze. Smith (2002: 4) points to the same when she notes, towards the end of her piece:

> I wept for Sarah Bartmann, I wept for every black woman degraded and humiliated by men obsessed by the hidden secrets they carry between their legs. And I wept for every brown South African reduced, degraded and humiliated by being called 'Hotnot' and 'Amaboesman'. I also wept tears of joy, and gratitude, that I had been chosen to witness a brief and victorious moment in history.

This relationality is important for Smith's text. Without it, the humanising project cannot be complete. Part of the objectification of people has historically involved denying them spatial and temporal context. To treat Bartmann as ahistorical, or as an interesting floating symbol, is to use her in the same manner as the theoretical impulse Magubane critiques. For the projects above, it bears noting that 'all representation and knowledge production are mediated, and that feminist research and practice, if it is not to betray its progressive thrust, is always relational and partial' (Lewis 2002: 7).

The historicisation of Bartmann that Magubane urges is an urgent matter; one which, after her, must go beyond the usual disclaimers about the constructedness of all identity, and which requires that Bartmann be located within a context in which her enslavement was possible, and her display, dissection and caging were celebrated in the name of science. It requires that she not be placed outside history, but embedded in the histories of colonialism, slavery, apartheid and other ongoing systems which stem from this history of racist terror. After all, what made her humiliation possible is not exceptional, as Smith reminds us. It was part of the widespread belief and academic knowledge-making to justify the inferiority of Africans, and the ultimate superiority of Europeans.[16] Its consequences continue to plague the contemporary moment, a factor that Smith's essay will not let us lose sight of.

Homi Bhabha (1994: 31) writes:

> The Other is cited, quoted, framed, illuminated, encased in the shot/reverse-shot strategy of a serial enlightenment. ... The Other loses its power to signify, to negate, to initiate its historic desire, to establish its own institutional and oppositional discourse. However impeccably the content of an 'other' culture may be known, however anti-ethnocentrically it is represented, it is ... the demand that ... it be always the good object of knowledge, the docile body of difference, that reproduces a relation of domination.

In these texts, Sarah Bartmann does not remain the 'docile body of difference'. She is not the icon of alterity that Magubane so skilfully critiques, but appears as self-loving in Nichols, rescued by Ferrus, mischievously stubborn in Smith's essay and indefinable in Wicomb's novel. The main question all of these texts address is the difficulty in speaking about how Blackwomen's subjectivity is constituted.

The literary texts here discussed unsettle the Eurandrocentric perspective as norm by imaginatively illustrating the inescapable marrying of perspective and discursive construction. Thus, the logic and aesthetics of colonial valuation, biased in the interest of white supremacist patriarchy, are unravelled in the refusal of linear narrative strategies (timelines). Collectively, these historic feminist texts offer a revision of prevalent literary representations of the past. Bartmann is not used as illustration for some alternative ideology. Rather, her narrative is engaged with in ways that are irredeemably contaminated by her past of violation. For David, then, whose story starts with Bartmann, it is an elusive beginning; his story is incomplete, non-linear and bungling. It is not a history that resides somewhere, which can be accessed with relative certainty and reliability. Similarly, Smith's essay and Ferrus's poem point to some of the difficulties of engaging in and with this history, but offer very different solutions.

All writers analysed here gesture to what is not knowable, invite us readers to 'wrestle with ways of unifying concepts which [we] had come to believe were polarised opposites, or could be placed into neat hierarchies, such as is the case with speech/silence' (Motsemme 2004: 4). What has emerged is the manner in which representing Sarah Bartmann within the African feminist imagination moves far beyond drawing attention to history's silences about her. All literary texts analysed in this chapter suggest that rather than speaking about her obliquely, it is possible to gesture to Sarah Bartmann's absent presence, and to contextualise and humanise her imaginatively:

> creating spaces which facilitate the telling of ... stories as connected as possible to [our own African feminist] centres of meaning, then we will have to take the risk of leaping into places which have become unfamiliar to many of us fed on the restricted diet of the power of articulation and the text. (Motsemme 2004: 5)

In other words, they move beyond writing back to older traditions. Instead, they uncover and discover the textures of crafting 'epicentres of our agency', suggesting that relying on the same recycled motifs is intellectual and creative laziness. Widely varied in style, tone and register choices, these writers illustrate the vast possibilities available to imagining historic subjects as human without focusing on their bodies as their sole point of reference.

CHAPTER 3

WHITENESS REMIXED, OR REMEMBERED IMPURITY, SHAME AND TELEVISION

> Shifts in identification that have been taking place under the sign
> of whiteness since the end of minority rule can be ascribed, in part,
> to the fact that previously sanctioned stagings of whiteness are
> increasingly registered as untenable in the everyday post-apartheid
> inter-racial encounter. (Strauss 2006: 179)

This chapter is concerned with what happens when a country's changing
political landscape destabilises older claims to identity and power. In a newly
democratic South Africa, not only is it noticeable that 'whiteness just isn't
what it used to be', to borrow Melissa Steyn's (2001) title from her seminal
study of South African whiteness post-apartheid, but the vocabulary for
speaking about whiteness in relation to colonialism and slavery undergoes
considerable revision. This is in line with Strauss's citation, on which I opened
this chapter, which stresses the emergence of new forms of identifying and
functioning as a white person in a changed political reality.

The meanings of whiteness in contemporary South Africa are a hotly
debated issue within white society as well as from without. Various media
platforms regularly give space to the contested meanings of whiteness:
from invitations to inhabit different white subjectivities to claims to white
marginalisation. While in the post-apartheid context 'black and white are
no longer synonymous with rich and poor' (Nattrass & Seekings 2001:
47), due to some of the successes of legislatively enabling measures, it is
widely accepted that B/black citizens are significantly more likely to be
poor than white citizens (Kingdon & Knight 2004).

However, race is not only highlighted in the verifiable statistics of
income. As Melissa Steyn (2001) relates in the preface to her study of

the shifting experiences of whiteness in post-apartheid South Africa, it is important to pay attention to the changes and the continuities, as well as to probe emerging elusive meanings and expressions. This is the task of this chapter, which reads specific new ways of negotiating Afrikaner/white identities with reference to claimed slave ancestry.

The shifts and 'remixes' that I analyse below occur against the backdrop of larger discussions about the meanings of whiteness in a democratic society. Steyn (2001: xvii) traces her own location in a changing country in this way:

> Personal immersion in another Western society had sharpened my appreciation of the fact that race is certainly not just skin deep. Indeed, it is generations deep and continents wide. I continue to struggle with the multiple fences of white identity that my heritage constructed to define me. But bits of flesh remain caught in the barbs. A white skin is not skin that can be shed without losing some blood. Yet the further I move from my white conditioning, the more I find community with an ever-growing group of South Africans of all gradations and pigmentation, who care about creating a fairer, more equitable society in which we all can grow in human dignity.

Steyn's insights above have direct relevance for my analysis of mutating white identities and the impulse to claim a different past than was celebrated for white South Africans under apartheid.

She identifies the sense of personal embattlement that accompanies an interrogation of what it means to be a white person in South Africa and the world. The condition of being raised and marked as white is not one that can be escaped through a denial of whiteness and privilege; whiteness follows her across time and continents. However, for Steyn, being white offers possibilities for redefinition of the performance of white identity. Rather than deny whiteness and historic meanings which continue to shape its materiality, Steyn chooses a critical stance to whiteness – acknowledging its pasts and imbuing it with different meanings that do not reinscribe its historic blindness and privilege. She chooses different alliances at the same time as being attentive to her historical marking. Such a stance rhymes with Strauss's invitation to construct a white identity responsive 'to the fact that previously sanctioned stagings of whiteness are increasingly registered as untenable in the everyday post-apartheid inter-racial encounter' (2006: 179).

Both Strauss and Steyn envision that the white subject is an active, self-reflexive agent in the rethinking and reshaping of white identity performance. Their shared vision differs from that of Antjie Krog's persona in *Country of My Skull* (1998) and from the recently released *Begging to be Black* (2009), the latter of which is posited as the third in a series of autobiographical books starting with the former. Krog's is arguably the most visible post-apartheid white imagination on contemporary South Africa,[1] with critical acclaim and high circulation of her writing on memory and nationalism in a democratic South Africa.

Krog's stance in *Country of My Skull* repeatedly stages her 'apprehension that she may not be invited into the new country of her imagination, that which is popularly called "The New South Africa" ' (Coetzee 2001: 685). In that text, the writer signals a shared white idiom of what J.M. Coetzee (1988) has called 'white writing' through the evocation of a 'disembodied' romantic landscape. Carli Coetzee (2001: 686) continues:

> Krog's country of her skull is a landscape from which she feels herself barred, as a white South African, on account of her whiteness, on account of the name of her father. It is a landscape familiar from her childhood, the landscape of the fathers and the brothers; but she can never again enter it. And at the same time it is a landscape into which she wishes to be invited by her fellow South Africans. But the figure in the landscape is distinctly different

from Coetzee's lone figure unable to imagine another presence. In Krog's work, there is a self-conscious desire to address an audience that includes black South Africans. ... At times it seems clear that the text invokes fellow-Afrikaners as readers, precisely those whom Krog wishes to convince of our/their guilt and complicity in South Africa's injustices, as recorded by the proceedings of the Truth and Reconciliation Commission [TRC]. At other times, the text is explicitly addressed to those whom Krog invests with the power to allow her into the country of her imagination and heart.

In Krog's text, then, the changing white subject is an insecure and somewhat passive one in its engagement with its historic Other; although provocative to imagined Afrikaner readers, it awaits invitation from Black people. The connection and desire to belong differently is enacted through the conflicted language of the empty landscape, even if we go along with Carli Coetzee's argument that Krog invests her landscape with insecurity that marks it as different from conventional Afrikaner narratives of land(scape). Krog's narrating subject insecurely addresses white audiences as she calls them to question and revisit older ways of being white/Afrikaner. However, her Other is an invented all-powerful, active collective with the responsibility to invite her to a sense of belonging to the imagined country.

Responses to Krog's text have varied. Krog's critics take issue with her chosen self-representation against the backdrop of the TRC. Claudia Braude's much cited *Mail & Guardian* (12–18 June 1998) review of Krog's book faults the writer for her stance on truth. For Braude, Krog's fluctuation between dismissing 'truth' and resistance to recognising the existence of truth is misplaced in this context. Such a 'postmodern' posture links too closely with the apartheid denialism of Afrikaner men with institutional power when they appeared at the TRC. Such a questioning of the place and devaluation of 'truth' by Krog can be extended to her stylistic choices to merge proceedings at the TRC with flights of fantasy in ways that sometimes blur the boundaries within *Country of My Skull*. Ashleigh Harris (2006), Jo-Anne Prins (2002), Sarah Ruden (1999) and Zoë Wicomb (1999) have shared some of these reservations and moved beyond this critique. They, like Laura Moss (2006: 86), note how the TRC narratives work as 'backdrops for the reporter-narrator's unsettling journey through the process of telling truth' and at other times take on 'an allegorical role in the healing of the nation' (see also Fester 2000).

More directly, Moss writes '[w]here I gently criticize the South African edition for both privileging the narrator's responses over the stories told in the testimonies themselves and for turning individual's stories into allegories of the nation, I find the American edition is even more culpable' (2006: 99). All of these critics problematise the manner in which Krog uses testimonies at the TRC, especially those of victimisation, as the background to her own angst about belonging. Such problematic setting, they argue, foregrounds Krog at the expense of those who are at the TRC. For Harris (2006), Krog's choices are unethical for two reasons. First, because they allow her to partially erase the voices of the people whose testimonies are used for the writer's opportunistic narrative of self-presentation. Second, Harris argues that Krog plagiarises these narratives since she occludes their sources in order to make her word 'quilt'. Sarah Ruden's (1999) review similarly questions the moral codes which inform Krog's self-construction. Ruden's (1999: 171) questions include, '[d]id Krog get permission to use this verbatim text at such length, or to alter its format, and what compensation did she offer the indigent author?' Finally, she equates Krog's appropriation of TRC testimonies to 'theft'.

From the above, then, it is possible to see Krog's prose as courageously:

> divided against itself, doubling up on itself given that the author is
> at pains to distinguish herself from the men of her race (as she calls

them), and the voice becomes one in search of a new ear, a new genealogy into which she can write herself; because for her it has become impossible to speak any longer only in the language of the fathers. (Coetzee 2001: 688)

The imagined land/country to which she awaits invitation is, therefore, both yearned for and awaited. It is also worked towards. Shane Graham's (2003) analysis rhymes with Coetzee's, stressing the difficulty of Krog's negotiation of her connection to and distance from the legacies and institutions of Afrikaner/white men. However, such work – although critical of the older Afrikaner/patriarchal established traditions – is not uncomplicated, as Krog's critics show. Tellingly, even Krog's defenders recognise the messy terrain of self-representation within her text. Graham calls the text Krog's '*memoir*' in which the writer 'is sensitive to the victims' loss, handling their testimonies gingerly without, I believe, exiling them to the margins of her book' (2003: 21, emphasis added). Susan Spearey (2000: 65, emphasis added) called it a text whose '*autobiographical* elements become increasingly foregrounded'.

For the purposes of this chapter, Krog's texts and self-positioning are beside the point. I find them useful metaphorically because they permit the exposition and introduction of the fraught terrain of revised Afrikaner/white self-writing with reference to Black subjects/history. Krog's work and position is important for the larger contemporary memory project and its figuration of the possibility of differently cast white subjectivities. Her work and some of the debates it has elicited are useful entry points into the contested terrain of another era in the memory project: that of slavery.

I now turn to my real interest in this chapter: reading explorations of white identities that index Khoi and/or enslaved ancestry. Such analysis aims to grasp an understanding of the specific work achieved by slave memory in relation to mutating white South African identities. I comprehend such racialised mnemonic identitiary activity as engagements with the meanings of changing nation and national belonging.

In her essay 'Krotoä Remembered: A Mother of Unity, a Mother of Sorrows', Carli Coetzee (1998) traces how Krotoä's life is mythologised in post-apartheid theatre and argues that this move works to reposition Afrikaner identity in a changing political landscape. Krotoä, also known as Eva, worked for Jan van Riebeeck as an interpreter between the Dutch and the Khoi and married into the Dutch community in the seventeenth century. However, Krotoä's status was dramatically altered upon the death of her husband, Pieter van Meerhoff. Her children were forcibly taken from her and raised as Dutch, and she herself was banished to Robben Island where she later died. Coetzee's essay focuses on a 1995 play in which Krotoä was referred to as 'onse ma' (our mother), performed nationally to supportive Afrikaner audiences. For Coetzee, a shift from representations of Krotoä as undesirable to her embrace as founding mother provokes questions such as:

> [h]ow is it that this woman, whose contribution to white South African identity (especially white Afrikaner identity) has been disclaimed for nearly three centuries, has come to be remembered by Afrikaners as 'our mother'? (1998: 113)

Rather than being an anomaly, Coetzee reads this shift in attitudes to Krotoä as part of a larger global trend in which colonised women are used by artists 'as metaphors for alienation and a perceived lost wholeness' (1998: 113). Interestingly, the criticism in Coetzee's 1998 essay is remarkably similar to the argument advanced by Harris (2006), Prins (2002), Gail Smith in *City Press*,[2] and Wicomb (1999) against Krog's text(s), discussed above. As Coetzee demonstrates, according to this kind of narrative, when Afrikaners claim Krotoä as a foremother, they can symbolically reposition themselves in the present.

Coetzee is not alone among South African feminist scholars in problematising the treatment of Krotoä's history/memory. More recently, Meg Samuelson has built on Coetzee's essay to note that in the South African transition, 'Krotoä-Eva has been the subject of an astonishing amount of historical revisionist writing, genealogical claims and fictional reconstructions' (2007: 15). Some of the enquiry by Samuelson and Coetzee partly responds to historian Yvette Abrahams's suggestion that Krotoä's historiography needs to be rewritten to ask questions about the silences which characterise her role in South African history. Coetzee cites Abrahams's work to challenge how Krotoä has been framed as a mythic figure of folklore in Afrikaner circles. Krotoä's new status as the Afrikaner *stammoeder* (founding mother) is opportunistic and, as Coetzee (1998: 114–115, emphasis added) further notes:

> [t]he political gain of this move is the acknowledgement of mixed blood and the Khoi contribution to South Africa. This is especially useful to Afrikaners, many of whom had long denied their 'non-white' ancestry publicly. By reclaiming as their foremother the Khoi woman Krotoä, these South Africans *can gain what seems like legitimate access to the new rainbow family* ... The dangers are clear: Krotoä's life serves as the image of a promised sense of fullness and completeness, a return to an origin, to fulfilment and reconciliation.

Krotoä's 'reclamation' as the Afrikaner mother who needs to be remembered requires the paradoxical forgetting of the events of her life and her specific relationship to colonial Dutch and later Afrikaner identity formation. It requires deliberate 'forgetting' of her banishment from Dutch society after her husband's death, as well as her historic inscriptions as an unfit mother whose children needed to be taken 'back' into Dutch society and away from her. For Krotoä's new use, the falsity of the claim to white racial purity needs to be laid bare.

Samuelson's scholarship is particularly important in highlighting this aspect, reminding us of the ways in which, although Krotoä was a talented translator and cultural broker, she resurfaces in transitioning South Africa through 'genetic transmission: Krotoä-Eva the translator becomes the rainbow Mother' (2007: 16). Indeed:

> [t]he Krotoä-Eva we encounter in cultural texts produced during the South African transition by white South Africans claiming belonging in the rainbow nation through identification with her is a domesticated figure. (Samuelson 2007: 18)

While Abrahams, Coetzee and Samuelson use different primary texts, they reach very similar conclusions about the contemporary uses to which Krotoä's evocation is put. Further, all three engage in an anti-racist feminist project which critiques Krotoä's representations and domestication: her appropriation in the post-apartheid moment is gendered in very troubling ways.

In addition to their readings, I note that such appropriations of Krotoä offer Afrikaners entry into a legitimate African identity which has been asserted throughout Afrikaner nationalism as a given. The very naming of this community as no longer Dutch but 'Afrikaner', and its adopted language as 'Afrikaans', has been premised on this Africanness as entitlement. That this 'white African' identity and belonging now need external legitimation points to emergent instability within Afrikaner identity formation and shifting positions relative to other South African identities.

Claiming Krotoä as founding mother is achieved through an admission of that which previously needed denial for Afrikaner survival: 'racial mixing', inverting collective self-representation by Afrikaners in colonialist, slavocratic and apartheid narratives. Krotoä as *stammoeder* contradicts dominant Afrikaner responses to the published academic work of the Hesses in the 1970s, 'a father and son team of historians' who demonstrated that 'the present-day Afrikaners had a high percentage of Khoi and slave ancestry'; their work 'was angrily dismissed by many Afrikaner intellectuals and political leaders' (Coetzee 1998: 119).

Clearly, what Coetzee and Samuelson analyse in literary texts is part of the Afrikaner response to the destabilisation of identity that accompanies transitional political periods. For Afrikaners, the end of apartheid marked the loss of the security ensured by membership of the dominant group, and a scramble in the new dispensation for new positions to inhabit. The appropriation of Krotoä is not a deconstructive movement away from an ideological location whose feasibility waned, but rather a battle for power. It marks sudden awareness of a shift from 'a culture of authority to a culture of justification' (van der Walt 2000: 59). A culture of justification is a means to survive without significantly questioning the tenets of apartheid thinking. It is not the response invited in the work of Strauss and Steyn on which I opened this chapter. Such a culture invents a different language to maintain structural power at a time when previous claims to power have lost state backing.

A similar impetus can be read into other tendencies within conservative Afrikaner politics, as evident in a speech made by a representative of the New National Party (NNP) in 2002. During the transition period from apartheid to democracy, the National Party was renamed the NNP in anticipation of its move from apartheid party in power to an opposition party in a democratically elected Parliament. In her speech on 27 April 2002, South Africa's National Freedom Day, the public holiday which marks the anniversary of the first democratic election in 1994, NNP Member of Parliament Anna van Wyk admitted that 'almost all' white people in South Africa have a slave ancestry, arguing that this was a 'well-known fact' and maintaining that slaves left a 'good legacy', citing buildings, and asserting that 'this should be celebrated'.[3] Her address was delivered in Cape Town outside the South African Cultural Museum, the historic Slave

Lodge. That an NNP Member of Parliament could make this assertion in contemporary South Africa and frame it as a 'well-known fact' serves as further illustration of Coetzee's stance. The absence of an explanation for the shift from 'denial' to 'well-known fact' echoes Krotoä's rehabilitation in the making of Afrikaner identity discussed above. Both are divorced from the NNP's dependence on white racial purity as a central tenet of white supremacy, which was enshrined in apartheid legislation. The assertion of known and embraced 'mixed blood' and ancestry becomes the new truth in the phoenix-like fashion of 'context-dependent' truth in Susan Williams's (1999) formulation. Such truth is constantly revived and remixed to create a relevant 'shared reality' for significant decisions and 'making claims for decisions that work in a practical sense rather than merely serving a symbolic function' (Williams 1999: 7). The shared reality is a reformulated lineage of racial mixing, while the symbolic function is tied to a negation of a differently remembered South African past which celebrated white racial purity and demonised Khoi presences. Williams (1999: 35) continues:

> [a] central feature of the relationship between the knower and the known is that the knower exercises control over the known. The external world, the things to be known, are conceived as passive, not in the sense of being inactive, but in the sense of being reactive rather than self-initiating. They are, therefore, subject to prediction and often manipulation.

The known in this instance becomes both Krotoä and the 'well-known fact' that van Wyk evokes above. Krotoä is the known through her domestication and the claim to intimacy suggested by her new status as 'foremother'. The 'well-known fact' becomes truth merely through its confident assertion as such by powerfully positioned individuals who speak with institutional authority.

Coetzee's observations about the practice of claiming indigenous 'roots' as a means to access specific kinds of African identity and relationships to land are useful. These new ways of identifying as Black or white are contaminated by foregoing historical processes even as they carry implications for the materiality of the contemporary moment. Further, as Samuelson has noted, 'narratives of "blood" not only reproduce apartheid racial obsessions and appeal to a dangerous mix of folk wisdom and eugenics ... but also silence and even dismember women' (2007: 21). Following Samuelson, then, van Wyk's newly recognised slaves and Krotoä are both useful and evoked to rationalise and legitimate a revised narrative of Afrikaner/white identity as constituted from diversity. At the same time Krotoä and this newly admitted past are rendered 'subject to prediction and often manipulation', as Williams argues above.

An additional tendency that resonates with Coetzee's and Samuelson's analyses is illuminated by a dramatised television series aired on public television in 1999. Called *Saints, Sinners and Settlers*, the series presented several key historical figures as the legally accused in a court of law. Each of the accused personalities needed to defend themselves against the populace of the new dispensation, represented by the state prosecutor. The historic figures on trial were drawn from South Africa's colonial, slave and apartheid eras. Framed as a history lesson which moved away from the staid tradition associated with South African history teaching, the television series participated explicitly in the memory process. The advertisements for *Saints, Sinners and Settlers* invited audiences to imagine and re-imagine how these historical figures would position themselves, faced with the ideologies of a post-apartheid society. Like the TRC hearings, blame could be accorded, but there was no available sanction for those found guilty of whatever charge was laid in front of them.

The judge, played by renowned actor Nambitha Mpumlwana, had the final say over whether the accused was a saint, a sinner, or a settler. In accordance with the reconciliation motif of the rainbow nation narrative,

116

historic enemies could be seen to reconcile after the proceedings, regardless of whether 'the people' had decided on a guilty or innocent version. All of the characters were recognisable controversial historic figures but, given the desire to entertain at the same time as participating in the larger programme of 'coming to terms with the past', the series formed part of the South African Broadcasting Corporation's emphasis on edutainment (educative programmes which are informative and assist in the task of reconciliation between the races). Each week's episode was advertised by S'thandiwe Msomi in the role of television journalist. She offered snippets of what was to come and presented 'live' coverage interpreting the day's events. This echoed the format of reportage on the TRC hearings, and was an intertextual reference that could not be lost on the television viewers.

Although the larger series offered many insights into the working and public enactment of memory in a democratic South Africa, two particular episodes had specific relevance for memorying colonial and slave pasts. The first, called 'The Reluctant Settler: The Trial of Jan van Riebeeck', and the second, 'The Trial of Hendrik Verwoerd', will be analysed in what follows.

The title of the first episode for analysis challenged both the hegemonic and the counter-hegemonic discourses on Jan van Riebeeck. Apartheid history textbooks credited van Riebeeck with the heroic 'discovery' of South Africa in 1652, and presented him as the standard-bearer of European civilisation and religion. According to this history, when van Riebeeck arrived, he found the country unoccupied save for a few 'Strandloper Hottentots'. He has been denounced within Black politics as the first coloniser at the Cape, and in this discourse his 'founding' of South Africa is rejected as the backbone of white supremacy and its legitimation.

Against this backdrop, the introduction of the adjective 'reluctant' in the title of the episode jars with both these narratives of van Riebeeck as hero or villain. His defence attorney presented a rehabilitated van Riebeeck: merely a corrupt opportunist who disappointed the VOC – called by its Anglicised name, the Dutch East India Company – that had sent him on a money-making mission by bungling his orders. This changed van Riebeeck, portrayed by the actor Tertius Meintjies, as a failure who is further puzzled by the proceedings he is required to partake in. Rather than being powerful and brutal, he is a solitary, greedy and incompetent fool. Consequently, neither the Company which authorises his colonial quest, nor the structured violence it unleashed over three centuries – as slavery, colonialism and apartheid – is interrogated. The effects of his colonising mission, described in his diaries as 'the van Riebeeck principle'; his successful attempts at displacing indigenous people from land; and his enslaving projects are disavowed and seen to be the chaotic violence of a single man who has no institutional power. In this manner, the rest of colonial Dutch, and later Afrikaner, society cannot be held responsible or accountable for colonialism or the ensuing privileges. The absence of any link between this early coloniser and other European colonisers who settled in the interior is also telling. The allocation of blame for colonial and apartheid violence to an individual, here evident, was also in keeping with the TRC hearings, where specific generals were brought to book for particular human rights violations, thereby allowing the beneficiaries of the system as well as the politicians who enabled and legitimised the violations to escape unscathed. This casting of the past as peopled by cruel individuals who brutalised specific people, also rendered in the singular, is the dominant manner in which a historical consciousness is performed in post-apartheid South Africa. This according of blame to individuals leaves the structural privilege which accrues to whiteness uninterrogated in as much as it also falls short of recognising the institutional power which makes slavery, colonialism and apartheid more than interpersonal relations.

In the same episode, van Riebeeck's relationships with Krotoä (called Eva van Meerhof) and Autshumao, her uncle and the interpreter for the Dutch before her, are brought to light. Autshumao is called 'Harry Hottentot', van Riebeeck's 'only friend'. When both Khoi figures take the stand, some measure of contradiction and narrative uncertainty is introduced. The evidence that van Riebeeck kidnapped and imprisoned Autshumao on Robben Island disrupts the text of valued friendship between the two men in question. That the site of Autshumao's banishment is Robben Island triggers associations of resistance to colonial and apartheid rule, rather than acquiescence and complicity that would support a reading of rare friendship.

Interesting dynamics emerge when Autshumao and Krotoä take the stand. Jan van Riebeeck explains Autshumao's kidnapping and imprisonment on Robben Island as the result of a series of misunderstandings that are made all the more elusive because of the 'chaotic' nature of van Riebeeck's diaries. In contrast, the prosecutor, Pule, played by Lindelani Buthelezi, insists, 'That is why journals are kept: to provide evidence when memory fails.' Autshumao's account of their relationship is in stark contrast to the friendship that van Riebeeck testifies to. His narrative is of manipulation and resistance; it places van Riebeeck in the position of an invader who needs to be outsmarted.

More baffling is Krotoä's testimony (played by Esmeralda Biehl). Taking the stand, she appears uneasy. She fidgets constantly as she testifies to the manner in which she was 'not treated like a slave': van Riebeeck 'treated [her] like a daughter'. Her evidence is that he taught her to read from the Bible, and she played the role of interpreter between various Khoi languages, Dutch and Portuguese. She speaks English in the courtroom and appears on the brink of tears during most of her testimony. She does not dispute that she was van Riebeeck's slave but argues that 'I was his favourite'. The camera moves to reveal van Riebeeck smiling at this and immediately returns to her face, showing that she has started crying.

It is not clear whether her tears are linked to her testimony about her relationship with van Riebeeck and her uncle, or whether it is the memory of her bereavement, her separation from her children and her banishment which is painful. This uncertainty is unresolved, and the following scene shows a white-haired van Riebeeck walking out of the courtroom, with stooped shoulders, alone.

This ambiguity in the representation of Krotoä and her relationship to van Riebeeck mirrors her depiction in the historical record. It is precisely this uncertainty which Coetzee, Samuelson and Abrahams interrogate, arguing it was used to different political ends by Dutch colonists and later by segments of Afrikaner society. These representations invite an engagement with Stuart Hall's (1997: 7) questions:

> Do things – objects, people, events in the world – carry their own, one true meaning, fixed like number plates on their backs, which it is the task of language to reflect accurately? Or are meanings constantly shifting as we move from one culture to another, one language to another, one historical context, one community, group or sub-culture, to another?

A reading of Krotoä's representations reveals the many symbolic uses to which she can be put. A reminder of the presence of African 'blood' within Dutch, later Afrikaner, society, she is banished and the memory of her is used to cast her as a degenerate, untrustworthy slave. Later, when she can be differently exploited, she is the haunting presence of the *stammoeder*. The timing of this repositioning coincides with the need for a renegotiating of white identities in a post-apartheid South Africa. It also follows on the heels of discussions on land redistribution.

Several readings of Krotoä are made possible in the episode discussed above. Her words suggest that she was content in the van Riebeeck household, that van Riebeeck was kind to her even though she was his slave, and that she received preferential treatment from him. She embodies a 'mild slavery', and testifies to not being an unhappy slave. Thus, her experience seems to fly in the face of the characterisation offered by the man van Riebeeck characterises as his friend, Autshumao,

Krotoä's uncle. The anxiety experienced by Krotoä is unresolved, nor is it presented as in need of unpacking. It suggests that there are unknowable dynamics to her personality and history. The absence of an exploration of what these might be reinforces the sense that there is a part of the story that remains untold. It invites imaginative engagements which are further encouraged by her visible unease as she testifies to her life in the late seventeenth century. While such narrative instability is introduced, it is also carefully managed in the interest of an established and tidy text of national reconciliation and rainbowism: through the individualisation of historical agency. At the end of the episode, van Riebeeck walks away alone but it is not clear what happens to the two Khoi subjects. Indeed, they are not the focus of the investigation or the court case: slavery and colonialism are small technicalities in the larger evaluation of the character of an important figure.

The episode which focuses on Hendrik Verwoerd, commonly referred to as 'the architect of apartheid', provides an interesting complementary narrative to the van Riebeeck episode. Most of the witnesses called to the stand are academics and they contribute to the portrayal of Hendrik Verwoerd as a highly learned man with a DPhil. Pierre van Pletzen portrays Mr Louw, Verwoerd's teacher, who pleads for an understanding of Verwoerd's ideologies as a means of indigenising himself and other Afrikaners. Again, Verwoerd's bigotry, like van Riebeeck's, is cast as logical if the correct interpretive lens is brought to bear on it. The only appropriate lens, these academic testimonies suggest, is a sympathetic one. Rather than judgement, what Verwoerd requires is understanding, which can only be engendered by a sensitive examination of his ideology. Indeed, many of the witnesses cast him as a man whose legacy of cruelty is not justified. Mr Louw argues that Verwoerd's policies make sense because:

> [u]nlike the English or the French we can't return home. On this very soil of Africa we must either stay or perish with our history, culture

and language. He understood that if the Afrikaner was forced to live under the Bantu's rule, it would cease as a nation.

The audience is asked to sympathise with Verwoerd, a highly problematic invitation given that the bulk of the audience has been violated precisely because of Verwoerd's policies. Indeed, most adults watching the programme would have had to suffer through the indignities of the Bantu Education policies he spearheaded and his leadership of the Department of Home Affairs and later government as state president. The main part of the narrative is in Afrikaans with English subtitles, so that Afrikaner academics are able to justify apartheid logic in its language. To counter this account of Verwoerd as tragic victim of cultural insecurity who overcompensates, the prosecutor, Johny Modise, played by Sechaba Morojele, introduced the famous case of Linda Boschoff.

Linda Boschoff was born to white parents in the Transvaal in 1956. She was brought up in a conservative Afrikaner family until she was expelled from school at the age of eight because she 'looked coloured'. The school applied for her reclassification, which was granted by the government. After this, the police forcibly removed her from her white family and community and allocated her to a coloured family. The case has been used to signal how Afrikaner/white identity had to be heavily policed in South Africa under apartheid. It has also symbolised the suppression of slave and other Black ancestry for white South Africans. Indeed, proclamations about the unpredictability of Black blood fuelled the larger issue of *swartgevaar*[4] which was used to justify the separation of the races.

The response to Linda Boschoff illuminated the response to the presence of a Black family in white Afrikaner history, quite contrary to what van Wyk, the NNP Member of Parliament, argues above. Boschoff's case demonstrated that the casting of Verwoerd as a tragic victim of cultural insecurity was untenable. This was further reinforced when Dimitri Tsafendas, Verwoerd's assassin, was called to the stand to testify to the bigotry of the man now being cast as sensitive and misunderstood. Ironically, while Tsafendas is a household name precisely because of his role as Verwoerd's assassin, he – unlike Verwoerd – died in obscurity in 1999.[5]

The prosecutor's case focused on showing that, far from being a series of attempts to move towards self-definition, the apartheid project recognised that it could survive only if it was brutally and rigorously enforced. Apartheid definitions of whiteness rested on the denial of any kind of 'contamination' by Blackness. The impulse that Coetzee discusses above, therefore, is new even as it parades as an awareness that was previously embraced. Indeed, apartheid could not have succeeded without the suppression of 'racial mixing' and denials of Black ancestry within white families.

The white South African resistance to white racial identity discussed in relation to Coetzee's work above intersects with other processes of 'mixing' in contemporary public and identity politics. For some within the Afrikaner community, the opportunistic assertion of an indigenous parentage participates in denials of the meanings which attach historically to white racial identity. These are linked not only to processes of erasure but also to a specific relationship with whiteness – that is to say, a denial of it – which has become fashionable beyond Afrikaner ranks in South Africa.

These assertions of indigenous African ancestry are ways of accessing not only 'authentic' African identity, but also of denying the implications of living as white people and adults in contemporary South Africa. They are as much about identity legitimisation in relation to Africanness as they are about a refutation of privilege based on race in colonialism and apartheid. Politically, such claims are motivated by a denial of privilege and complicity, of entanglement, and function as a means of dodging critical engagement with whiteness as a racial marker with associated connotations. The timing of these reinventions is coupled with debates about land redistribution to indigenous communities, from whom it was plundered during colonialism and from which Black populations were forcibly removed in a system of laws which guaranteed white ownership of land. These expressions of African descent, therefore, have material outcomes in as much as they have socio-political saliency.

Furthermore, to have a Khoi/slave woman as ancestor is to claim a Black identity, an African indigeneity and entitlement in the blood-based discourses which supported colonialism and apartheid. While the definition of racial subjectivity, 'non-whiteness' and Blackness, specifically in anti-apartheid struggle politics, was premised on the social, political and economic implications of living under apartheid, dominant white definitions of race in South Africa have always been based on blood, and on race as bodily evidence. Those Black South Africans who were classified 'coloured' were inscribed with discourses of 'racial mixing' and 'miscegenation'. Contemporary claims by Afrikaners to have a Khoi ancestor see Afrikaners as occupying the same discursive location that colonial and apartheid discourse relegated to coloured people. These claims contradict earlier racist meanings attached to being coloured, given that the 'miscegenation' led to the construction of coloured subjects as 'leftover', 'without culture' and 'lost'. Rather than deconstructing this earlier impulse, recent Afrikaner claims to coloured positioning are not attendant to implications of this repositioning in relation to historical subjects constructed and classified coloured.

While appropriations of Khoi and/or slave women as Afrikaner ancestors permit the rehabilitation of both memory and identity in contemporary South Africa, they also fall short of doing the work of postcolonial memory. Consequently, although claiming a woman of colour as foremother superficially undermines white supremacist narratives of white racial purity, this subversion paradoxically works to mask historic and current meanings of whiteness.

A third project which addresses itself to the wide presence of slave ancestry in Afrikaner families is the documentary *The Commander's Slaves: A Different Kind of Landed Gentry*, aired on e-tv in 1998 and produced and directed by Ramola Naidoo. The women whose lives and lineages are traced in this film lead to the highest, most privileged of Afrikaner families. These slave women were sold to commanders and generals at the Cape in the seventeenth and eighteenth centuries. In her review of the documentary for the *Daily Dispatch* of 1 July 2000, Barbara Hollands remarks:

> [i]t should be quite an eye opener, because what most of us don't know is that these slave families ended up in a variety of enterprises like agriculture and wine farming and exerted considerable influence in the Cape.

Here, Hollands's comments show the splitting ability of race consciousness in white South Africa: the ability to make both the claim of always having known, in van Wyk's vein above, and the collective ignorance of 'race mixing' indexed by Holland here. It is part of the 'new' phenomenon that Bishop Tutu would talk about in relation to apartheid amnesia, post-1994, where '[w]e were soon to discover that almost nobody would really now admit to having supported this vicious system' (1999: 15).

Ramola Naidoo's project proposes more than the fallacy of white racial purity. By tracing slave women as the grandmothers and great-grandmothers of apartheid South African presidents like Louis Botha, the filmmaker goes further than this. She locates the presence of slave ancestry not only in the highest Afrikaner families, but also makes it clear that the white supremacist project of 'racial purity' assertion was a *conscious lie*. It was fabricated deliberately, and relied on the active repression of the memory of specific, known members of these families.

In his discussion of the documentary on the South Africa L-Archives in July 2000, Mansell Upham points to certain glossed-over facts in Naidoo's representations of the slave women. It is not clear from Naidoo's documentary that the women on whom her narrative focuses posed contradictions. These freed women at the centre of Naidoo's text – Angela van Bengale, Catharina van Paliacatta, Maria Everts – are not shown to have been slave owners themselves later. Suppressed is also the presence of their 'criminal convictions, their greed, ruthlessness, dishonesty, connivance, sexual armoury' (Upham 2000). Upham further questions Naidoo's choice not to represent other slaves who were not privy to such fortune. All in all, for Upham the production was an 'elitist and neo-classist, re-caste but promo-friendly documentary by an Indian South African woman of non-Cape heritage' (Upham 2000).

The identified problems with Naidoo's documentary point to the challenges of engaging in a project which dynamically deconstructs racial purity narratives in insurgent ways. Naidoo chooses to challenge this representation and the power struggle it entails. While it has become customary to assert that racial purity, the foundation of all white supremacist regimes, is a fallacy, Naidoo's project goes beyond mere assertion and illustration. Her documentary, the shortcomings identified above notwithstanding, shows the racial purity position in colonial and later apartheid narratives to be a self-consciously crafted position. If the leading Afrikaner families knew that there was slave ancestry in their families, then claims to racial purity and securing privileges based on the coupling of white racial purity with white supremacy, were a deliberate lie.

Naidoo's project offers a useful counter-narrative to those accounts of Afrikaner racial mixing examined above. Her documentary relies on the metaphor of excavation rather than on the currently fashionable claims to the already known, albeit troublesome truths critiqued by Coetzee and Samuelson. The slave women she traces to the heart of leading Afrikaner families do not work to further enshrine white racial privilege. They are not rescued from the recesses of history in order to legitimate Afrikaner claims to African political and material entitlement. Indeed, Naidoo's documentary raises questions of legitimacy which complicate the appropriation studied by Coetzee and Samuelson.

This is the point that Upham's review misses: Naidoo's documentary may be flawed because it does not further probe the complicities of previously enslaved people in the institution of slavery. While recognition of such complicities and labyrinths is important to the larger memory process, its absence from Naidoo's film does not nullify the insights offered by *A Different Kind of Landed Gentry* about the malleability of information used to harness and enshrine hegemony.

Superficially, the uncovering and recognition of Khoi and/or slave women in Afrikaner families is similar. Yet the forms and effects of such uncovering differ markedly. The tendencies discussed in relation to Coetzee's and Samuelson's scholarship, and van Wyk's pronouncement, earlier in this chapter sit uncomfortably alongside Naidoo's film, even as they all emphasise the same previously repressed knowledge. The former regenerate previously inconvenient truths, formerly confined to the level of repressed and unsanctioned knowledge, into the realm of recognised truth in order to protect historic material power. The latter destabilises the meanings of such knowledge by asserting its presence across history in the Afrikaner imagination. Naidoo's documentary is counter-hegemonic and questions the new-found usefulness of such knowledge and, by extension, the political opportunism that leads to the current embrace of that which has been known within Afrikaner circles all along. The evidence uncovered by Naidoo and made public knowledge serves to question the motives of the convenient 'remembering' of slave ancestry by Afrikaners in a post-apartheid dispensation, where their material as well as identitiary privilege is ostensibly threatened. Naidoo's project partakes in the production of postcolonial memory, questioning and destabilising authoritative slavocratic and apartheid epistemes.

Afrikaner identities are not the only South African white identities which opportunistically denounce racial purity in post-apartheid South Africa. Although Afrikaner identities do so most explicitly in the sites identified above, there is evidence of such tendencies in other white South

127

African sites. In what follows, I briefly turn my attention to forgetting whiteness and claiming indigeneity within the academy.

In an article on ways of inhabiting Blackness and whiteness in the South African academy, Zimitri Erasmus has documented the pervasiveness of white denial in South Africa and revealed its influence to lie beyond those considered Afrikaner. Commenting on the epistemic and other kinds of violence directed towards many insurgent Black intellectuals[6] at South African tertiary institutions, Erasmus cites an incident during which, in response to a paper by a womanist historian, she observed 'white liberal scholars passionately avoiding the terrible fate of being marked as *white*' (2001b: 187). This became unambiguous when:

> [i]n an attempt to participate in the discussion, a white feminist prefaced her contribution with 'I am not black, but ...'. She was interrupted by a white female archaeologist who asked her, incomprehensibly, 'How do you know that you are not a black woman?' To her credit, the former speaker did not reply. (2001b: 189)

Erasmus proceeds to demonstrate that such assertions of relationships to whiteness are not unusual. Although different from the example discussed in relation to Afrikaner identities, examined jointly these analyses overlap. Denial of whiteness and a gesticulation towards a position within Blackness is not confined to Afrikaners, as Samuelson also shows, or to public culture. Rather, it permeates even the arena of social science and humanities scholars, who resist using the critical theoretical vocabulary of their disciplines to critique biologist body- and blood-based articulations of racial identity. The archaeologist cited by Erasmus can only ask her question if she believes that being Black/white is about biology, genealogy and blood. Any other conviction makes nonsense of her interruption.

In contrast, in Erasmus's narrative, the white feminist who acknowledges her racial positioning, albeit circumspectly, *knows* that she is not Black because she has lived actively as white all her life, has been assumed to be and read as white, and has participated in South African society as such. Her refusal to engage the interruption suggests that she acknowledges her distance from being Black as due to lived experience.

These fashionable and opportunistic white appropriations of Blackness in South Africa trivialise precisely what they ostensibly celebrate. In conflating Africanness, Blackness and linked identities with the presence of an aboriginal African woman and/or slave ancestor, they depoliticise race and ahistoricise power relations. They undermine the discursive social and political constructions of racial identification. In this manner, attempts by progressive white and Black South Africans to meaningfully come to terms with the country's racial past in order to forge forward are thwarted. Reconciliation becomes impossible because there is no acknowledgement of a past of conflict, violence and white collective privilege. In the midst of a progressive drive towards imagining new ways of claiming agency (Steyn 2001), and of a growing body of scholarship that interrogates whiteness (see Nuttall 2001; Posel 2001; Reynolds 1994; Steyn 2001; van Rooyen 1994), these denials of its existence are appeals to victimhood. They are as much about erasure as dominant white identities were during apartheid: there is no history to make sense of, no reconciliation to participate in, no engagement with white privilege for those who have ceased to be white. In contrast, forced into a different kind of usefulness and servitude, Black women historical subjects are trapped in the same relationship with white South Africans who have repressed their support of apartheid by forgetting whiteness in ways that mask its historic and ongoing effects.

This trendy Blackness is particularly troubling when viewed in relation to notions and responses to colouredness in contemporary South Africa. Black South Africans who were labelled and classified coloured in the various subdivisions of that category registered in colonial and apartheid discourse as 'half-caste', 'bastard', 'God's step-children' (after Sarah Gertrude Millin's 1924 novel of the same name) and their bodies were regarded as deviant, contagious and shameful. The anxieties of 'racial mixing' and 'miscegenation' plagued the colonial and apartheid imagination and a series of laws were enacted to legally curb its occurrence. In colonial and apartheid terms, these were people who should not have existed. Having inscribed coloured bodies with regimes of shame, the reliance on a register of 'mixed ancestry' exoticises this position and trivialises the memory of three and a half centuries of racial terror and pain inflicted on these as well as other Black communities. In the same manner that slave memory was erased from formal history, and that Afrikaans, formed as a creole by the slaves, was appropriated and became a white language, so the presence of Black and white ancestry has now become the domain of white South Africa, as segments of it reconfigure themselves in further self-interested participation in a changed political climate. The relationship of mainstream white South Africa to coloured South Africans appears caught in a continuous spiral of appropriation and erasure.

Further, a national narrative that relies on individual testimonies and experiences at the expense of deconstructive structural power offers such appropriation and erasure an alibi. Indeed, when the complicated terrains of white racial privilege, complicities and other white political agency are reduced to the roles of identified white men, much remains uninterrogated in the cracks. Such uninterrogated material further buttresses the anxiety Helene Strauss (2006) says plagues contemporary white South African identities, given the failure of previous forms of white assertion in the post-apartheid moment. Strauss's scholarship reveals the manner in which 'white South African cultural workers have been working hard to revise available categories of identification and to offer new vocabularies for thinking through inter-subjective relations and racial embodiment in a democratic South Africa' (2006: 179). This chapter has shown that rethinking the tools available to assert identity by white people is indeed a fraught process with vastly different kinds of effects. Against such contested terrain, critical readings of claims to rethink and remix white identities are necessary, as was also clear in the varied reception to Krog's attempts to self-represent.

'AS A SLAVE YOU HAVE TO HAVE FAITH OR YOU'LL GIVE UP': CAPE MALAY/MUSLIM IDENTITY CLUSTERS IN CAPE TOWN

From far away, trailing just out of reach. Echoes. Messages distorted, yet vaguely familiar. Memory. (Chude-Sokei 1997: 14)

Recent theorisations of diasporic patterns centre on the politics of home(lessness), migration and displacement. Because of the differing character of global relocations, however, the indiscriminate application of one set of diaspora theories to make sense of the Cape Malay diaspora examined in this chapter is untenable. Using a blend of diaspora theorisations to filter meanings seems a more productive lens through which to decode the enactment of Malayness in contemporary South Africa. For, while extensive attempts have been made to conjecture the shifting dynamics of African slave, South Asian colonial indenture and Muslim diasporas, these have been theorised for the most part as mutually exclusive in academic literature, with notable exceptions in the theorisation of West Indian diasporas. Where intersections emerge, they do so in relation to more contemporary clusterings of certain identities. Deciphering the functions of diaspora for the articulation of Malay identities in Cape Town exists at the nexus of the aforementioned forced migrations, since Cape Malay or Cape Muslim communities, in their self-identification as such, foreground their South East Asian Muslim foreparents enslaved by the Dutch and British and transported to the Cape.

Most scholars of diaspora trace the history of what Sonita Sarker labels 'Diaspora (with an upper case D)' (2002: 2) to Jewish dispersal from Palestine by both Babylonians and later Romans. They nonetheless note how the term has become 'mobile', as Vijay Mishra posits, to incorporate within its 'updated' meaning later streams of forced and voluntary migrations (1993: 34–35). The latter has increasingly come to refer to diasporic formations of Africans, South Asians and Caribbean peoples 'to the "West" ', movements which cannot be read as separate from European colonial undertakings (Cohen 1997; Sarker 2002). In spite of the increasing looseness of what the term has come to mean, Robin Cohen argues that diasporic people are not just outside of their 'natal (or imagined natal) territories' but also share cultural baggage, often in the form of language, religion and resultant culture. It is within these arenas that collective memory is shown to be the organising principle behind diasporic identity. Processes of yearning for and mythologising about the homeland are used via memory to maintain strong ethnic consciousness over a long time, as well as to problematise the community's relationship with the 'host' place.

An examination of several cultural and religious narratives which emanate from and seek to define Cape Malay/Muslim communities illustrates the above postulations. Indeed, the conflation of Capetonian Muslim and Malay identity, or the use of the two labels interchangeably in the Western Cape, testifies to the manner in which these two seemingly disparate labels are seen to function similarly in a specific local setting. The historian of slavery, Robert Shell, argues that the label 'Malay' followed from the use of Malayu/Melayu as the lingua franca of both the Indonesian region and one widely used until the mid-nineteenth century in the western Cape.

Positing a different view in his 'Re-classifications: Coloured, Malay, Muslim', another historian, Shamil Jeppie, suggests that the 'origins' of the label 'Cape Malay' are more elusive and complex. He bases his argument on the historically shifting naming patterns (Jeppie 2001) in relation to western Cape Muslims. The historical records available cannot be taken as reliable sources on the self-identification of this community from its arrival, predominantly as slaves of the Dutch. For Jeppie (2001: 80):

[b]ecause poor and politically powerless peoples' voices are seldom heard it is hard to say for sure what they called themselves between the arrival of the first Muslims in the latter part of the seventeenth century and the late nineteenth century proliferation of names for them.

This swell of names has included 'Maleier', 'Muslim', 'Malays', the derogatory *'slamse'* and 'coloured Moslems'. Jeppie traces the historical course of this naming, linking it to slavery, colonialism, apartheid and the democratic era in South Africa to show the loaded meanings which attach to identities at the same level across eras, and to occasionally inconsistent ends. Contesting the appropriateness of the 'Malay' label, Jeppie subjects it to scrutiny for both its historical value and the accompanying ideological implications.

This marrying of historically produced dispersal ensuing from slavery with the signalling of political intent is not uncommon in diaspora studies. Jemima Pierre traces the usage of the term 'diaspora' in relation to African peoples in the context of the trans-Atlantic slave trade as a consciously political project of Pan-Africanism. The gesticulation towards diaspora enables Africans in the Americas to show their contribution to the shaping of new cultures, institutions and ideas in the 'new' locations (Pierre 2002). An examination of the multifaceted debates around diaspora identification in the United States and Caribbean contexts leads her to the observation that it has always symbolised a politics: 'a source of political action' for a movement against injustice, racism and colonialism. Diasporic political identification politics has also been historically constructed:

in opposition to still vital/racialist/racist ideologies that depicted Africans/Blacks as inferior: a people without culture, significant history, or national/territorial connection (i.e., Black people in the diaspora had no 'roots', no 'homeland'). (Pierre 2002: 15–16)

Its usefulness, she concludes, is rooted in its deployment as both a historicised conceptual tool and a politics that impacts on identity/ community belonging to transcend national/immediate cultural and historical boundaries (Pierre 2002). Pierre's last point links with the contradictory relationship between recognitions of diaspora location and the politics of nation-states. In a case like South Africa, where Cape Malay/Muslim communities' identification was necessarily negotiated in relation to slavery, colonialism, apartheid and, recently, democracy, it should not be surprising that the same associations have been used to disparate ends. Few cases illustrate the changeability and ongoing needs to negotiate identity like Cape Malay/Muslim (re)positionings in relation to the nation-state. The apparently regional and linguistic signifier 'Malay' at dissimilar stages points to the 'dynamics of location and re-connection' to 'offer a new and more contradictory set of questions and responses', to borrow Carole Boyce Davies's (1994: 14–15) formulation.

Historically, as Jeppie shows, Islam was the dominant religion among the slave and exile community. This was a strand which most resembled the one practised in South East Asia. It could therefore work as a cohesive force within the enslaved communities, at the same time as it signalled difference from the articulations of Islam among Indian indentured communities in KwaZulu-Natal. Islam became central to the identity of Cape Malays to numerous ends. Indeed, there are records of some difficulty in the classification 'Malay' in the (Cape) colony: was the Khoi convert 'Malay' or Muslim? Jeppie suggests 'the Muslim-as-Malay came to be constructed against the Coloured-as-Christian in official and dominant discourses in the nineteenth century' (2001: 82). By 1925, 'Malays' were politically organising in ways that emphasised their differences from both the indigenous peoples and the 'Asiatics' (Jeppie 2001). From the very onset, the identity 'Capetonian Muslim/Cape Malay' was fraught with contradictions and the struggles both from within and without to clearly demarcate the borders could not be taken for granted. Malay/Muslim identity was distinguished both from other Muslim groups and from other (previously) enslaved peoples.

This use of diasporic identity as a separating marker from others in the same geographical colonial space, later nation-state, as well as from indigenous groups, is recognised by James Clifford (1997). This attribute makes diasporas as international as they are transnational. Part of this (re)fashioning of identity relationally involves a (re)negotiation of which experiences to reject, replace and/or marginalise. This is a particularly fraught position for the descendants of slaves whose foreparents played a crucial role in shaping the character of the contemporary 'host' space. Hence, a complete denunciation of the 'new' space in favour of the original homeland can carry the contradictory consequence of effacing the very ancestors contemporary diasporic subjects seek to recognise. This is because current identity formations are always historicised and narrated in relation to memory. Consequently, identification solely with the motherland effaces/denies the contributions made by the forebears to the 'new' location. It therefore serves to collude with the slavocratic, white supremacist system which led to their diasporic (dis)location in the first instance.

However, a denial of diasporic identification via a negation of homeland and links with co-ethnics elsewhere functions to negate the trauma of rupture caused by enslavement and forced transportation elsewhere. Clifford refers to the phenomena described in terms of the mediated tension at the core of living diaspora. It is an inescapable part of the separation and entanglement of living here and desiring another place. This tension, which he sees as defining the experience of diaspora, attaches to loss and hope simultaneously and it can be a source of both support and oppression. Diaspora consciousness is entirely a product of cultures and histories in collision and dialogue. Although he speaks somewhat romantically of this anxiety as having an 'empowering paradox', where 'dwelling *here* assumes a solidarity and connection *there* [even if] there is not necessarily a simple place or exclusivist nation' (Clifford 1997: 269), his framework nonetheless remains an extremely useful one through which to read diaspora.

The particular difficulty of Cape Malay/Capetonian Muslim diasporic identity is well illustrated by the engagement of (sectors of) this community with not only the changing South African state and citizenry, but also with the South East Asian region. In the same manner that post-apartheid South Africa has opened up the terrain of race/ethnic belonging to a variety of meanings, it has permitted the revisiting of earlier positions by Cape Malay/Muslim on multiple belongings. In this respect there is a link, rather than a rupture, between the rejection of a Cape Malay identity during the anti-apartheid struggle and its later rediscovery and celebration in contemporary South Africa.

Muhammed Haron (2001) uses the example of Achmat Davids (1980), a leading historian of Islam in Cape Town, who was once among those who rejected the label 'Cape Malay' as inaccurate and loaded with colonial and apartheid baggage. An identification as Malay was seen among some left-leaning activists and thinkers as a retrogressive step, too closely allied with the efforts of apartheid apologists. It echoed too intimately the conservative impulses present in the work of anthropologists like I.D. du Plessis, who celebrated the high culture of the Malay 'race'.

In the early nineties, however, it was the same Davids who would claim Indonesia as 'ancestral homeland' for most Capetonian Muslims/Cape Malays since they, according to him, would be able to trace their roots 'to one or other island' (Zegeye 2001) in the South East Asian region. Davids' performance indicates the capacity of diaspora identities to generate rival effects. His earlier position suggests that left-leaning, progressive anti-apartheid politics disqualifies a Malay diasporic identification, whereas his subsequent position reveals that the two politics can be wrapped in a relationship of embrace. Viewed in isolation, Davids' about-turn can figure as an exceptional case of an individual who changed his mind. However, there is evidence of a larger communal about-turn having occurred around the same tension of embrace/disavowal of South East Asian belonging, and its claiming as originary homeland.

The instance involving the invitation by Tunku Abdul Rhaman in 1961 is one such case. As the prime minister of Malaysia at the time, he called on Cape Malays to set up home permanently in Malaysia as free rather than as oppressed under apartheid. Rhaman's invitation was seen as both dangerous and unfeasible:[1]

> [i]nstead of a gracious acknowledgment of the invitation there was a muted response to this call. The leading community organizations of the local Muslims simply ignored the invitation, and young political radicals rejected it outright. (Jeppie 2001: 82)

Across the political spectrum, it appeared as though the invitation was unwelcome. That there was no rush to take up the offer even from the more conservative sectors of Cape Malay/Muslim society speaks volumes for the confluence of meanings which attached to disavowing South African citizenship as entitlement, on the one hand, and to acknowledging relationships to a slave past in apartheid South Africa, on the other. For radical progressives, this rejection was in keeping with their identification as Black South Africans engaged in a just, winnable fight against an oppressive regime. This response also demonstrated the ways in which participation in revolutionary activity (anti-apartheid activism) was not only a recourse due to the absence of personal escape (moving to an ancestral homeland). The dismissal of Rhaman's invitation by activists in the western Cape was a conscious underscoring of choice and agency in revolutionary activity. The enticement suggesting that Capetonian Muslim/Cape Malay historic subjects could 'choose' to be unoppressed by changing their geographical location was at odds with anti-apartheid, struggle politics. The young radicals took issue with the underlying ideology behind the call: that there was a limited series of ways in which belonging could be codified in relation to descent. The apartheid state was arguing that South Africa was a white country from which all others needed to be excluded from participation except in service to its 'valid' citizens. By definition, Capetonian Muslim/Cape Malay people were excluded from the category entitled to full citizenship. An acceptance of the Malaysian prime minister's invitation would have been a concession that Capetonian Muslim/Malay people 'belonged' somewhere other than in the republic. Within the binary logic of the National Party regime from 1948 onwards, it was not possible to successfully articulate a nuanced sense of belonging which simultaneously asserted both Black South African and Malay diasporic membership. The latter could be assumed more readily, whereas the former needed constant declaration, validation and defending.

Behavioural patterns in recent years suggest a shift from this earlier rejection of Malay diasporic identification. The new dispensation has seen a proliferation of exchanges between South Africa and South East Asia, accompanied by loud claims of shared parentage and affability[2] on both sides. This has found celebration in renewed articulations of Cape Malay/Capetonian Muslim identities, which are heavily critiqued in the scholarship of many young Capetonian Muslim scholars.[3] Jeppie (1987, 1996, 2001), Gabeba Baderoon (2002), and Ismoeni Taliep (1992) fall among those who disarticulate a Cape Malay identity as part of the recital of Capetonian Muslim/coloured history and identity in the Western Cape province. These scholars read the recent upsurge in diasporic identification as part of a conservative drift in coloured politics, and fault its participants for being inadequately attentive to the ideological basis for diaspora politics. All three are irritated by the failure of the proponents of a Cape Malay diasporic identity to recognise that the convergence of narratives they participate in has political implications for whoever else lives in South Africa and South East Asia. To identify as Cape Malay in the celebratory manner which foregrounds mutual recognition and sameness across the diaspora, negates the 'African' dimension in location as (Black) South African. Diasporic identities are always defined as much towards a community as they are against another, and the rehearsal under discussion is predicated on more troublesome moves. In this ambit:

> a series of ideological projects has attempted to subsume this variety of origins [for enslaved people] into a single identity ... construction of an overdetermined 'Malay' identity [which] can be traced to the ethnographic work of I D Du Plessis. (Baderoon 2002: 7)

This 'overdetermined' identity in Malay diasporic celebrations, because it is posited as 'a single identity', actively functions as a denunciation of contemporary South Africa as a valid/valuable home. Amidst conservative expressions of black domination and coloured marginalisation, thus fracturing Black alliances which pre-date democracy, this rejection is highly troubling for it validates these racist narratives. However, if the same impulse is seen as a desire to open up the terrain of Black internal and multiple belongings simultaneously, it gestures towards creative and progressive ends.

A helpful model for thinking through the above tendencies in this manner is Louis Chude-Sokei's (1997) concept of an 'echo chamber', used to describe how traces of cultures from the motherland, left because of slavery and exile, now interact with contemporary formations crafted in the 'new' space. The echo chamber occurs when 'the echoes [of home] that are new world black cultures have now bounced back creating a complex scenario that can be grasped by the metaphor of an "echo chamber" ' (Chude-Sokei 1997: 7). The echo chamber coined here specifically for diasporas emerging out of enslavement and transportation of Africans, zooms in on the relationship of cultural activities on both sides of the Atlantic. Its transfer value for the communities emerging out of enslavement, but from Asia and Africa, is self-evident. Read like this, it foregrounds the relationships between the original homeland in memory, the contemporary, current synthesised cultures in the homeland, as well as current cultural practices from both diasporic and homeland spaces. The connections are threefold: 'home' and 'new' space are connected to each other historically and through memory; the two spaces are then linked to each other. Chude-Sokei's model speaks to the inseparable relationships diaspora holds with history and with the present simultaneously, and therefore to the task of rememory. This memory, at once concerned with the past as with the present and the synthesising of those two in double-helix fashion, also encapsulates 'black exile, homelessness, racial oppression and an overwhelming desire for a mother-or an other-land' (Chude-Sokei 1997: 4). Finally, Chude-Sokei's echo chamber is a process and place of translation and of 're-translation (an echo of an echo)' (1997: 8–9, 14), and in its straddling of both temporal and spatial dimensions and the synthesisation of these, it works in chronotopical fashion.[4]

Thus it is possible that the 'preservation' that Achmat Davids speaks of as characterising the moment of recognition as Cape Malay and South East Asian people examine one another is Chude-Sokei's echo chamber. The echo chamber is also suggested in Davids' casting of the exchange as a mutual beholding, a gaze received and returned. It is important that part of this gaze is a moment of recognition, an echo, and a shared surprise. The chamber enables this, for Davids speaks to both a geographic and a temporal recognition and to a conversation which then further fuels the mutual interests between different parties.

This chronotopical dimension of diaspora is also evident in how Sarker discusses diasporic phenomena. Sarker stresses that diasporas engender an engagement with origin/belonging, duality of identity and different kinds of transnational identities generated through transnational migrations. Indeed, since diasporas foreground the relationships between those in diaspora and others living in the 'homeland' space, they emphasise the 'implicit belief that cultural practices supersede the changes across time

142

and space diaspora purportedly wrought' (Sarker 2002: 4). Viewed in this light, it becomes clear that both the Malaysian and Indonesian/Cape Malay community exchanges are about mutual recognition and acknowledgement. They are subversive since they challenge the complete success of the rupture intended by slavery. They also bear testimony to the power and resilience of collective memory of home to regulate diasporic identity. Thus, this recognition of 'preservation' is an acknowledgement that there are clear and 'hidden', in Hall's formulation, presences of the 'homeland' in the diasporic culture.

More likely, the impulse and recognition contains the diasporic tension Clifford theorises. Thus, in keeping with reading human behaviour along an axis, both tendencies are likely to encounter one another at unusual slants.

This celebration of Cape Malay identity is problematised for its occlusion of historic points of origins for the said community and its rejection of creolised identity formations. It is attached to a 'series of ideological projects [which] have attempted to assume [the] variety of origins and practices into a single identity' (Baderoon 2002: 7) through which 'the Muslims of the Cape are given cultural roots that are not local at all, nor "creole" ' (Jeppie 2001: 81). Baderoon's and Jeppie's criticism of this inclination towards Malay diasporic celebration flags two complementary and mutually reinforcing energies. The ambiguous naming 'Malay', echoing as it does 'Malaysia', the country, leads discursively to the fashioning of historical origins to confirm the South East Asian region broadly, but Malaysia specifically, as originary homeland. When this is used, as Baderoon argues, to reinforce notions of a simple and singular identity, it is conservative. This conservative thrust works in favour of denying the impact socio-historically and culturally of the African continental location. In Jeppie's formulation, it is an erasure of specificity brought about by western Cape location. Further, when Cape Malay and Muslim are used as though they mean exactly the same thing, this removes the influences which derive from non-South East Asian locations.

This idealism critiqued by Baderoon and Jeppie denies the creolisation which occurs to produce Capetonian Muslim society from slaves and exiles from the Indonesian archipelago and, slaves from East Africa, Mauritius and the southern African interior. It denies the exchange in cultural and linguistic currency between South East Asian enslaved peoples and indigenous African slaves and colonised Others. As such, then, the Malay diaspora celebration discourses critiqued by Baderoon, Jeppie and Taliep proceed as though Malay culture was transported to the western Cape, and remained untouched until recent developments permitted more creative exchanges between Indonesian and Malaysian citizens and Capetonian Muslim/Cape Malay people.

The above is illustrated by Achmat Davids' comment on the initial set of voluntary exchanges between the western Cape and the Indonesian archipelago: '[w]hen we discovered each other there was total amazement on both sides that the culture had been so well preserved in South Africa' (*Mail & Guardian* 25–31 August 1995). Davids' statement is unsurprising for elements of the home culture are always present and processed in the emergent creolised culture in the 'new' location. Stuart Hall (1990) has argued against the fallacy that homeland cultures are absent in new diasporic creolised cultures. Using the Afro-Caribbean context, he shows that this claim is one belied by Africa's pervasive presence in the consciousness of the Caribbean. Although '[a]pparently silenced beyond memory by the power and experience of slavery', it is discernible across time in:

> the everyday life and customs of the slave quarters, in the language and patois of the plantations, in names and words, often disconnected from their taxonomies, in the secret syntactical structures through which other languages were spoken, in the stories and tales told to children, in religious practices and beliefs in the spiritual life, the

arts, crafts, musics and rhythms of post-emancipation slave society. Africa, the signified which could not be represented directly in slavery, remained and remains the unspoken unspeakable 'presence' in Caribbean culture. It is 'hiding' behind every verbal inflection, every narrative twist of Caribbean cultural life. It is the secret code with which every Western text was 're-read'. It is the ground-bass of every rhythm and bodily movement. This was – is – the 'Africa' that 'is alive and well in the diaspora'. (Hall 1990: 398)

Hall's reading of the memory of the original continent in the rememory and cultural presences of African diasporic people in the Caribbean resonates beyond the specific regional space he concentrates on. In many respects, most scholarship on diaspora processes verifies the survivals of home culture in diasporic societies at varied levels of intensity, both subtle and overt. In Hall's terminology, diasporic society reflects home culture in narrative as well as in less obvious epistemic forms. That these are 'hiding' in language and the meaning-making system it shapes has been observed about Capetonian Muslim/Cape Malay identity in some recent scholarship. The research of Anne Lyon (1983) and Kerry Ward (1995), for instance, has gone some way towards demonstrating the typicality of the Cape Malay diaspora. Their respective studies have confirmed the discernible diasporic echoes Louis Chude-Sokei's opening quotation above intimates.

Lyon's research has shown the echoes and traces which are moments of recognition among several South East Asian diasporas, while Ward demonstrates that Cape Muslims are re-examining identities in contemporary South Africa as 'an indication of the political fragmentation of political identities in the aftermath of [the] ANC's [African National Congress's] banning and the diffusions of the struggle against the apartheid state' (Haron 2001: 4). This appears to be in keeping with Stuart Hall's work, not only on the processes which constitute identity but also on the ways in which '[d]iaspora identities are those which [are] constantly producing and reproducing themselves anew through transformation and differences' (1991: 52). Read together, this corpus of scholarship suggests that the location of the memory of South East Asia can be recovered from the cultural, linguistic and artistic crevices in contemporary Capetonian Muslim spaces. The extent to which these presences are 'hiding' in 'secret code' points to the synthesisation, which is to say, creolisation, of this memory and presence.

Given this understanding and recognition of echoes processed through memory at various stages from slavery to the present, the criticism levelled against conservative recognition of Malay diasporic identity makes sense. The difficulty with Achmat Davids' statement on the preservation of Malay culture in the western Cape, and how *well* this has been accomplished, points to a denial of the processing of these echoes by Capetonian Muslim/ Cape Malay historic subjects. Davids denies this creolisation in a move which also appears to break with an African-linked identity. It is the absence of an African reality at the precise moment of the overdetermination of the Malay diasporic subjectivity which gestures towards the conservative impulse critiqued by the likes of Baderoon and Jeppie. When the roots of Capetonian Muslim/Cape Malay subjectivity are seen to be solely in South East Asia from whence they were transferred wholesale under conditions of slavery, and remain still identical to contemporary cultural manifestations in the homeland, the suggestion is that they were not affected, impacted upon in transit or upon arrival in the western Cape. It is a stress on a return to the homeland which should be unsurprising for a diasporic community, given that it testifies to that defining tension discussed in relation to Clifford's theorisation of other diasporisation processes.

This desire for return is also evident in the 'Three Hundred Years of Islam in South Africa' festival which was hosted in the western Cape in 1994. Interestingly, while there are different Muslim communities in South Africa, the festival focused specifically, and exclusively, on western

Cape Muslim history. This is due to the coupling of this festival with the Capetonian Muslim/Cape Malay society's relationship to the South East Asian region. This focus meant that the other significant Muslim population within the country, to be found among communities descended from Indian indentured labourers transported to the sugar plantations in KwaZulu-Natal in the nineteenth century, was excluded. It also occludes the influence of Islamic strands from the African continent brought by slaves from Muslim societies of East African and Mauritian origin. The conflation of the history of Capetonian Muslim societies with that of 'Islam in South Africa' further reveals the intertwining of religion and region in constructions of identities for Cape Malay communities. It also demonstrates that this identity is often maintained in ways which highlight specificity, and set it apart from other similar and/or parallel communal identities circulating in the South African populace.

More recently, Haron (2001) has suggested that tendencies within Cape Malay communities towards recognition of diasporic identity invite a fuller and relational reading of coloured subjectivities. He suggests that when the entire continuum of coloured identities is examined, these formations reveal themselves to be a terrain which can be mediated 'without having to reject the one for the other; bearing in mind that the conflict of identities remains problematic without a satisfactory solution in sight' (Haron 2001: 1). Nonetheless, the conflict remains a creative one, and one that opens up more powerful and nuanced possibilities for coloured subjectivities and collective identity constitution. The creativity of conflict does not detract from the difficulty of inhabiting constantly refashioned identities, however, even if the communities themselves participate in this repositioning. Importantly, for Haron attentiveness to emergent discourses is in step with other re-evaluations of racialised identities in a post-apartheid South Africa. Indeed, the constant layering of rupture means that collective trauma is an attendant part of the series of renegotiations of identity from slavery, through colonialism, apartheid and in response to contemporary political factors. Haron's comment on the relationship between conflict and the absence of a 'satisfactory solution in sight', rather than being a romanticisation of resolution, draws attention to the materiality of the oft-theorised 'creative conflict' to reveal instability as ensuing. Haron's analysis also demonstrates the trickiness of engaging the flux in identity processes without trivialising the attendant layering of pain as part of that insecurity. In reading the above tussles with positions in relation to an accepted Malay diasporic identity, the flexibility of all identity formation processes is underscored. The examples above which show a shift, or apparent about-turn, in politics of self-location vis-à-vis the Malay diaspora show this quite forcefully.

It seems particularly apt to take note of Carole Boyce Davies's prescient caution on scholarship which interprets migratory subjectivities. Noting that '[t]he ongoing inquiry into meaning has to resist closure as it holds itself open to new meanings and contests over meaning' (Boyce Davies 1996: 15), she authenticates this by talking to the tendency of migratory subjectivities to set up several defiant 'home places'. These are series of imagined communities, networks of kin which can sometimes have a foundation in essentialist categories. In light of the foundational bias, these categories need to be subjected to complex consideration given that they can 'also become a kind of flirting with danger as they too have the potential of being totalizing discourses' (Boyce Davies 1996: 7). The above intricacy notwithstanding:

> reinterpretations or reinterrogations of questions of identity offer opportunities to rethink a variety of categories with which we work and which we identify as 'automatic' categories, as if meaning remains constant and understandings of identities never change. (Boyce Davies 1996: 19)

It allows a reading of Capetonian Muslim articulations which reveals various representational layers to better reveal the category 'Cape Malay's' multiple textured surfaces. This is in tune with Zimitri Erasmus's (1997) invitation that a reading of coloured identities needs to be especially mindful of the attendant hy-bredie-sation processes at play. This nuanced appraisal of creolisation developments, and appraisal of these identities in various relationships of hy-bredie-ty, would move away from historical oversimplification of coloured subjectivities. Such an approach would not occlude these conservative impulses even as it uncovered a range of creative self-significations.

RELIGIOUS DIASPORA AS 'HOME SPACES'

If the celebration of diasporic identity relates to exilic desire for and attachment to home, as much diasporic theory cited above suggests, the use of 'Muslim' interchangeably with 'Malay' indicates that Islam, or more appropriately being Muslim, is made to function in ways similar to South East Asian origin. There has been an upsurge in explorations of how religion can be, and is, mobilised across various contexts to function as a home space for those in the diaspora.[5]

Julius Dasmariñas (2003) has postulated that religion can allow co-ethnics in the diaspora to facilitate connections and contestations with regard to the larger community of that religion. Here, the religious place can be the bridge between spiritual home and homeland, facilitating more successful negotiation of bicultural allegiances. In such cases, religion can be framed as a safe, familiar locale which can grant shelter from certain pressures present in the larger society.

Enslaved peoples carry the convictions and religious systems of their motherland with them and continue to synthesise them upon arrival in the 'new' place. Other slaves in the African diaspora, especially those transported to the Americas, held on to African Traditional Religions (ATRs) to produce Santeria and so forth. Alternatively, Africans in the Americas incorporated ATR rituals and precepts into Christianity alongside Amerindian/Native American belief systems, or emerged with creolised religions such as Rastafari. South East Asian and East African Muslim slaves, political exiles and many converts from regions of East Africa where the dominant religion was *not* Islam imbued western Cape adherence to Islam with the variety of purposes and meanings discussed above. Even if the dominant form of Islam practised by slaves was that from the South East Asian region, converts and Muslim slaves from elsewhere did not leave the practice and experience of Islam unmarked. The further complications which arose when Indian and Mauritian immigrants arrived in South Africa in the last decades of the nineteenth century injected further meanings and places into Muslim life in the western Cape.

In Rayda Jacobs's celebrated novel *The Slave Book* (1998), the character Sangora Salamah from Java is a devout Muslim. In his introduction to the reader, his Malay and Muslim identities are not only coupled, but also jointly foregrounded. These remain the key characteristics through which Jacobs's narrators unravel and clarify his behaviour. Within the first chapter, in a scene which details his transportation from the auction block, Islam is presented as a place within himself to which he can retreat. In a scene whose trauma is echoed throughout narratives of enslavement, autobiographical and fictional, he has just been separated from his wife, Noria, and the reader's eye is drawn to how:

> [t]the wagon was loaded with all the goods that the farmer had bought, and Somiela and Sangora rocked back and forth between the barrels and the sacks. She didn't have to look at Sangora to know his thoughts. In his head he would be saying a prayer. In his eyes, nothing would show. (Jacobs 1998: 20)

The two slaves, Sangora, and his stepdaughter, Somiela, are loaded onto Andries de Villiers's wagon en route to the wine farm which acts as setting for the bulk of the novel's narrative. Their position on the wagon emphasises their status as his property, two of the 'goods that the farmer has bought'. This contrasts sharply with what are revealed to be the inner workings of the slave characters themselves. If slavery works to subjugate and violate the enshackled through its excessive emphasis on their corporeality, it makes sense for a novel which seeks to be an imaginative 'scratch at the surface'[6] of slavery at the Cape to direct attention to the mental, emotional and social aspects of slave characters. Somiela's and Sangora's thoughts reveal more than slavocratic society would like to know. The 'goods' rocking back and forth in the wagon are two thinking beings: one speculating about her stepfather's thoughts, and the second deep in prayer. Significantly, he has the ability to pray without being detected. This ability to mask and reveal himself at different times is a skill linked to him in a variety of ways.

The capacity of Islam to offer a special space for slaves is reinforced through the slave Arend. In conversation with Somiela, his mother Rachel remarks on the links between Muslim identity and various forms of subversion which are explored further in the novel. During a veiled warning to Somiela, Rachel announces about the slave-owning class:

> They'll punish us if they think we listen to the religious nonsense of the Mohametans. They don't mind the Mohametans working for them – we have one here called Salie van Celebes – but they don't want us listening to them. There is a house in Dorp Street where the Mohametans teach people. ... My son, Arend, the interpreter – the people in Dorp Street have converted him. He has a Mohametan name also, Ali, but they don't know in the house. They don't know he's converted. We're not allowed to turn Christian, so what god do we have? How can we marry? The Mohametans will marry you. God recognizes this marriage even if the law doesn't. (Jacobs 1998: 30–31)

This conversation, which occurs quite early in the text, points to several attributes which will later be cemented with Muslim identity. Islam is opposed to Christianity – one as the religion of the slave owners whose membership is heavily policed, and the other the religion of the enslaved. Rachel's query about the need for some kind of deity and sacred scheme is solved by conversion to Islam by the slaves in Cape Town. It is only Islam that allows the slaves to be fully spiritual beings. Christian membership is prohibited to the enshackled, and the protracted debates throughout slavocratic societies in the western Cape and the Americas in the eighteenth and nineteenth centuries demonstrate the necessity of prohibiting Christianity for slaves. Islam offers an alternative for the slave characters in Jacobs's novel, suggesting a similar role in the lives of the unfree in the western Cape. Islam is also linked to literacy. Part of the subversive activity that the Muslims ('Mohametans') engage in throughout is accessing literacy, which is then kept hidden from the slave masters. At the moment of freedom, even the otherwise authoritative slave narrating subject, who is revealed at the end to be Sangora, notes surprise that so many skills had been obscured under slavery, most hidden even from friends.

Dasmariñas (2003) postulates that '[m]igration is, therefore, a theologizing experience' in cases of traumatic migration to societies hostile to the arrival of people from elsewhere. This theologising encounter provides an escape from the oppressive environs in the 'new' place of arrival. However, the ability of religion to work as home space is best illustrated through the collective accessing and uses to which it is put in the 'new' residence society. In these instances, religion can be used to secure and create a home away from home, a liberated zone (Dasmariñas 2003). The above conversation suggests that Muslim places in the slavocratic society of the novel function as free locations.

Given that part of the machinery of the slavocratic order is the objectification and dehumanisation of the enshackled, Muslim spots in the novel work as sites where slaves acquire book literacy and acknowledgement as spiritual and cerebral beings. This is the subversive aspect of Islam as it is made to function in Jacobs's novel, echoing colonial slave society in the western Cape. Thus Muslim districts, like 'Dorp Street', acknowledged and recognisable as religious, can be reformatted in the service of other social and historical needs and organisations at different junctions to meet (a)rising needs. Islam represents a form of rebellion and a spiritual home for slaves who can convert.

The coupling of Malay origin and Muslim identity in Jacobs's narrative lends credibility to the belief in the slave-owning class that 'the Malays were the sly lot, taking every opportunity to rebel' (Jacobs 1998: 14), even as there are suggestions that there are large-scale conversions occurring from the slave ranks. In accordance with the dominant ideology of the slavocratic society portrayed in the novel, there is a hierarchy in the valuation of slaves. For the slave owners, Malay slaves are the most difficult to contain, to successfully subordinate. According to this stereotypical thinking, they are unpredictable and are known to lose control 'without provocation'. This makes the Muslim slaves particularly troublesome for the slave-owning class.

If the colonial slave society bars access to Christianity, literacy and whiteness, as part of the regime of slave objectification, the novel inverts this valuation system in favour of Muslim/Malay identity. In the novel, Islam is used as trope through which to redeem the slave characters from overdetermination by the discourses of the master class. This is in line with Louis Chude-Sokei's (1997) postulation when he discusses diaspora formations and the competing identity dynamics they give rise to. He argues that the artistic and cultural formations emerging from these enslaved peoples and their descendants often take place in ways which challenge knowledge-making under slavery. The Malay slaves, as those born into Muslim society, are the most sympathetically portrayed and occupy the highest rung in *The Slave Book*'s judgement. In the revelation of the most authoritative narrating position being Sangora's, Muslim/Malay positioning is also cast by Jacobs as authorising trope. The revelation that the introductory voice and final narrator in the novel is Sangora demonstrates that the reader has, at the end of the novel, come full circle. This is an impression that the 12 chapters serve to reinforce. In addition to being mentally adept, Malay/Muslim characters are said to be 'master crafters', an allegation that emerges at several points in the novel. It is this mastery which explains the 'high' price the males fetch as slaves.

Sangora, most symbolic of this group, is the most sensitively represented character in the novel. He is also the most complex, and best educated, 'a carpenter and could read and write. They didn't know he came from a line of caliphs and sheikhs and had a high religious background' (Jacobs 1998: 110). He is endowed with a questioning mind and a humane nature which surfaces sporadically to surprise the other slaves. For example, he defends the stereotypically depicted East African slave Kananga,[7] who brutalises other slaves: 'Don't you see? He's forced to act against us. That's another way to keep slaves apart' (Jacobs 1998: 56). This comment demonstrates his sophistication and ability to observe the institutionalisation of slavery while the other slave perspectives against which he argues focus on the minutiae of their condition.

Collective Muslim identity is defined as that which is both humanising and supra-human. This representation seems to capture the sentiment ascribed to Sangora in the narrative, that '[a] normal man [sic] needs his God. Now what about a slave? As a slave you have to have faith or you'll give up. You don't have anything else' (Jacobs 1998: 157).

Research into religious diasporas, here Muslim rather than Islamic,[8] has shown that belonging can be premised on an identification with a shared history and understanding of an individual's place 'in a community of believers (*Ummat-al-Islam*)', and it is this which enables the communication of (comm)unity in religious praxis across regimented spaces (D'Agostino 2003). The Muslim slaves in Jacobs's novel share this recognition and it is important that those who convert are taught various means to access this space. For slaves, Islam offers recognition as human, with all the ensuing associations. While religion can be said to function quite centrally to various societies' self-definition and constitution, Islam at the Cape took on an additional series of significances. Particularly for Malay slaves, transported as they were from Muslim locations, it was a direct connection to pre-slave pasts. Islam functioned to support the slaves' link not only to the homes from which they were wrenched, but also to one another; to older senses of community as well as to newer clusterings with other slaves with different geographical origins, but shared religion. It offered for the enslaved a connection to an identity prior to capture and exile: a home. Islam offered for the converts a worldwide family in the *Umma(t)*.[9]

The allegiance to Islam, and belonging to the *Umma*, explains how religious home space not only allows diasporic co-ethnics to recommune, but also invests the constitution of a multi-ethnic community with a sense of transnational ties. This allegiance can be unpacked through translation (theory), where it is made to function:

> as a tool for shaping memory and creating a connection to Muslim diaspora that transcends the individual's ties to a national homeland, by placing the focus on the transnational aspects of the religious community. (D'Agostino 2003: 7)

Thus an allegiance to the *Umma* can be galvanised to differing ends to organise trans-ethnic as well as co-ethnic subjectivities and to support these politically. Given the varying geographical locations from which peoples enslaved and made to work in the Cape were drawn, the prominence of Islam as the religion of the majority of slaves offered an already pre-existent identity which pre-dated the enforced character of those enslaved. That the religion of the enslavers, Christianity, was part of the machinery used to deny the slaves humanity and subjectivity further worked to cement the variety of ways in which Islam could work as counter-discourse to slavocratic doctrine.

Equally important, given Christianity as the religion of the enslaving Europeans, Islam gave the Asian and African slaves a significant and visible form of difference from the ruling class. Precisely because their religion stemmed from a different place, it carried dissimilar implications for emergent political and social affiliations. Given the dehumanisation undergone through the process of capture and ongoing enslavement, Islam also offered the slaves a spiritual/mental space of retreat through which they were reinvested with full humanity. The long tradition which accompanied their religion, and the new ways in which it was able to familiarise people from various locations, restored to the Muslim slaves a source and place of pride which contrasted sharply with their current position, where they were shamed.

Islam was able to reinforce this fully human position and pride in numerous ways. The presence of other *free*, which it to say *not enslaved*, Muslims in the western Cape in places like Bo-Kaap enshrined the ability of Islam to work as a freedom index. In Jacobs's novel, these are represented by the 'Dorp Street' community discussed earlier in the chapter. Significantly, this is the 'blood' family that Harman Kloot, the white convert to Islam, discovers. Upon realising the truth of his brother's warning that 'Black blood's a funny thing. You never know when it will surface' (Jacobs 1998: 137), Harman is challenged by the knowledge that Boeta Mai and his family are *only one* of several Black branches of the Kloot family whose existence is kept hidden from Harman and his siblings. Confronted by Boeta Mai with clear evidence of earlier interaction between his father, Roeloff Kloot, and this Black side of the family, Harman wonders:

Why had he done it? Was it to let Harman Kloot know that he, Boeta Mai, had white relatives, or that the Kloots, who had hurt his mother, had slave blood? In either case, it was born out of arrogance and he was not such a man. (Jacobs 1998: 160)

156

Later, Harman realises:

> It certainly wasn't his father's intention to tell him about these
> relatives. Why had he kept it from Harman? His father had told
> him about his real mother, how she had walked away from her new-
> born son, left him under a tree for the jackals; why not this? Was it
> a greater shame than having a half-breed son? But Harman knew
> what it was. A half-breed son spoke of a father's carelessness – he
> could be forgiven the indiscretion of his youth – not of slave blood
> running through the veins of the family. (Jacobs 1998: 161)

Interestingly, when Harman finally unearths a place where he
experiences 'belonging', it is through entry into a Muslim community
headed by the Black Kloots. Significantly, the leadership of Boeta Mai
again echoes the male Muslim leadership in ways that run counter to
the brutal Dutch/English masculinity on offer. Like Sangora, Boeta
Mai is gentle, cunning and generous. When Harman embraces them,
he finds communality and family symbolically and literally. As with
all other markers of identity, the religious arena used as home space
by the diasporic community is made to function to inclusive and
exclusive ends for the co-ethnics in diaspora. Indeed, even for those
characters who are not first generation Malay slaves, Muslim identity
offers a connection to a mythic homeland which elevates them above
other slaves in characterisation. Islam ultimately holds the potential
to redeem and re-humanise the objectified. It also offers a site for the
performance of a gentle and intellectual masculinity which contrasts
sharply with the regimented, heavily policed and armed Christian
presence in Jacobs's narrative.

A Malay identity, along with an embracing of Islam, is both a positive
marker of identity and a celebration of pre-slave memory. Given how
much had been taken away from the human beings who were enslaved, it

was important for Islam *not* to be the religion of the dominant class, and therefore one of the few dimensions of which they could not be robbed through the process of enslavement. In the inverted world of Jacobs's novel, 'Muslim' becomes the highest order of achievement for any of her characters. This remains the case even if Sangora repeatedly and graciously asserts that Harman, prior to his conversion, is also a man of the book, meaning the Bible. However, precisely because this second 'book', the Bible, is used to justify slavery, Salie and the other slaves are sceptical of Sangora's assertions. Salie fumes and replies: 'Who do you think locks us up at night? Don't be so naïve, Sangora. It's the people of the Book' (Jacobs 1998: 132). The contrast between the two books is emphasised here, despite the importance of book literacy for both the slave and the enslaving strata of society.

Salie's anger at Sangora's plea is historically justified, for:

> [d]uring the process of colonization ... the book was perceived by the [Europeans] as a carrier in which knowledge from the New World could be deposited, as a carrier by means of which signs could be transmitted to the metropolis, and, finally, as a text in which the Truth could be discerned from Falsehood, and the Law imposed over chaos. (Mignolo 1994: 261)

The exchange between Salie and Sangora also demonstrates the extent to which choosing Islam is still caught up in the rationalising logic about worth which justified enslaving people deemed 'inferior'. Given the prominence of the book, primarily the Bible, but also other forms of writing in the slaving missions and doctrines of European powers (Cliff 1990; February 1981; Mignolo 1994; Walvin 1986) from the fifteenth to nineteenth centuries, the long legacy of Islam and its written tradition in Arabic served as powerful antidote, even if purely symbolically, for those slaves captured from Muslim locations. Since the book was used as the primary icon of colonial knowledge systems, and as 'evidence' of numerous forms of European 'superiority', the *Qur'an* and *Hadith* and their role in Islam, along with the ancient Arabic written script, could be drawn upon as counter-discourse to the claims of European superiority. This emerges quite clearly when one considers the staunch adherence to Islam throughout slavery to the present in the western Cape, and the accompanying claims to Malay (and sometimes even Arab) identity in the contemporary Capetonian body politic. Since Muslim/Malay identity, both collective and individual, is cast as inversion and subversion of the Dutch/English Christian colonial slave order in the western Cape, it works to unsettle claims of slave inferiority. However, to the extent that the inversion does not alter the terms, it challenges the resultant ideology which propped up slavery but not its apparatus. Cape Malay/Capetonian Muslim is still shown to be 'not inferior' through the attribution of a long literate history, an inscribed religious tradition and demonstrable artistic mastery represented by the repetition of 'master craftsmen' as a descriptive attribute for Malay men in the novel.

For converts in Jacobs's novel, the embrace of Muslim personhood needs to be demonstrated and earned at several levels. For instance, even after Harman has revealed himself to have committed 'race treachery' by siding with the Koi-na against the Dutch in a battle which sees him fleeing to the western Cape for safety, this is not enough to redeem him from the category 'Christian'. The slaves at Zoetewater are unconvinced that his defence of the Koi-na is significant enough to alter their opinion of him. This may make him a white man unlike others, possibly because his mother was herself Koi-na. However, it is not enough for Salie, Arend and the others to fully consider him an ally. Significantly, upon his conversion to Islam, they at last deem him deserving of their faith and their unguarded friendship. Revealingly, the choices are presented in order of increasing importance, so that Harman's conversion to Islam also sees his final exit from the prospect of enjoying white privilege, even in a different locality. It is a space he needs to denounce in order to be welcomed into the Muslim sphere. However, as he abandons his previous life, he is required to act more honourably by embracing that branch of his family that is Cape Malay. Again, it is only through his entry into Capetonian Muslim society that he is represented as a man within a community, rather than as the isolated individualist he was represented as prior to his conversion. In Muslim society he finds commonality among men who are principled, and loyalty to religious family. His entry into Muslimhood coincides with his marriage to Somiela, ex-slave, and his admission into the Black branch of his family. Both are shortly followed by his fatherhood. The crafting of Muslim space, sanctity and authority in Jacobs's text serves to reinforce the ability of institutionalised religion to function as much to connect as to mark difference. This separation from the Christian slave owners, and connection to the larger *Umma(t)*, shapes the significance of Muslim identity as subversive identity in Jacobs's novel.

Although Aysha Gamiet moves, like Jacobs, from the same coupling of Muslim/Malay identity to signal subversive histories, she synthesises this resistant tradition differently in her essay 'Moslems of the Cape: Descendants of Indonesian Freedom Fighters' (1985: 15; see also Ali 1986). Gamiet uses historical and diasporic connection as an authoritative position from which to enter into international and local politics. She focuses specifically on historical sources and memory accounts from contemporary Cape Town to participate in both South East Asian and Black South African identity cross-political currents. As an activist-writer, Gamiet stresses the resistance of her forebears in the face of European conquest and enslavement as a way to problematise the action of other members of the diaspora, this time in 1985 Indonesia.

Her essay highlights the manner in which shared pasts and memory do not automatically produce a community of ideals and shows that this cannot and should not be taken for granted. Thus a shared history of resistance does not neatly and automatically translate into revolutionary politics in the present. Through this argument she points to what James Clifford would later detail as the tensions inherent in diasporas, *given their entanglement in global histories*. Thus, the mere fact of shared ancestry is seen to be insufficient to ensure Indonesian rebuttal of the supporters of apartheid, as Gamiet would hope. Her work demonstrates that diasporic co-ethnics cannot be relied on to cohere in predetermined and thus predictable ways (infinitely), even if Islam and the identities which accompany it signal community. Gamiet notes that Muslims still visit the *Kramat*, Sheik Yusuf's grave, every Easter as a ritual of memory:

> [t]hey come to pay homage to the man they revered as one of South Africa's first revolutionaries. They cover the grave with coloured, embroidered silks and flowers, burn incense and recite prayers from the Koran. (Gamiet 1985: 15)

For Gamiet, this is a particularly constructive legacy given that the positioning of Sheik Yusuf as an early revolutionary links directly to the liberation struggle she participated in against apartheid at the time of writing and publishing her essay.[10] Her essay demonstrates clearly the manner in which embracing a South East Asian diasporic subjectivity can be achieved at the same time as holding an identity deep-rooted in South Africa. For Gamiet, there is no sense in which these need to compete.

The visit to the *Kramat* every year has become for Capetonian Muslims/ Cape Malays one of the ways in which slave memory is processed. In Jacobs's novel, Sangora flees to Hanglip, the navigational mark used in Sheikh Yusuf's grave. While rituals performed during *Ramadaan* and *Eid* stage the belonging to the *Umma(t)*, they are intoned in locally inflected ways which are influenced by the history of slavery referenced by Gamiet above and Jacobs (1998). Muslim areas of commonality in *Umma(t)* fortify the ability of identities to work in the service of religious diaspora.

161

This is further supported by, for example, the learning of Arabic, as well as rituals around food and cleanliness that are shared across Muslim communities. These similarities, as well as other Islamic practices, offered a space of commonality under slavery even when home languages differed. The adherence to Islam and the manner in which virtue could be coded signalled physically in precisely the opposite way to the racist framing of slaves as dirty, exceptionally earthly and sexually lascivious. Indeed, some of the rituals required of Muslims at certain times, like *Ramadaan* and *Eid*, as well as certain forms of dress – even though not (necessarily) performed for impact upon the slave master class – worked to challenge dominant racist discourses on slave characteristics.

Restraint, regulation of pleasure, abstention and other ways of visibly adhering to Islam were direct testimony to the presence of self-will in the slaves. They also signalled agency since slaves could, like the characters in Jacobs's novel, be part of those who 'converted and refused to do certain things because they interfered with their new beliefs' (Jacobs 1998: 31), and at other times Islam could be the invisible internal retreat, as demonstrated by Sangora's praying discussed earlier in this chapter.

Islam, as noted by Jacobs's character Rachel, also validated relationships of love, marriage and family for slave communities in ways that Christianity did not. The recognition of consensual (heterosexual) unions permitted the enslaved re-entry into recognised human status which challenged the slavocratic order. The acknowledgement of their choice signalled their location in the continuum of pleasurable and willed activities which evidence the humanity they were told they lacked as slaves.

Read together, Jacobs and Gamiet, although referencing the same era in divergent genres, suggest a confluence of memories produced and (re)produced through practices of remembering and storytelling (Brah 1996). Brah suggests that a reading of diasporas as partaking in and reproducing contradictory dynamics gains from an attentiveness to how history affects the narrative and narrativity of memory to differing ends. The pairing of diaspora and the collective memory used to work in its service reinforces both the link with co-ethnics elsewhere and, as shown by Jeppie's reading of Achmat Davids' 'preservation' discourse, some of the most virulent assertions to purity.

'IS THE SECRET IN COOKING?' CODED FOOD, SPICE ROUTES AND PROCESSING MALAY IDENTITIES

This chapter builds on the discussion on diaspora started in the previous chapter with literary texts and other written narratives. I now turn to analyse Cape Malay/Capetonian Muslim food and Berni Searle's installations as visual sites that individually and collectively encode diasporic slave memory. There are both overlaps with literary embedding previously discussed, and distinct strategies evident in the exploration of diasporic meanings within these two visual texts. In this chapter I am interested in the kind of meanings suggested by visual cultures that are not immediately associated with each other but both of which, nonetheless, receive much public attention. In many respects, these visual texts challenge received notions of how diaspora and slavery are articulated by their location and through chosen framings. Through attention to detail and the interpretative frameworks posited by the communities themselves, in the case of Cape Malay food, more engaged possibilities emerge that are in keeping with the continuum approach evoked in relation to Carolyn Cooper's theorisation in the previous chapter.

Viewing the Malay diaspora through different artistic channels illuminates the territory of diasporic articulation. Olu Oguibe and Okwui Enwezor (1999) have invited a commitment to reading 'contemporary African visual cultures' without privileging appraisals that focus on 'the construction and contestation of identities; identities fashioned by others and foisted on Africans; identities contested and rejected by Africans' at the expense of 'African perspectives on the question of identity, and on the parameters of cultural narration' (1999: 12). Mindful of the vast literature on diaspora and slavery in creative forms, I am nonetheless concerned here with excavating the kinds of meanings that are directly suggested by the visual cultures under analysis, and in answering the question: how do the texts theorise?

Similarly, Gabeba Baderoon (2002: 4) asks: '[i]s the secret in cooking? In recipes, shared or hoarded? Or do the secrets of food lie beyond taste?' Here, she gestures to the connections between food and political processes, subjected to much academic scrutiny in recent years. Her questions invite an engagement with food that stays with the materiality of food even as it moves beyond the mere corporeal engagement with Capetonian Muslim eating spaces. In other words, Baderoon alerts us to the ways in which what is meant by food's contexts is layered beyond the immediately obvious. She also introduces the importance of thinking about food processing as a site of deep social activity, as Fraser and Gunders (1999) also stress. Thinking through food as metaphor reveals these layered contexts of connection to others, creativity and continuity.

Public, written sites which link Cape Malay identities with food abound. They range from popular cook books, most notably those by Cass Abrahams, to numerous websites which claim to provide various clues on Cape Malay culture more broadly. They hint at key shifts in the shaping of subjectivities and collectives.

The variety of forms and ideologies of these sites testifies to the knotty relationships between Cape Malay identities and food. An example of this is the Knowledge Network's page on the Cape Malay. The education/information engine renders Cape Malay cuisine central to examinations of Cape Malay distinctiveness and culture. Tellingly, in the background historical section, the information given on post-emancipation society posits:

> [t]hey came to be known collectively as Cape Malay, since despite their diverse origins as far afield as East Africa and Malaysia, and

166

[sic] they all spoke the 'traders' lingua franca' – Malay. When they were freed, they settled on the land on which they'd been living, and the Bo-Kaap in Cape Town is where most of them now live – *and cook*.[1] [Emphasis added]

Later referred to as the 'rich culinary heritage of their slave forefathers [sic]', Cape Malay cuisine is declared to be 'as exciting, colourful and varied as the Cape itself [and] widely recognized as a unique aspect of South African culture'.[2] Importantly, unlike prevailing depictions of Cape Malay cuisine, the Knowledge Network grants more nuanced consideration to the dynamics of food-space as memory landscape. The history of enslavement is contextualised alongside rules which govern *halaal* and *haraam* foods without undue stress on these facets of Cape Malay food customs.

Indeed, along with an acknowledgement of the creolised origins of Cape Malay (food) culture as a merging of (South East) Asian, (southern and East) African and European influences is a rooting of contemporary Cape Malay articulations within a South African context. This format harmonises with that adopted by Cass Abrahams, food historian and cook book writer. The reprinted version (C. Abrahams 2000)[3] of her most famous Cape Malay cook book – *Cass Abrahams Cooks Cape Malay* – stresses the connections between the cuisine and its South African location. Subtitled *Food from Africa*, the book is touted as a hybridised cuisine, distinctly South African. It is, after all, *Cape* Malay. Introduced in the foreword by M.C. D'arcy – a medical doctor and columnist on art from a Muslim perspective in *Muslim Views* – as offering an array of feasts for the reader's and cook's delight, it is a compilation from a community about which he writes, 'nowhere on this planet is there a community so fervent in thanks to the Almighty for the blessings of the table'. To accentuate the combination of tasteful artistry, the blurb declares that, in this expanded edition which includes a few select dishes from other South African communities:

> Cass hopes to take dishes which have been passed down from generation to generation for well over 300 hundred years out of the family kitchens and on to the menus of the restaurants of South Africa so that everyone visiting our shores will be able to savour the flavours of the unique Cape Malay cuisine.

This attention to detail in Cape Malay cuisine, to exceptionality which is nonetheless anchored to South Africa, is echoed by other commentators. Shamil Jeppie observes that for Muslims in Cape Town, the 'premier art is food' (in Baderoon 2001: 4). Thinking about and describing Cape Malay cuisine in a myriad of aesthetic frames is typical of conversations around this food culture. Such anchoring of food consumption, discussion and processing in the aesthetic realm does not disavow its concrete meanings.

The materiality of food is most easily associated with the parameters which govern who can consume what, where and with whom – the terrain of power regulation and subversion. Food histories for Cape Malay/Capetonian Muslim societies connect with the history that the famous spice route was also the slave route; that the processes of cuisine differentiation for the European colonial project were linked with the brutal transportation of people from the same places. This is as true of the Portuguese slave raids in East Africa as it is of later Dutch trade through the Dutch East India Company. Thus, the blending of tumeric, garlic or cumin into Dutch/English colonial society, or the absorption of piripiri and allied peppers into Portuguese (and later Dutch/English) colonial cuisine went hand in hand with the enslavement of Asians and Africans.

Historically, slave communities have been pressurised to make the most out of available culinary resources. As previous scholarship cited in preceding chapters on creolisation evinces, conditions of necessity and survival also often give rise to expansive creativity. When the community under discussion is Muslim, the added layer of time and food type emerges. To the extent that food practices are inevitably caught up in the power dynamics which inscribe both those who offer and the consumers of food, these are valid areas of inquiry. The associated sensations for food relate to collective processes that avoid 'indigestion of identities', to borrow Elspeth Probyn's (1999) phrase. This becomes evident when food is used as a means to think through the inscription and rejection of identity as determined by shame, greed, hunger and (dis)pleasure. Against this backdrop, analysing the mnemonic terrain that is Cape Malay food recognises the histories of enslavement, colonisation and apartheid, at the same time that it should decipher the narrative possibilities for agency offered by representations of the cuisine. Embodiment is inescapable for living beings, and the lives of slaves were overwritten by discourses which stress their corporeality. Eating is part of this inescapable bodily presence. In this respect, it is logical that food cultures can provide stability for displaced communities living under conditions that deny them control over their lives, over their specific nourishment, and can therefore provide enslaved people with the power to heal or harm.

Baderoon (2001, 2002, 2007) speaks of food information as part of the negotiation of the sociality of food. There are obvious facets and secret crevices in food cultures, she suggests. The hoarded or shared recipe makes and recasts meaning and so food communicates more than just taste, suggesting that there are additional meanings just below the surface. Food is integral to how communities define themselves and how they demarcate boundaries of that belonging (Fraser & Gunders 1999). Consequently, a label such as 'Cape Malay food' signals relationally what it is *not* as much as it does what it is.

The role of the Capetonian Muslim/Malay diaspora connects with how Baderoon discusses the gendered textures of Muslim food in Cape Town. Her interviewees confirm the centrality of community to the transmission of knowledge about identity through food. Selection, preparation and textures determine the reception of food in as much as these processes are themselves inscribed by specific histories. Historic inscription refers to both meanings gathered through historic inheritance, as well as to the ways in which such historic weight continue to disrupt meanings in the present. For example, food can be used to counter current dislocation experienced due to the 'absence of a fuller Muslim presence in popular culture' (Baderoon 2002: 4) as well as offer a site for contesting dominant cultures during slavery, colonialism and apartheid. As Baderoon observes, food is never simply about consumption; taste is equally about images and memories. Nor, it must be added, can Cape Malay/Muslim food be seen purely as a response to a politics of rupture, dislocation and victimisation through the various systems of terror which pre-date democracy. A discerning eye recognises that making Capetonian Muslim food can chart a 'creative rather than nostalgic relationship' to home (Baderoon 2002: 4). The processes of mixing, inventing and discovery underscore all creolised cultural and artistic modes with detailed historicised meanings.

This creative process pertains to the terrain of identity at numerous levels. Remarking on the configurations offered by her interviewees that '[f]or the older people, cooking symbolises the structures through which important family traditions are sustained', Baderoon observes how food can function 'both as a means to overcome feelings of homelessness, and as the basis of a comfortable and creative relationship' (2002: 9, 12–13). Comfort and creativity are relevant for imagining community into being because:

> communities redefine themselves and are defined by others not by face-to-face relations but by (a) their right to define a collective past, a definition with homogenizes the different kinds of memories preserved in different visions of the community; (b) the right to regulate the body and sexuality by the codification of custom; and (c) the consubstantiality between acts of violence and acts of moral violence. (Das 1995: 15–16)

All of the above are evident in the constructions of Cape Malay diasporic identity broadly, but more specifically in relation to the terrain of eating. According to Veena Das (1995), diasporic communities are able to shape a creative mnemonic narrative for a variety of ends. These demonstrate the manner in which Capetonian Muslim/Cape Malay communities function as political actor rather than as a face-to-face realm of relations. Here Das's reading rhymes with theorist Jemima Pierre's (2002) conceptualisation of the political value of diaspora living.

Writing of another diaspora, the Palestinian–American one, Lisa Suhair Majaj (2001) has suggested that when food acts as a vehicle for memory, it mediates the experience of rupture inherent in diasporisation. The preparation, selection and sharing of food becomes a space for sustenance of cultural memories in diaspora. Where food is this vehicle, or one of them, the burden often falls on women. In this regard, Suhair suggests that domestic spaces may take on contradictory empowering and disempowering features for women, who have to negotiate competing individual and collective demands.

Baderoon's research testifies to the continued gendered dynamics of food as memory-space even when those responsible for the preparation are not always women. Indeed:

> [t]he ability of women (and some men) to wield power through food when they themselves are subject to forces outside their control is displayed in these stories ... the food itself carries evidence of mutability, of dynamism and complexity in the present and the past. (2002: 14)

All her respondents accord value to the transmission of food knowledge, demonstrated, for example, in the disdain for buying Cape Malay recipe books rather than resorting to family recipes. It is not only the relationship to quantities and forms which matters here, even if these act as containers of creativity. The creative memory terrain of Cape Malay cooking is circumscribed by a sophisticated relationship to networks of knowledge. It is not only whose knowledge that matters, but also where and how it is accessed.

A preponderance of images of Muslims alongside food in Cape Town nonetheless coexists with a near total absence of Cape Malay dishes in most Capetonian restaurants, leading Baderoon (2004, 2007) to coin the phrase 'ambiguous visibility' to describe this disjuncture. Ambiguous visibility describes how the narrow spectrum of representations of Cape Malay/Capetonian Muslims is shorthand for proper knowledge. Thus there is at once hypervisibility of Cape Malay 'culture' and erasure of complex Capetonian Muslim histories beyond the visual and linguistic idioms permitted in constructions of visibility. Ambiguous visibility functions in the aid of stereotype, where the discursive implications of this visibility and its parameters remain unexamined. Baderoon's (2003) theorisation of the ambiguous visibility of Cape Malay cooking is linked with dominant approaches to Islam. Since Cape Malay is often used interchangeably with Muslim in the Capetonian context, it was able to function as a means of dealing with Muslim presences in the western Cape. This would have been reinforced under apartheid when this region was the stronghold of the United Democratic Front, a united coalition of anti-apartheid activists and organisations formed in 1983.

When considered as an artistic tradition, Cape Malay cooking, its registers and gesticulations, can be analysed in conjunction with other genres of artistic engagement emanating from similar spaces. Indeed, V.Y. Mudimbe has suggested 'that we consider African artworks as we do literary texts, that is, as linguistic (narrative) phenomena as well as discursive circuits' (1999: 32). At the same time, as both Baderoon and I have suggested separately elsewhere, Cape Malay food, its registers and its public appearances offer careful readers a type of archive that requires multifocal readings. Whereas Baderoon (2004, 2007) has argued for the recognition of Capetonian Muslim food as an archive with specific demands that the researcher has to be sensitive to, I have insisted on the importance of reading Cape Malay food for the kinds of agency that are occluded in conventional archives, which are nonetheless very limited for women slaves in the South African context (Gqola 2004, 2007).

Mindful of the above, against the background of Cape Malay spicing and cooking cultures I now turn to a critical appraisal of selected works by the internationally celebrated Cape Town-based artist Berni Searle. The installation components chosen as part of this chapter speak to the processes via which diaspora, gender and geographies convene and detach. They reference spice routes as/and slave routes in manners which resonate with the Cape Malay cooking negotiations discussed above. I read her installations as linguistic and visual texts which foreground the preparation and synthesisation of diaspora and competing identities.

Kobena Mercer speaks precisely to the performance in Searle's work when he writes of the paradoxical finding of freedom through the exploration of a prior loss as 'the body becomes a site for translation and metaphor' (1999: 284). Against the backdrop of Cape Malay cooking, Mercer's observation applies as accurately to the preceding Cape Malay cuisine discussion. It serves to highlight the relationality between the different art forms analysed as spaces for the exploration and processing of Cape Malay/Capetonian Muslim identities as diaspora culture.

SPICED BODIES IN MOTION:
TRANSLATION IN BERNI SEARLE'S ART

> Less an external substance than a cultural co-efficient, spice behaves like a computer program, simulating value. To paraphrase Shakespeare, some commodities are born spicy, some achieve spiciness, and some have spiciness thrust upon them. (Morton 2000: 3)
>
> Creating is making visible. (Lakoff 1994)

Provocative in both her themes and her media, Berni Searle's creations speak directly to the topic at hand. Her substantial installations have a resolute presence which she plays with. In equal measure she gesticulates towards what might be absent, missing, suggested or lost. Her materials are small, everyday matter: spices, bottles, film and boxes that at once signal to the recognisable and serve to destabilise meanings. The individual objects she plays with are commonplace and seem mundane in their meanings. At the same time, they have weighty suggestive capabilities. Their apparent simplicity belies the incredible sophistication of Searle's artistic techniques and burning implications. Desirée Lewis reads Searle's work 'under the rubric of "conceptual art", a practice in which core assumptions of realistic art are questioned' (2001: 108), a reading that rhymes with Salah Hassan and Olu Oguibe's (2001) more extensive definition. They note that conceptual art as a category makes sense when its three key characteristics are seen as propensity towards self-reflexivity, moving away from clear categorisation (as either 'object' or specific genre, such as painting), and shift to the authority of framing and context over the actual parts of the artwork. They continue to note that 'conceptual art has never been a monolithic practice or unified artistic discourse but a contested field of multiple theoretical practical positions' (Hassan & Oguibe 2001: 70).

Resisting materials which most audiences expect to see in art, and replacing these with more transient products and forms, Searle's installations operate more by hint than by direct quotation. It is possible, in the examples analysed here, to discern a series of commentaries through attention to the repetition of (Black female) body, spice and colour, even if her work contests space and opens up text to a series of multiple significations.

The names of the sequences articulate dimensions within the struggles for identity explored within the exhibition. Searle's art installations are suggestive of 'a cognitively attractive view of human creativity' which triggers a series of associations because '*inspiration* is a matter of knowing what to borrow, and *creativity* is a matter of knowing how to reuse and blend that which is borrowed' (Veale 1996: 1).

Her installation 'Girl' (Figure 1) offers a side view of the same horizontal woman's body lying on her back. This is the artist's body, repeated three times, with each row quartered. The artist's body is in the frame and the sequence gestures to Jacques Derrida's notion of iterability;[4] although 'repeated', the sequence with the 'girl' lying in horizontal frames changes with each repetition. What is important is both the emerging pattern from the similarities, and the new accruing meanings which emerge from the introduction of difference with each frame. This works at various levels. From top to bottom the colour of the spices is red, brown, yellow. Closer attention reveals that the intensity of the colouring varies as well so that the yellow spiced body has a larger presence in the bottom frame than either the red or the brown seasoned ones before it. Here some of the intextual references made include histories of spice as metaphor. In western texts there is an old association between women's bodies and spice/s/ing, anchored in the book 'Song of Songs' in the Bible and again later in another tradition by William Chaucer in his *The Miller's Tale*.

Both these traditions conceptualise of woman and spice as separate entities, and the spice is seen to alter her in some way. In these same traditions, the 'spicing of the body appears to move in two directions at once, forward and backward, to resurrection and to youth' (Morton 2000: 5). Different and continuing creative traditions would use spice as vehicle for ideologies which sought to inscribe women's bodies differently. Indexing these traditions and later Orientalist ones, Searle invites an engagement with these forms of knowledge generation around bodies and, to use Zine Magubane's (2001) formulation, with 'which bodies matter', when and to whom.

Viewed from left to right, the installations repeat a segment of the body in decreasing percentages of overlap. Frames one and two have breast and upper arm repetition; two and three have lower abdomen and pelvic area duplication; three and four have a negligible part of the lower shin/leg recurring. Finally, the bottles on top of each of the 12 frames, although repeated, are arranged to form different patterns.

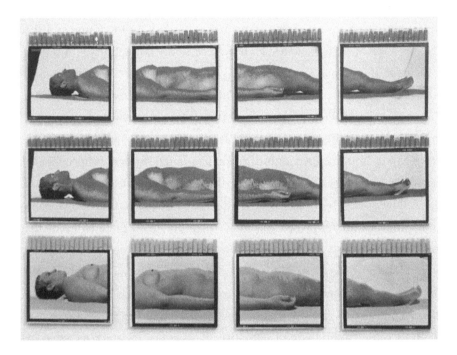

Figure 1: *Girl.* From the 'Colour Me' series. 1999.
Images, courtesy Berni Searle.
Medium: Mounted colour photographs, glass tubes, spices.

This repetition invites an engagement with the conceptual metaphors where creating is making visible through various re(-)presentations. If repetition can be used to foreground both similarity and difference, as in Derrida's iterability, concentrating on small details leads, by suggestion, to an awareness of what is important in the whole. However, given that the whole is itself fragmented, there is the constant displacement or deferment of closure. The merging of creation and exemplification in Searle's work is in keeping with the manner in which sites and means of creation/creativity are indexed and destabilised in equal measure, sometimes at the same time. This is further illustrated by the manner in which the (processed) artist's body is incorporated into the installation.

Rory Bester (2003: 9) observes that:

> [t]he racialised body often intersects with the gendered body. Explorations of the gendered body, especially in relation to questions of nakedness and nudity, can be distinguished by the difference between self-representation and the representation by others.

The confluence of histories against which Searle's inserted body can be read include both the histories of colonised and enslaved bodies on display, on the one hand, and the artistic tradition of transforming naked women's bodies into the nude, which begins with European oil paintings and finds echoes in contemporary practice. About the latter, John Berger (1972: 53–54) has observed:

> [t]o be naked is to be oneself ... To be nude is to be seen as naked by others and yet not recognised for oneself. (The sight of it as an object stimulates the use of it as an object.) Nakedness reveals itself. Nudity is placed on display.

Searle's art choices are an engagement with some of these traditions, as well as feminist artists' responses to this artistic tradition where the woman artist's body 'was often deployed as an act of reclamation' (Coombes 2003: 246).

Lying on her back, open to the gaze of the audience, the woman in the artwork appears helpless, still; an impression which the frames seem to confirm. However, the installation at the same time evokes a range of intertextual associations. It gestures towards two apparently divergent associations. The first connection hints towards one of the most famous of magic tricks where a magician 'slices' a woman into several parts. That the different body parts in Searle's piece will not fit into one box but rather create a 'spilling over', drives home the illusory nature of the compartmentalisation. The use of her own body in her installations, or traces of it, interrupts bodies of knowledge and offers her body as evidence. Searle's choices in this regard further undermine the expectations of passivity in the artistic tradition of the nude and of the obedient poses assumed by the magician's assistant. The use of her body locates 'Girl' within the terrain of artistic and ideological representation where these two are posited as stubbornly tied. It also resists the positioning of the artist/creator outside the observed piece and focuses the eye on multiplicities of positioning. This is appropriate given the second association evoked by 'Girl'.

The other (famous) image suggested by 'Girl' is that of the cross-section of the stowage deck of a slave ship. Coombes (2003) has further noted that such compartmentalisation gestures to colonial 'scientific' inquiry which preserved and presented body parts as 'evidence', as discussed in Chapter 2 with reference to Bartmann and O/other exhibited bodies. The colours of the spices suggest connections to slavery and trade in spices during European expansion from the fifteenth century onwards. The image in question is made famous in relation to the trans-Atlantic slave trade, which is to say the enslavement and transportation of African peoples. This work's upshot is a connection to this slave trade and a broadening of its imagery to other aspects of the same slave trade beyond the transportation of people to the Americas and, in fewer numbers, Europe. The particular inflections that are introduced because Searle uses her own body spiced in a slave ship foregrounds the reality that diaspora and other:

> issues of exclusion, political mobilization on the basis of collective identity, and narrations of belonging and otherness, cannot

be addressed adequately unless they are located within other constructions of difference and identity, particularly around gender and class. (Anthias 2002: 620)

Anthias suggests that questions about which particularities in diaspora serve to silence women are necessary, as much as she stresses the need to investigate how patriarchy, capitalism and other power hierarchies stifle specific forms of diaspora experience for women. Her work is particularly well suited for a reading of Searle's art, given that the installations under discussion engage with precisely the difficulties of representing Black/ diasporic women's experience and the processing of those experiences. This becomes an urgent project, especially for those subjects located as Black/diaspora women in overdetermined tropes where they mean symbol and little else. Anthias cautions against the superficial inspection of diasporic cultural and artistic spaces, since ways of looking and being looked at are themselves immeasurably implicated in the value and ideologies of the results they uncover. While Hall (1990) underscores the value of probing the minutiae of diasporic people's collective lives, laying language and artistic production to extensive scrutiny, Anthias's analysis underlines the centrality of interrogating the interpretive lens itself since societies are always influenced and stratified according to the differentials of power at work in the world system (even if the specific manifestations are localised).

According to Sharmilla Sen (2002), the solipsist reductionism against which Hall and Anthias caution can best be avoided through attentiveness to the overlapping of diasporas suggested in Searle's installations, which draw on African/Asian slave iconographies. Sen points to the complicated nature of diasporic processes and identification, since the same diasporic space can be occupied by various competing claims and inter-temporal contributions. Importantly, diasporic belonging and claims can overlap and compete so that the descendants of slaves in the Western Cape can not only claim a South (East) Asian and African diasporic identity, but different sectors can foreground dissimilar aspects to a variety of ends. Thus, claiming a Cape slave foreparentage suggests both African and Asian descent, but the extent of the suggestions *means* differently. Furthermore, the relationship of the two is complicated by the chosen form of self-naming in as much as it rests on collective positioning in relation to imposed labels of identification such as 'coloured'.

The artist uses her own body in many of her works, challenging the dynamics of power and highlighting her agency, corporeality, as well as the ways in which she has been written on, coloured by processes which she evokes from the past. The spices do not cover her evenly, as '[s]pice is a linguistic and ideological operator rather than an essentialised object' (Morton 2000: 3), nor do the boxes/frames capture and enclose parts of her satisfactorily. The suggestion of movement, the spilling over of body parts, the uncontrolled repetition which implies that the bottles will never be rendered uniform, and so on, all suggest uncontained/uncontainable movement. This presentation foregrounds multiple associations, hinting at the ability of the mind to create, explore and move even as the body is tied down, or boxed in under slavery, like Sangora praying in the wagon (see Chapter 4). These suggestions also blend well with the hint of a magician's trick to engender a reading of movement and slipperiness. Spice and body are particularly useful media to explore this slipperiness, as is the label 'colour[ed]' echoed in the title of the series ('Colour Me') of which 'Girl' is a part. Here 'coloured' in its many meanings, gradations, instabilities under slavery through colonialism and during apartheid, stirred into the mixture of displayed Blackwoman's body, works well for fluidity with spice since the latter is 'itself more a flow than a solid object: as pulverised substance, it has already been liquefied' (Morton 2000: 5). Both Blackwoman's body and spice are over-inscribed in systems of slave and colonial significations, since:

spice also binds Searle to a cultural heritage that is located in the 'border' space between migration and Diaspora, between colonialism's forced migrations and apartheid's refusal of diasporic identities. (Bester 2003: 15)

In 'Girl', then, Searle makes connections with the classification 'coloured' under apartheid, stirs in her gesticulation towards diaspora location, and dishes up its contribution to her identity as a gendered process. This is as much through the use of spices as it is through her reference to a clearly adult woman's body as 'girl'. Here she references the tradition of critiquing the widespread racist references to adult Black women and men as 'girls' and 'boys' under apartheid. The varied spices suggest process, preparation and change; in other words, they vibrate with cooking processes. Indeed, this reading is supported by Searle's own words to Bester, where she notes that '[t]here is always some kind of transformation that the body undergoes in the process of making the work, which is often taken further when it is exhibited' (2003: 16). The echoes of slave ship stand for movement and location, while the hint of magic suggests that all is not as it seems. The spices, varied, are spread over her but do not cover everything: the experience of slavery/apartheid/ oppression is not all she is. The spices also suggest her fashioning of herself and the synthesisation of her own identities, gesturing at the self-reflexivity that Hassan and Oguibe (2001) reference. This reading also supports the working of Derrida's iterability since older identities stemming from displacement are layered over by more recent experiences of 'colouring' and displacement under apartheid.

According to the information which accompanied this installation at the South African National Gallery in Cape Town, Searle's 'maternal great-grandfathers' came from Mauritius and Saudi Arabia and 'married Malay women'.[5] In a later statement she was to reveal:

[m]y great-grandfather from Mauritius was a cook and I have indirectly experienced his expertise through the food that my mother cooks, pointing to food as cultural signifier. Apart from my physical features, very little connects me to this heritage, one of the tentative aspects being food. ... This effectively means that the local or potential indigenous part of me can be traced by looking at my lineage of my maternal and paternal great-grandmothers, i.e., women.[6]

The above reverberates with overlapping diasporas, cooking in the Malay diaspora as explored above and especially in relation to Baderoon's interviews, as well as with the synthesisation of diasporic belonging. Spice here performs as both a sign of trauma/slavery and echoes the process of diasporisation in the form of an echo chamber. In this respect, it remains an ambiguous and ambivalent medium. Again, this is consistent with the uses and histories of spice for the descendants of slaves, but also, as Timothy Morton shows in his comments on the lingering creative engagement with spice through 'tropes, figures and emblems':

[s]pice is a complex and contradictory marker: of figure and ground, sign and referent, species and genus, love and death, epithalamium and epitaph, sacred and profane, medicine and poison, Orient and Occident, and of the traffic between these terms ... Literary criticism, aware of the complexities of figurative language, is able to demonstrate aspects of this topic which have not been pursued in cultural anthropology and histories of the commodity. It is able to treat issues of rhetoric, representation, aesthetics and ideology including notions of race and gender, in ways that make us sensitive to the power and ambiguity of sign systems. (Morton 2000: 1)

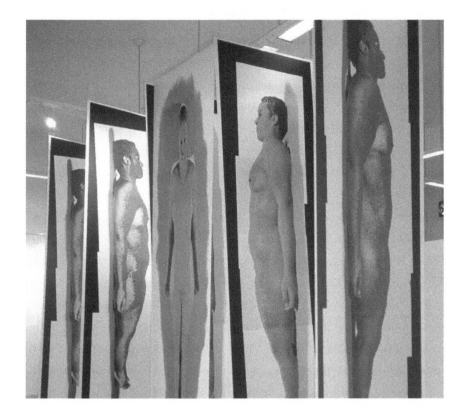

Figure 2: *Red, Yellow, Brown: Face to Face.* From the 'Colour Me' series. 2000. Images, courtesy Berni Searle.
Medium: Digital prints on architect's tracing paper, spices.

Thus, in her 'Colour Me' series, Searle evokes and deconstructs the paradoxes of this history of spice as metaphor, in addition to questioning the means through which these significations can be approached. The spices the artist uses signal both rupture and continuation, gesturing to the processing of bodies, identities and cultures in the process of creolisation which attaches to diasporisation. In line with this, Bester remarks that Searle's use of spices in her 'Colour Me' series matters also for the further associative meanings which emerge from the techniques chosen by Searle. Consequently, the artist presents 'spice that marks her body, spice that marks the space once occupied by her body, and spice that provides a fragrance in the exhibition space' (Bester 2003: 16), further complicating the meanings of what can be discerned in the visibility/invisibility continuum discussed with reference to Baderoon's writing earlier in this chapter.

Figure 2, 'Red, Yellow, Brown: Face to Face', has connection with Figure 1 ('Girl'). Also from the 'Colour Me' series, 'Red, Yellow, Brown: Face to Face' is a play on identities and the fabrication of these. It maintains the rationale reviewed above. Its subtitle proposes confrontation as process. While much of what is said about Figure 1 can be applied to Figure 2, the latter additionally introduces an encounter with compound personifications. When the various tints engage 'face to face', this is as much a bodily contact as it is a conference of ideas. The divergences in information, experiences, expectation and so forth were already hinted at in the citation from Morton's *Poetics of Spice* above. The artist's body is again seasoned with brown, yellow and red powder, this time on digital vellum prints suspended from the ceiling horizontally. Below each, on the floor, is the suggestion of spices that have flowed downwards, again stressing the impossibility of containment and the inevitability of movement. The suspension of the spiced body in this manner ensures that the repositioning of enslavement is not portrayed as a matter taken lying down. Here, spice is used in the same way that Searle later employs clay in 'Julle Moet Nou Trek' (Figure 3), discussed in more detail below: to mark a vacated space.

The different colours are again an allusion to racial classification under apartheid, as well as the ensuing contact and collision of multiple identities. The coloured outlines around the shape of the artist's body also hint at associations beyond, but which are nonetheless linked to, bodily and discursive subjectivities. Together, these prints play with a series of conceptual metaphors which trigger one another off along a train, as much as they reinforce one another. The move between the conceptual metaphorical frameworks is cyclical. The presence of the artist's/woman's body not taking things lying down evokes bodily and psychic presences, embodied knowledge and forms of control. If movement is process but also part of creation (because, Lakoff [1994] reminds us, bringing into being is a creation conceptual metaphor), changing position from here to there is the colouring (also rendering as coloured) process. As much as the installations suggest cooking and processing as movement, they also resonate with taking things apart and examining them in their minutiae. The persistent questions then, which cannot be answered under the rubric of Searle's conceptual art, pertain to the consequences of reassembling these chunks, the same slides and body parts, differently. Does this result in the reconstruction of the same body, at different angles, and can the same knowledge processes be engendered?

In the same way that presence of body distils concepts, as discussed above, its absence in the next figure discussed is compelling. If the body as evidence locates the proof of existence, thereby equating visibility with existence, what happens under, during and through displacement in slavery, colonialism and apartheid? What kind of subjectivity and reality is shaped under these circumstances? And how is it representable? If the body as presence is evidence, how does the absent body map and negotiate subjectivity?

The visual that both animates and stumbles over these questions is Figure 3, 'Julle Moet Nou Trek', from the *Bloedlyne* exhibition. 'Julle Moet Nou Trek' is Afrikaans for the command 'You must move now'. The speaker is separate from the collective s/he addresses in the second person plural, and is therefore secure where they are unsteady. S/he can stay put. The utterance in Afrikaans echoes evacuation directives from the National Party under apartheid. It further conjures up other forms of displacement which tie in with the name of the piece. The evacuated body is represented by the imprint it has left on the sand. The clearly discernible hands suggest an attempt to hold on, thereby showing that the move is not willed, but forced.[7] In addition to the less

185

forceful indentation of most of the body are the pronounced breasts. The reflected movement suggests resistance and stumbling. The body is offered at an angle which suggests that it has been elongated, pulled into the kind of shape it is (in). It is not a resting or comfortable body but a fighting one. The traces of the body on the sand are uneven, suggesting different degrees of impact. The materials used in the piece are in keeping with the title, which is an order; a verbal act of displacement. The interaction of the language which issues an order to move ties in with the themes of dislocation and perpetual motion explored in Figures 1 and 2.

Figure 3: *Julle Moet Nou Trek.* 1999

Images, courtesy Berni Searle.

Installation: Clay powder, glass, feather dusters.

The materials used (sand, ostrich feathers) also root the piece in a particular geographical region. Sand suggests a connection with the coast, and ostrich feathers locate the displacement in South Africa since ostriches are only found here. More specifically, the displaced are in the Cape. The use of ostrich feathers also hints at the inability to escape the situation, since ostriches cannot fly. The combination of ostrich feathers and sand is evidence of coastal South African positioning, even though ostriches were exported from the Cape Colony en masse in the nineteenth century for use in accessories as well as feather dusters. Again, Searle uses commonplace 'domestic' products in her installation to index displacement.

The ostrich feather duster works to signal in a manner parallel to spices in the earlier artworks. It marks displacement through objects transported across continents as symbols of how the exotic and capital flow merge. These goods are used as much for their ideological value as for their association with aesthetics, as 'luxury' commodities in previous centuries. As Coombes (2003: 250) has asserted:

> [m]uch of Searle's work has focused on challenging the ways in which the inscription of color on the body was used as a technology of apartheid. A trademark feature of many of her installations is the manipulation of substances and pigments already resonant with colonial referents and the tropes they produce, such as the spices of the *Colour Me* series (which evoke discovery, exploration, exoticism, sensuality, and slavery) and the Egyptian henna of the *Discoloured* series.

These 'luxury' and 'exotic' commodities rested on an aesthetic valuation premised on unfree labour and displacement. More importantly, the 'Julle Moet Nou Trek' is part of a series on identities, named 'Bloodlines', yet foregrounds disruptions, not continuities, within family. The line drawn links different forms of displacement which ruptured families. On the other hand, bloodlines link the importance of this violent displacement to the maintenance of the fiction of white racial purity and superiority, as well as the status of lineage within patriarchal familial mapping. Bloodlines are about race, genealogy, pedigree and species; they are the stuff of biology and the bedrock of patriarchal race science. Their discourses have been used to rationalise slavery, colonialism and apartheid, to authorise the directive 'julle moet nou trek' and to grant it vicious force. Here, although the name focuses on the utterance, the visual version centres on the displaced and her resistance.

As in previous installations, Searle focuses on the displaced, usually marginal perspective. The experience made sense of is that of the alienated, the disempowered, who nonetheless does not take her lot passively. These visuals not only link with the vulnerability of collectivities under attack and the delicacy of ensuing identities, they also ask questions about the current implications of past processes. In other words, they are mnemonic devices that invite reflection on the meanings of the past in the present.

Figure 4, 'Lifelines', is from the reverse series to the 'Colour Me' series, 'Discoloured'. In addition to the reference to the naming and cataloguing of the Black body, and in the South African case specifically the Blackwoman's body, Searle foregrounds action and the focus on the hands highlights agency (it is in my hands) in the formation of identity. Dis-coloured suggests a deconstructive tendency as well, unlike un-coloured, which is erasure. The series is therefore not about undoing but about breaking down, and also *dissing* 'coloured' as discursive construct that overdetermines.

Hands are important in this representation of colouredness. Given the underlying theme of bodies not taking things lying down, the hand introduces another metaphor for the working of identity. The hand in the frame has a series of overlapping colours, with the effect that the greater part of the hand is black while the margins have a purplish tinge to them. Again, the print is presented in blocks, not as a whole, this time 24 squares in total.

Figure 4: *Lifeline.* From the Discoloured series. 1999

Images, courtesy Berni Searle.

Installation: Digital prints on architect's tracing paper.

This installation plays with juxtaposition, separation and mixing. The colours are blended on the hand held open to the gaze: an allusion to the discourses of racial mixing that have overdetermined coloured identities as much as the notion of coloured body as spectacle.

Literally stained with Egyptian henna, the visible palm conjures up a working hand, perhaps dirty, stained by the dyes used in whatever labour it was involved in. The suggested link with the 'Colour Me' series suggests that it is the artist's hand, which would be in keeping with Searle's presentation of herself bodily within her artwork. The combination of artistic creation and dirty labour that contaminates is striking and no doubt deliberate.

A working hand has agency, so although an open palm suggests vulnerability, it is not a helpless hand that we are faced with but a busy hand. Colouredness and the mental effects of displacement multiply, overlap, join and separate visually here. The dirty hand is a discoloured hand: at once a b/Blackened hand and a colourful one. The colour has not been taken away; it is not colour-less. It is *discoloured*, suggesting that it is not the colour it usually is. This signifies two different levels of meaning which enter into public discourses on race in South Africa historically and contemporarily. With 'the menacing effect of the darkly shaded henna clearly establish[ing] a narrative of trauma within the work' (Bester 2003: 26), a dirty coloured hand cannot be an idle (lazy) hand in accordance with the stereotype of coloured people. A discoloured hand is represented as a hand given more colour, a mix of colours, signifying Blackness in the South African context where white (both as race and hue) is often said to 'not be a colour'. That the hand is dirty from work suggests connections with manual labour with the attendant connotations of working class, unless the hand is read exclusively as the artist's. She could also be seen as indexing the oft-quoted assertion by Hendrik Verwoerd, the 'father' of Bantu Education and former apartheid state president, that Black people were to be educated to make them most useful to white South Africans.[8]

Writing on the representations of land ownership and labour in the white South African creative imagination, J.M. Coetzee has noted that white ownership and relationship is problematised by the Black labour that tills it. As a means of dealing with this, then, Black bodies and their labour are absented from the pastoral tradition of imagining white ownership of land. For:

> [i]f the work of hands on a particular patch of earth, digging, ploughing, planting, building, is what inscribes it as the property of its occupiers *by right*, then the hands of black serfs doing the work had better not be seen. Blindness to the colour black is built into the South African pastoral. (Coetzee 1988: 5)

Given the centrality of land to identities in South Africa, it is unsurprising that Searle makes reference to the position of Black hands to land as part of the dis-colouring process. For, if white entitlement to land is one of the key means of self-construction, for Afrikaner identities specifically but colonial British ones as well, then questioning that entitlement is through an insertion of Black narratives on land. Indeed, displacement and its contestation have been definitive of anti-apartheid liberation movements, and before them of indigenous African resistance to colonial violence.

Further, as Njabulo Ndebele has pointed out, the absence of Black labour from land, and its importance to the *plaasroman* tradition analysed by Coetzee, has significant implications for collective white South African identity formation beyond the ranks of Afrikaners. Extended, it offers a means of justifying all white existence in colonial and later apartheid South Africa:

> Indeed, the South African pastoral was not just a way of writing. It crystallised a way of perception which was studiously cultivated into a way of life. The pastoral is the clinical tranquillity of the contemporary white South African suburb with its security fences, parks, lakes, swimming pools, neighbourhood schools, and bowling greens, all in place without any suggestion that 'they are the product of' human labour. Instead, western civilisation has miraculously brought everything into being. Always hidden behind this legacy of imperial achievement has been the unacknowledged presence of black labour and the legitimacy of its political claims based on that labour. (Ndebele 1990b)

Part of the racist narrative of colonialism, slavery and apartheid links with this denial and erasure of Black participation in the construction of all the facets of privilege and 'civilisation' white South Africa prided itself

191

on. It was part of the underlying justification for violent displacement so that the land could be said to have been 'discovered uninhabited' upon Dutch and British arrival. Later it was to feed into forced removals under apartheid and the constant brutalisation of farm workers. To present, which is to say, make visible, the existence of Black people and their labour in the work of Berni Searle is a counter-narrative to this. Searle highlights the importance of labour to the experiential location of Black subjects in South Africa, first under slavery and colonialism and later under apartheid's racial capitalism.

If the hand is read as belonging to the artist, it links her to this tradition of unrecognised Black labour. It further highlights associations between creativity and hard labour. (Self-)representation is hard work, especially for those who have historically been spectacles. Hands also appear prominently in conceptual metaphors of control, both to confirm and to resist/deny its forms (Lakoff 1994). The hand here gestures towards the dis/ability to handle the colour baggage. The representation of hard work also signals the recognition of the work of survival, the work of memory, and the tradition of work *dissing* coloured constructions. This is supported by the series name, 'Discoloured', 'an obvious semiotic play on a series of visual acts against "Coloured" identity' (Bester 2003: 25). An open hand is also a gesture offering and signalling openness to sharing: an invitation to collective process.

Berni Searle's work tackles the recognition that 'one of the legacies of knowledge is that we who were once the objects of that clinical gaze find it difficult to transcend' (Chude-Sokei 1997: 2), not through a mere observation and comment on this as fact, but through a destabilising process. This is achieved most notably in the installations which feature her own naked body, as she uses the installations to 'draw attention to the legacy of scrutiny, objectification and violation of black women's bodies' (Lewis 2001: 109). So we see how the:

sinister violence of racial classification is registered in the deep staining of the body, convoluted tracings on hands and feet, coloured substances that seem irrevocably to contaminate human bodies, and constant allusions to the relentless inscription of conquered bodies. (Lewis 2001: 109)

Her spices make allusions to processes of displacement and dispersal, and the naming of 'Red, Yellow, Brown: Face to Face' suggests multiple connections with various diasporas of colonised and/or enslaved peoples globally. By locating her body within the arena of representation, Searle opens up the space to invest observation with authority. She positions herself symbolically to ask about the meeting of creatively portrayed positions with represented subjectivities. Her engagement with displacement, destabilisation and diasporisation is an invitation to enter into a myriad difficult questions about identity, process and representation. Clearly, the lines are blurred when the artist herself is embodied as a Blackwoman engaged in a process of representing Black identities in transit and process. What are probed are the histories which locate Blackwomen's bodies specifically, but also Black bodies in general, as spectacle, commodity and object of knowledge. Through offering her body as a layer in her exploration of these themes, she intervenes in artistic and epistemological representation histories. The result is a complex and tricky engagement with what it means to be a Blackwoman artist uninterested in a project that validates the violent distance of representer/represented. Finally, Searle's installations unpack the prospective of representing displacement corporeally through a Black female body in a manner that is not predictable. For, how does a Blackwoman represent the embodiment of diaspora artistically, given the histories of 'grotesque' spectacle and 'exotic' Oriental that attach to dominant historic representations of African and Asian bodies in creative and epistemic regimes which support diasporisation?

As diasporic representations, her installations refuse to be contained and rearranged in the process of exhibition, in a manner akin to other African and African diasporic artists who use conceptual art to problematise notions of origin and authenticity (Hassan & Oguibe 2001). Here Searle chooses media which are multidimensional and which suggest the charting of movement and places opened up by an examination of memory and diaspora. This is the memory-space she enables through her textualising processes.

Read against and as part of the re-imagination of diasporic identities in the Western Cape, Searle's work forces its audience to engage its multidimensionality and its discomfiting tendencies. It requires inventiveness with tracing physical as well as memoried topographies, especially in the absence of oral or other records. Searle has spoken to this as follows:

> [t]racing this lineage is an ongoing process, often hampered by a reluctance of relatives to talk about where they come from, especially those who were reclassified white. Often, amongst 'coloured' people, tracing this lineage is avoided because of the negative stereotypes surrounding indigenous people and slaves that were brought to the Cape. A further complication is the lack of documentation such as birth, death and marriage certificates, which forms an essential part of this process of 'tracing'.[9]

Her representational strategies are at odds with those implicated in the histories which she critiques and unravels. Thus, whereas the work of Graham Huggan (1989, 1990), for example, has shown the manner in which mapping is more than recording and marking, Searle's art does not easily settle for one way of making sense of the past. Huggan points to the static flatness of maps as models of containment that indicate the simplification and privileging of certain readings of the world. In this manner, maps are both spaces which authorise and appropriate knowledge as well as that which is contained on the page.

Maps' representation, as Huggan demonstrates, is not only two-dimensional; it proscribes a more complex, dynamic depiction of experience. This is because colonial mapping 'not only conforms to a particular version of the world but to a version which is specifically designed to empower its makers' (Huggan 1989: 127). It requires what Huggan has defined as the mimetic fallacy to operate successfully. The mimetic fallacy is perpetuated when a/the 'approximate, subjectively constituted and historically contingent model of the real world is passed off as an accurate, objectively presented and universally applicable copy' (1989: 127).

In her work, Searle destabilises the book and the written word or printed map, choosing instead to represent locations as shifting and slippery. This proposal is deferred constantly through the presentation of the artwork as a photograph of movement rather than its repetition. Resisting the flatness of the authoritative text in typical conceptual artistic style, Searle's exhibitions, and especially the installations discussed here, hint at the process of plotting and tracing, rather than presenting authoritative texts in the manner of the colonial mapping strategies described by Huggan.

Searle's work creatively recharts the terrain, suggesting mobility and creative possibilities in the combinations offered by her material, most notably the spices which are at once brutal histories of objectification and a source of connection with the larger diaspora. The creativity of process and change is implied by the presence of spices as an ingredient in cooking. Thus, there is the suggestion of more than one series of subjectivities being processed.

Huggan's theorisation of maps as enablers and as knowledge systems designed to give power to their charters is extremely helpful in thinking through Searle's conceptual mapping of the diasporic identity terrain. Staying with the conceptual terrain as landscape, difficulties are often metaphorised as landscape or navigational challenge. If conceptually Huggan and Searle suggest the reading of geographies of problems, it is useful to ponder, albeit not resolve, the direction in which Searle's navigation leads.

WANDERING STRANDS AND DRIFTS

The foregoing discussion has demonstrated some of the ways in which Cape Malay/Capetonian Muslim diasporas find expression in creative forms. It has revealed that diaspora is not a contained series of engagements, but rather generates and is fashioned in rapport with various historicised power differentials. What has been revealed is the necessity of subjecting a variety of creative forms to scrutiny. It is equally important that the tools of the analysis be receptive to uncovering, discovering and scrutinising the compound enunciations of memory in (contested) diaspora.

Diasporas are untidy identity formations and gesture in numerous directions at once. The Malay diaspora is represented as an overlapping diaspora in all the work examined here, to differing degrees. The extent to which it is so, and the manifestations of that overlay, however, remain contested. This is inescapable and the creativity evident in the articulation of the Capetonian Muslim/Cape Malay diaspora is part of what 'becomes socio-cultural and political manifestations of (post)modernity, embedded in [over] three centuries of dislocation' (Sarker 2002: 2).

The diaspora theory examined here, as well as the examination of the creative forms that theorising diaspora can take, reveals that while diasporas are varied and differently theorised, some of the interdisciplinary work generated in diaspora studies is useful and transferable. While participating in this transfer, it is crucial to be mindful of the specificities. Indeed, the sites examined above demonstrate that the same diaspora, Cape Malay/ Capetonian Muslim, can be called in the service of diverse significations. It remains vital to ask what a diaspora discourse permits subjects to do when evoked, given that the Cape Malay diaspora appears as interested in the homeland in South East Asia/East Africa as it is in maintaining roots in the Western Cape. It seems to challenge and Clifford's (1997) premise that a desire to return always characterises diaspora, since the only return explored here is imaginative. As emerged with the discussions of food in Baderoon, the return *can* only be imaginative.

The relationship of diaspora to rememory, needing constant attention and reworking as suggested by Nkiru Nzegwu's (2000) work, is applicable to Baderoon's and Searle's projects in this chapter, as well as Gamiet's in the previous one. Such imaginative labour also extends to the contradictions thrown up by time in the articulations and associations of Malayness and Islam in the Western Cape. The constant shape shifting and fluidity of the helix-shaped memory permits an engagement with a variety of identities within and through which to claim Cape Malay identity – this need not preclude a simultaneous, progressive Black South African identity, again as Chapter 4 shows.

Indeed, the innovative promise of the identity 'Capetonian Muslim/Cape Malay' seems to multiply even more. It becomes possible for celebrations of Malay diasporas to signify differently across spatial and temporal planes – apartheid and post-apartheid. Like all identities, they can be progressive or intransigent depending on the uses to which they are put, given that location and identity have more shifting symbolic/metaphoric value than fixity and consistency (Huggan 1990). Consequently, when Achmat Davids made that somewhat provocative statement about several Black constituencies seeking distinct identities and having the grounds to explore their specific subjectivities within the Black South African collective in a democracy, in other words, outside of the racist associations which apartheid made synonymous with Black precision, he may not only have been right but may also have invited a useful paradigm shift.

Indeed, if, as Andreas Husseyn has suggested, language is the only home for those in the diaspora, then examination of the applications of words and visual language is a worthwhile pursuit. The blend of primary material analysed for traces of diasporic memory and its processing takes its cue from Husseyn's declaration that 'today, we cannot discuss personal, generational or public memory separate from the enormous influence of the new media as carriers of all forms of memory' (2000: 29). Perhaps, as the history of spice as metaphor has shown, for diasporas arising out of enslavement, even older technologies continue to matter, like spice with a status as 'cultural marker, and a strange one at that, halfway between objects and sign, goods and money' (Morton 2000: 4).

As this chapter and Chapter 4 reveal, to claim Cape Malay identity emerges from the analysis of historic uses of Capetonian Muslim identity, food culture, websites, a novel and several installations, as a gesture toward claiming *both* an African and an Asian ancestry. 'Cape Malay' testifies to the creolisation which defines the experience of surviving slavery in being both 'Malay' and from the 'Cape', in a hyphenated identity resonant with other qualified collective identities by displaced peoples globally. It is the worked-at-ness that spice represents for this diaspora process, given that '*[s]pice is the very form of the idea of the commodity itself*' and '[i]n its derivation from *species*, both in the sense of money and in the sense of sheer appearance, and with value and wealth, *spice* requires us to explore the paradoxes inherent in the dialectics of substance and subject, appearance and reality' (Morton 2000: 4–5). The spice metaphor in food, and in Searle's installations, reminds us that spice is language, context-specific and unstable. When spice is seen as part of the narrative of Searle's text, its ability to act to suggest the process of creolisation as part of the experience of diaspora is illuminated. The attachment of creolisation to diaspora is visible in many of the texts chosen for analysis here.

However, even in the recognition of creolisation, it is worth taking note of the warning sounded by the writer and scholar Maryse Condé (1999). She uses the example of the Martinican literary movement of *Créolité* to show that creolisation discourses can themselves be used to marginalise the place from which slaves were wrenched historically. Condé further

198

highlights shortcomings in the conceptualisation of migrant communities as dysfunctional, devoid of means of synthesising the confused conglomerations of their own identities. To do this would be to trap these communities in binary oppositions which require that they choose conclusively either the one or the other. Rather, the space of diaspora can be creative, and the possibilities and combinations it advocates can arise, as the case of the Cape Malays analysed above proposes. She links this creativity to explorations of authenticity, so that, as she suggests, legitimacy ceases to be something that is opposed to hybridisation and thus allied to purity, but instead is itself a shifting signifier, being remodelled all the time. Therefore, when Jeppie, Baderoon and Taliep (1992) question some of the impulses in favour of celebrating Cape Malay origins in South East Asia, they recognise a rather hesitant engagement with creolisation sequences and histories rather than a complete dismissal of the processing of identities through memory. Indeed, if, as Condé suggests, the celebration of creolity can work to displace the position of South East Asia in the Cape Malay/Capetonian Muslim imaginary, the resistance to forms of creolisation should be unsurprising. In the work examined here, it emerges quite clearly that '[e]mbodied intelligence provides rhetoricians with a way of putting the individual back into cognition without invoking naïve individualism' (Oakley 1998: 1).

To extend Condé further, it seems that the re-cutting, reformation and reformatting of the meanings and entanglements of the signifiers' identity and authenticity are themselves in a state of flux, which runs contrary to current theorisations of authenticity and ensuing discourses as undesirable. This re-examination is explored in relation to Morrison's rememory, and in so far as the rememoried terrain is not linear, it is conceptualised in terms of Dorothy L. Pennington's helix-formed memory, which needs constant attention and reworking, as suggested by Nzegwu's work. This is the work of memory, of working with and through the echoes which attach to memory and diaspora.

CONCLUSION

UNSHACKLING MEMORY, REMEMORYING AGENCY

Studies in post-apartheid memory abound, but these are usually limited to the study of colonial and/or apartheid memory. This book makes an intervention by reading slave memory post-apartheid, recognising that 'sites of cultural displacement and encounter may thus be seen to offer, albeit chaotic and unguaranteed, revised definitions of the self within a wider political, geographical and cultural dimension' (Thomas 2000: 12). In order to do so, I have explicitly chosen a postcolonial feminist location because it privileges subaltern compositions and valuation of meanings, rather than an outward-looking explanatory framework.

My chosen critical vocabulary, methodological stance and theoretical tools are well suited to uncovering the new ways in which slave memory functions in unpredictable, sometimes contradictory ways for different groups in contemporary South Africa. This multiplicity and conceptual untidiness has been read through frameworks that highlight movement, such as the echo chamber and helix-like postcolonial memory. My explicit discussions of Morrison's rememory, Pennington's helix-shaped memory and Williams's memory as a shadow – all three my key theoretical models – directly address the refusal (or failure) of memory to be flattened or made linear/truth. For example, the claims to an indigenous Khoi ancestry have worked to inconsistent ends for both Khoisan and white societies, as shown in Chapters 1 and 3. This shows that claims to historically indigenous identities are made for reasons that are not always progressive (Strauss 2009).

The paucity of written material by enslaved people dating from this era, as well as the short trajectory of the historiography focusing on slavocratic South Africa, mean that explorations of slave pasts need to be self-consciously excavatory. Perhaps this is why the archaeological dig has been so popular as a means of opening up this debate. Historians of slavery, such as Susan Newton-King, Patricia van der Spuy, Robert Shell, Wayne Dooling, Pamela Scully, Robert Ross, and Nigel Worden have done enormous work in this regard in a very short space of time. Nonetheless, that very few specific names come to mind in relation to this topic also points to the novelty of the subject within the South African context. The work of these historians of slavery contributes much to the possibility of imagining slavery, and representing it in ways that are accessible beyond the audiences of academic texts. It is no small matter that in the acknowledgements to the first novel penned by a descendant of slaves in Cape Town, *The Slave Book*, these historians are credited with enabling that imaginative project. While it has become customary to thank historians for all manner of things, the various discussions about the 'absence of any folk memory' discussed in the introduction bear testimony either to the incredible power of the shame associated with that past, or to the success of 340 years of white supremacist physical and epistemic violence to suppress other histories, stories, memories. Most likely, the fact that slavery is being 'discovered' by so many, descendants of slaves included, as a part of South Africa's social and cultural formation is due to a combination of shame and repression. That a slave past is only recently entering the consciousness of the larger populace has much to do with the ability to explore identities opened up by the onset of democracy.

The subject of slavery in South Africa is a fast-growing area of specialisation, and the fact that democracy has coincided with the increasing movement of knowledge globally has benefited these discussions. This historical coincidence has made possible a proliferation of resources on the Internet and the World Wide Web which offer information and links to sites where slavery is being researched. The subject of colonial Dutch and British slavery has therefore grown from a little-known fact, suppressed until 1994, to one with an ever-growing audience. In a few seconds it has now become possible to access a list of historians and their articles and books on the subject, networks which address themselves to the study of slavery, archives with various articles specific to South African slavery, and a variety of other sources. Fourteen years ago most people could walk past the plaque that marks the spot where the slave tree once stood and not notice it,[1] or assert with certainty that slavery was something which happened when African people from other parts of the continent were transported to the Americas. To the extent that people are awakening to the horrible reality of enslavement as part of a collective South African past, the memory industry is fruitful. It is a productiveness that could only have emerged in a dispensation where the pursuit of knowledge is not criminalised.

This book has revealed that creative renditions and rememoryings of slavery in contemporary South Africa offer fertile ground for examination. It has juxtaposed different explorations of identity in relation to slave histories. Whereas debates on coloured identities are prevalent in South Africa at the moment, few of these are historically positioned. Examinations of the history of coloured identity formation can learn much from a reading which is sensitive to a history of slavery. This is particularly so given the recognition that all identities are produced within specific historic contexts. Much is missing from an attempt to understand the movements within collective coloured subjectivity formation when these processes are read only against the backdrop of apartheid.

While I understand that there may be value in a more comparative study of slave memory in future, that is a separate project. It is also not one that would necessarily be best served by an elision of the South African context in favour of a larger 'global' sphere of meaning. Indeed, as Laura Chrisman's (2000) scholarship referenced in this study shows us, much is unseen in South African studies by this outward gaze. This outward reach for a (global/northern) reference point is akin to what Graham Huggan, the original supervisor of the doctoral dissertation on which this book is based, has called 'the postcolonial exotic' in his full-length study of the same name. Although Huggan is not speaking exclusively of the South African space, the kind of impulse that he analyses inevitably reduces complexity and the nuances of the specific/subaltern in favour of global interest, capital and simplification ('marketing marginality'). I am convinced that it is important to pay attention to shifts in post-apartheid culture and identity, without viewing South Africa solely as the terrain of application of theories and lenses that have been wholly developed elsewhere. Knowledge travels and this is why theoretical insights can have meaning where they do not originate. At the same time, new meanings continue to emerge and evolve, shaped by the spaces that give rise to them. A postcolonial feminist orientation allows for this conceptual conversation across geography, but in ways that illuminate South African expressions in the 'now', rather than pre-empt them based on global trends and interactions with the local ('the glocal').

IMAGINING PASTS, ENVISIONING FUTURES

> The emergence of an identity, with social values embedded in it, will in time solidify into memories of cultural practice, which can be both a blessing and a curse, that predispose us to replicate our values and social practices wherever we are in the world. When we reach that stage, having decided that its benefits somehow secure our future, we will have arrived, to begin perhaps yet another age of creativity. (Ndebele 2001: 81)

As the preceding chapters have demonstrated, a memorying of slavery involves an act of contestation. It also entails the refashioning of identities and group politics. This book has read some of the emergent cultural and creative artifices for this rememorying of slavery. It has confirmed Ndebele's sense of the ensuing meanings being at once 'a blessing and a curse' for different subjects at varying points. That the first 15 years of liberation have enabled the current efflorescence of research about slavery also marks the simultaneous arrival and beginning Ndebele prophesies in the quotation above.

One of the paradoxes revealed by this study is linked to the claims of Black ancestry by segments of white South Africa. Rejections of white racial purity stem from various quarters and work to a diversity of ends. While some are refreshing and are instrumental in the undoing of colonial, slavocratic and apartheid lies, as in Ramola Naidoo's documentary (Chapter 3), others are opportunistic. The latter remain interesting since they reveal as much about contemporary insecurities as they do about previous ones. Samuel Kiguwa had argued that '[r]ather than giving [whites] security, apartheid consolidated the white minority's fear of the black majority and this led to the banning of all black political organisations, sending their leaders into exile, execution, or long prison sentences' (2002: 192). Against this backdrop, it becomes clear that some of these repositionings are part of a larger, older tradition.

What is more, the new dispensation has allowed for a revisiting of identities, or has enabled more sublimated tendencies to surface. For Black people, this has meant opening up coloured subjectivity for a new kind of questioning, and reviewing what identifying as coloured can mean. It has also meant more worthwhile engagements with Khoi identities for those for whom coloured as an identity is too fraught with apartheid and colonialist baggage to be redeemable. The onset of democracy has made this a worthwhile project because, under apartheid, Khoi groups like the Griqua would have been subsumed under one of the sub-classifications of coloured. This is because '[t]raditional politics exercised before the 1994 changes served to silence the voices of the weak and oppressed, consigned their histories and experiences to the margins and subsumed all experiences under the dominant outlook' (Kiguwa 2002: 198). For Black subjects descended from slaves, the new dispensation has enabled the exploration of difficult, often painful processes of identity. It has become possible to claim and inhabit coloured identity differently, and to assert Khoi heritage proudly without automatically being assumed to be complicit with apartheid classification and affirming that system's strategies of divide and rule.

The texts analysed in Chapter 2 explore ways of confronting these silences when they maintain hypervisibility. Focusing on the case of Sarah Bartmann, about whom volumes of racist knowledge have been written, the chapter examines the trickiness of any dialogue about Bartmann's subjectivity. How do strategies informed by anti-racist and feminist, African-friendly politics intervene in the representation of the subject who was one of the most famous slaves? The chapter reveals that the difficulties of imagining Sarah Bartmann differently stem from her hypervisibility as well as her hypersexualisation. Trapped in the racist epithet 'Hottentot Venus', she is inscribed in history as all body. Given the variety of ends to which southern African indigenous bodies have been used for scientific racism, what southern African representational traditions emerge? These are the questions posed in this chapter, questions reconsidered in the creative and academic material analysed. This points to an unresolved dilemma, since:

> [w]hen the body becomes the site of torture and severe trauma, one of the important channels of experiencing reality becomes distorted. One's body is the only potential non-object. One can experience it as a non-object, a word that is used as a creative solution influenced by feminist and womanist readings of the body which criticise the objectification of the body of the woman. ... I thought of the word 'non-object' as a way of trying to break free of the dilemma of subject and object. Trauma to the body, the means by which one perceives reality, creates psychological trauma. Our body is the only reality we can possess. Therefore when the possession of this reality

is painful, one's perception of reality is traumatised. (Prins 2002: 355–356)

The chapter concludes that this search is a troubled one, and this is examined in relation to a history which justifies objectification and the exhibition of Blackwomen's bodies. The texts examined develop varying ways to participate in the situation of helix-like memory. When Wicomb, like Prins, connects imagined pasts with the contemporary, she resists the structure which posits a static concept of time and representation. Also noteworthy is the manner in which landscape emerges as a trope in both Prins and Ferrus. Land in literary signification usually symbolises alienation in Black South African literature due to historical reasons. However, the two poems suggest that land(scape) is being imaginatively rendered as a place of presence for historical and fictional Black subjects. In Ferrus's poem it is the return of Sarah Bartmann to her home*land* which begins the healing. For Abrahams, the writing of a Sarah Bartmann historiography, like the making of a film about her return for Smith, cannot be one where cold distance is maintained between the subjects placed on either side of the knowledge-generating exercise.

In this regard, the findings of Chapter 2 are echoed in the analysis of Searle's work. There are clear overlaps between the explorations of positioning Blackwomen's bodies, slave subjectivities and cultural origins. Within the larger discussion of diaspora in Chapters 4 and 5, Searle's work is examined for what it reveals about home, dislocation and process. Here it moves in tandem with other explorations of identity in relation to diasporic belonging. Searle, as in the material on Captonian Muslim/Cape Malay food and the role of Islam, illustrates the multifarious implications which ensue from diasporic presence.

In her critique of Paul Gilroy's *The Black Atlantic: Modernity and Double Consciousness*, Joan Dayan (1997) points to the challenge of making sense of an unreconstructable past, that of ordinary slave experience. For Dayan, this is a challenge which can be met *imaginatively* in both scholarly and creative work. The readings and decodings of this rememorying require more than Gilroy's preliminary recognition that these are offerings from slaves and their descendants, and that the processes of diasporisation are invested with 'some predetermined essence and value', for:

> Gilroy's world of double speak is ultimately categorizable in terms of those who know how to theorize and those who do not; those who seek solidarity in practical struggles along ethnic lines and those who play the games black people in all western cultures play with names and naming. (Dayan 1997: 3)

Gilroy's singular 'pre-slave history' is meaningless when considerations arise about the heterogeneity of the societies from which slaves came. Further, diasporic movements circumvent the 'need for a local movement' and, as Dayan asserts, fashionable theorisations of diaspora within academia need to be offset against concrete 'rhetorical practice outside academe'. Indeed, she proceeds, '[t]he juxtaposition helps us to understand how culture and politics are reciprocal, how they operate in tandem with each other' (Dayan 1997: 5), rather than reading diasporic activity simply as a series of responses to a specific list of stimuli. Essentially, after Stuart Hall (1991: 52, emphasis added), diaspora:

> does not refer to those scattered tribes whose identity can only be secured in relation to some sacred homeland to which they must return at all costs. *Diaspora identities are those which are constantly producing and reproducing themselves anew through transformation and differences.*

The Malay diaspora cannot be read solely in terms of its foregrounded origins in South East Asia. Rather, the complications which are introduced through relations to Islam, as well as to national politics both pre-1994 and post-democracy, offer a glimpse into the manner in which Malay diasporic subjectivities are processed 'anew through transformation and difference'.

Patricia J. Williams (1991) has convincingly argued that slaves, as chattels, can neither own property nor be invested with self-will in a slavocratic society. Islam as a tradition, and as a faith, challenged this tenet. Not only did the slaves have humanity in Islam, but they also had safety from the scrutiny of the slave-owning class which tried in vain to unsettle this faith. Studies on the trans-Atlantic slave trade have emphasised the importance of religion to slave cultures. Muslim slaves had a means to signal their humanity in a manner that flew in the face of white supremacist declarations of their excessive corporeality.

MEMORY'S OPENING PATHS

Dayan's criticism of Gilroy has been incorporated into the methodology of this study. In thinking through the emergent representational forms of slavery, I have explored some academic texts alongside more deliberately creative expressions. This has been done to resist the polarisation of creative texts as those which are interpreted through academic theoretical procedures, thereby positioning the former as the raw material and the latter as the complex apparatus through which the value of the former might be asserted. Rather, I have assumed both to be engaged in epistemological projects which gain from, and feed off, one another. This approach is also in line with the womanist and African feminist insistence on the situatedness of theoretical knowledge production.[2]

Indeed, a reading of Abrahams's historiographical work on Sarah Bartmann alongside more self-consciously creative endeavours like Ferrus's poem and Wicomb's novel, with the background of Pennington's helix-shaped memory, unlocks the manner in which academic knowledge-making and Dayan's 'rhetorical practices outside academia' are in tune.

The same can be said of reading Baderoon's articles and theorisation on the meeting places of Capetonian Muslim identities and Malay cooking alongside Searle's installations, which index similar narratives. This fluidity of boundaries works in the interest of the interdisciplinary nature of postcolonial studies, a field that this study draws from extensively.

Postcolonial feminist methodology as deployed in the manner I have just described also serves to broaden the terms of academic debates. Mzwanele Mayekiso has outlined the necessity for this debate in relation to traditional forms of knowledge creation within academia. He has argued that '[t]he need for this debate is reflected in the problems that academics have with community struggles, since they depend on other academics' interpretations, on limited interviews normally conducted in English, on questionable court documents, and on biased newspaper accounts' (Mayekiso 1993: n.p.).

Creative and theoretical grappling with the representation of slave subjectivities, and with the identities which follow on from enshacklement, have been read side by side. It is important to listen to and between these narratives, as well as to pay attention to the larger narratives of which they are part, so that we may be able to hear the conversations, the ruptures and overlaps which exist in the mythologising of the new South Africa. This should always be accompanied by a rigorous interrogation of systems which naturalise the pervasive denial of difference.

What has been uncovered during the course of the first 16 years of democracy in relation to slavery, contemporary identities and future possibilities, suggests that the field will grow rapidly in both size and complexity. Other studies can explore the developing textualities ushered in by another decade of freedom, as well as probably braver explorations of identity that an older democracy will engender. Further, for the generation coming of age in 2010, the distance to lived reality in apartheid is larger. Consequently, the potential of the imagination is greater. This is not to say that innovation is the sole domain of young people. However, historically the young have been the trendsetters in the ambit of politically inflected creative innovation. Homi Bhabha has argued that strategies of subversion which reveal subaltern signification may 'be both politically effective and psychically *affective* because the discursive liminality through which it is signified may provide greater scope for strategic manoeuvre and negotiation' (1994: 145). No doubt whatever turns this project takes will have attendant contradictions. One of the most disturbing contradictions of the new South Africa has been the surge of xenophobia against other Africans. This xenophobia can only exist in the refusal to remember history. Its presence points to the ability of memory processes to coexist with processes of forgetting and erasure.

This study has not attempted to fully capture the range of activities which seek to render slavery imaginatively. Nor has it come up with a conclusive analysis of the identity politics ensuing from these explorations. Like all research it has been selective, and the material, although not specifically selected to make set arguments, has nonetheless enabled certain coverage of the terrain. It has tried to read echoes in the complex cultural phenomena it has examined, and has revealed these to be unmoored from the simple binarisms of either complicity or resistance.

One of the advantages which comes from the timing of the study's completion pertains to the positioning of the texts it analyses as part of the structuring of a new reality for a new country. Because the nation-building exercise is still in process, as evidenced by the current widespread contestation of almost every identity, the memory terrain of the new South Africa has not been scrutinised in relation to ideologies of the nation *per se*. There are clear inferences to be made from how these ideologies participate in shaping or resisting a nationalist ideology. Patricia McFadden has spoken directly to the challenges posed when we try to think through the processes of nation-making in the South African context when she declares:

211

[i]t is in the interface between 'human rights' and the civic spaces that the new and critical meanings and energies for a different kind of social reality lies. Human societies have created their most lasting and most socially relevant institutions and 'spaces of belonging and identity' through the mobilization of human agency and knowledge. We have defined such moments as 'democratic' because they express and speak to the innermost desires for peace, fairness (justice), liberty and a consolidation of what makes us social. (McFadden 2000)

Because at the end of 16 years of freedom there are a multitude of meanings articulated under the banner 'South African', there is no consensus over the existence of a privileged national consciousness. Nation as an imagined community rests on the myth that:

what holds a nation together is a conscious decision on the part of every member to affirm his or her acceptance of that nation's collective identity and cultural heritage. Members share in their past a glorious heritage and regrets, and in their future, a programme to put into effect. Their sense of shared values and collective affirmation of such values is what constitutes a nation. (Kiguwa 2002: 195)

At the beginning of 2010, South Africans rest under no such illusions, rife as public discourse is with talk of four nations, two nations, the Zulu, or Khoi, or Afrikaner nation. Into this terrain can enter the further complicating talk of conspiratorial 'Xhosa nostras', xenophobic negrophobia, and opportunistic 'Zulu troikas'. Future scholarship on memory or contemporary identities will have to grapple with this multiplicity of competing belongings and allegiances. One of the most interesting discoveries of this study has been the pervasive presence of women within the terrain of slave memory-making. This is particularly striking when read against the predominantly male and masculinist Truth and Reconciliation Commission memory process. This is why, after all, there needed to be a special hearing for women.

I have not been able to establish the reasons behind this tendency for women's high visibility within slave memory. Perhaps women's memory-making lies in sources more conducive to the kind of exploration I have chosen to engage in here. No doubt the sources also reflect my biases in terms of genre as well as my ingrained feminist politics and approaches. Future explorations of the memory terrain might also examine other memory eras (colonial, pre-colonial) and other projects, such as Premesh Lalu's *The Deaths of Hintsa* (2008). I have limited myself here to creative renditions of slavery in early democracy. I have not explored the important male domain of carnival here because the work of Denis-Constant Martin (1999a, 1999b, 2001) has addressed itself to this extensively. The overlaps in the material analysed indicate that superficial claims about the likelihood of certain memories residing in specific genres are untenable. As such, intertextual references have featured prominently among the poems, documentaries, novels, art installations and scholarship analysed in these pages. These may yet develop into fully fledged creative traditions of their own, as the work of Yvette Christianse as well as the flourishing business of Sarah Bartmann suggests. These offer an exciting avenue for further research, as the memory project adjusts to the requirements and challenges of another decade of freedom.

ENDNOTES

INTRODUCTION

1 Private correspondence, 20 June 2003.

2 The most visible markers of the beginning of memory and its academic study in relation to history are often cited as Maurice Halbwachs's *On Collective Memory* (1980), initially published in French in 1951; the journal *History and Memory: Studies in Representations of the Past*, founded in 1989; and Pierre Nora's seven-volume *Lieux de Mémoire*. These texts define 'history' as academic history-making, in other words, as historiography. For Nora, it is the empirical, academic, critical, source-bound reconstruction of the past (Bailyn 2001). Historiography's central premise rests on the past as distant and different from the present. Consequently, in order to make sense of yesteryear, history becomes explicitly selective regarding factual information (Bailyn 2001). In contrast to history, memory is theorised by Nora as that which has a cordial relationship with the past. Its location is not in academic discourse in the form of a recognised discipline, but rather pervades the terrain of 'signals, symbols, images and mnemonic clues of all sorts' (Bailyn 2001: n.p.). This relationship which memory has with the past means that it is spontaneous, takes in unquestioned past experience, and is more likely to be absolute than tentative. Its area of influence is more pervasive than that of history because, as Nora demonstrates, it moulds us and our awareness, given its emotional format.

3 Toni Morrison, 'Living Memory'.

4 See, for example, The Western Cape Oral History Project, founded in 1985, which transformed into the Centre for Popular Memory, located at the University of Cape Town; the University of KwaZulu-

Natal's Centre for Oral History and Memory Work in Africa, founded in 1994; a conference ('The Eastern Cape: Historical Legacies and New Challenges') co-hosted by the universities of Fort Hare, Rhodes and Oxford in August 2003; a colloquium on 'History, Politics and Memory' held at Monash University's Johannesburg campus in October 2004; and tourist companies like The Direct Action Centre for Peace and Memory in Woodstock, Cape Town, use former activists as tourist guides, while the Robben Island Museum employs the prison's former political prisoners as guides on the island.

5   Gail Smith, 'Fetching Saartje'.

6   *Sechaba* is the African National Congress periodical founded in 1967.

CHAPTER 1

1   It is never quite clear what 'ethnicity' means in the South African context. This is due to the use of the term/concept to mean 'race', 'nation', 'culture' (which itself in some contexts marks race), etc. I use it here to mean what some refer to as 'nation' (different and distinct from nation-state), as a rejection of the racist 'tribe'. While 'ethnicity' as a category remains extremely troublesome in South Africa, for different reasons, I use it here because it is less ambiguous than 'nation', which is what I would use in another context where it would be understood differently from 'nation-state'. I prefer it to most of its alternatives even as I am unsettled by its historical connotations. For some of the most recent arguments in favour of using 'nation' in this manner, see Chinua Achebe's *Home and Exile* and Yvette Abrahams (1997).

2   See the magazine *Sawubona*, November 2001 issue. This advert plays around with associations of Africans as freak, referencing the well-known exhibitions of Africans on European stages in colonial and slave eras. However, it does not critique these in any discernible way, unless their mere referencing is seen to do this.

3   'Shangaan', like 'Bushman' and 'Hottentot', are legacies of colonial

misnaming of Khoi, San and Tsonga people. These labels nonetheless continue to have some use in contemporary South Africa, sometimes by Black people who claim ignorance of this history and at other times by those who claim the terms have been rehabilitated and reclaimed.

CHAPTER 2

1   A shortened version was published as 'Fetching Saartje' in the *Mail & Guardian* of 12 May 2002.

2   SABC, 04 August 2002, 'Bartmann enrobed for final journey', available at http://www.sabcnews.com/politics/government/0,1009,40056,00. html, accessed on 18 January 2003.

3   This is from a statement issued by the deputy minister, quoted on SABC news, available at http://www.sabcnews.com/politics/the_ provinces/0,1009,39990,00.html, accessed on 18 January 2003. See also http://www.info.gov.za/speeches/2002/02073014461003.htm.

4   President Thabo Mbeki's speech is available at http://www.polity. org.za/html/govdocs/speeches/2002/sp0809.html, accessed on 18 January 2002, and was widely reported on and quoted in the South African media. For the full text of the speech, see http://www.dfa.gov. za/docs/speeches/2002/mbek0809.htm.

5   Marang Setshwaelo has spoken about 'Saartje' as her nickname. See Setshwaelo (2002).

6   In the rest of the collection *The Fat Black Woman's Poems* (Nichols 1984), as in *i is a long memoried woman* (Nichols 1983) and *Lazy Thoughts of a Lazy Woman* (Nichols 1989), Nichols explores various discursive constructions of Black women from slavery, slave revolts, colonialism, anti-colonial imaginaries, nationalist movements, and twentieth-century 'global' culture.

7   She says this in an interview with Mara Vena archived at www. hottentotvenus.com.

8   Cuvier had argued that these groups shared the same characteristics.

9 For the context of this chapter, I use Black feminist and womanist interchangeably to refer to a Blackwoman-centric feminism. I have elsewhere, in much detail, explored the names which attach to different feminisms espoused by Black women in 2001 (see Gqola 2001b). The other essays in this special issue on African feminisms also address themselves to aspects of this topic. See also the essays in Nnaemeka (1995); Hill Collins (1990); Mirza (1997).

10 'Feminists of the African world' is used here to refer to writing and creative theorisation present in the works of feminists beyond the continent and into the diaspora. I wish to explore this in the work of some Caribbean feminists here, and although I find the use of 'African feminist' to describe them equally useful, for the sake of clarity I defer to the more conventional understanding of who is an African feminist, even if this is also sometimes contested. The essays in *Agenda* issues 50, 54 and 58, which were special issues labelled variously African Feminisms Volumes 1, 2 and 3 (2001, 2002, 2003), explore these contestations. See also the essays in Nnaemeka (1995).

11 Susan Bassnett, 'The State of Language and Teaching is Parlous'.

12 A *swirlkous* is made of cut-off pantyhose and worn as part of the process of making hair 'slick'. Coloured women and other Black women (used to) wear these as part of straightening their hair out. It is also worn to keep the hairstyle intact, and for these purposes scarves are also used. In the US context, for example, a *swirlkous* goes by the name of a do-rag.

13 The film won Best African Documentary at FESPACO African Film Festival and Best Documentary at the Milan African Film Festival, both in 1999.

14 Jessica Horn on *Other*, a BBC radio show, 20 July 2003.

15 Jean-Marie Le Pen, a conservative French politician, who is also founder and president of the far right-wing Front National, has run for presidency five times, and came second in 2002. Although he lost to Jacques Chirac,

217

the large number of votes cast for him in the first 2002 polling round, which placed him ahead of the left-wing's Lionel Jospin, suggested that there was significant right-wing support in contemporary French society. Le Pen has criminal convictions for racist, xenophobic, Islamaphobic and anti-Semitic actions, has advocated for the marginalisation of HIV-positive people, and complained about the number of players of colour in the French soccer team. Smith's juxtaposition of a historic France that placed Bartmann on display and celebrated her dissector, Cuvier, on the one hand, with a contemporary France in which Le Pen is popular, on the other, suggests that much in France remains the same across centuries. The juxtaposition is also a subtle critique of human development across time, and the ideals of the French Revolution.

16 These ranged from historian Edward Long's *History of Jamaica* (1774), where he argued that Africans were closer to orang-utangs than they were to Europeans; the surgeon Charles White's *Account of the Regular Gradation in Man* (1799); and *The Anthropological Treatises of Johann Friedrich Blumenbach*, tr. and ed. Thomas Bendyshe (1865).

CHAPTER 3

1 *Country of my Skull* won the Alan Paton Award for non-fiction (1999), an award from the Hiroshima Foundation for Peace and Culture (2000), the Olive Schreiner Prize (2000), and one of Africa's Best 100 Books for the 20th Century, with a 2004 film adaptation starring Samuel L Jackson.

2 Review of Antjie Krog's *Begging to be Black*, day month 2009.

3 Part of this address was flighted in the South African Broadcasting Corporation's Channel 1 Nguni news bulletin at 7.30pm.

4 *Swartgevaar* literally translates into 'fear of black' and 'black danger', where 'black' stands for Black people and all things associated with them. It inscribes Black people as *gevaarlik*, dangerous, and therefore justifies using immense levels of violence to 'protect' white people from

Blacks. It also finds articulation as fear of miscegenation, as in the oft-heard axiom 'you never know when Black blood is going to turn up', so it is better to keep it/them out (of your family).

5 This claim seems counter-intuitive. However, on the one hand, his name is recognisable to most South Africans alive today, and was recognised under apartheid, spurring a range of corruptions of his surname as synonyms for stabbing. On the other hand, he retains mythic significance and his death was neither widely covered in the media nor was he part of the TRC or any other nation-making process. Therefore, although his *name* is known, his personal circumstances and whereabouts were not widely known between the presidential assassination in 1966, his sentencing to imprisonment from which only the state president could release him, the onset of democracy in 1994 and his death in October 1999 in a psychiatric hospital. He lies in an unmarked grave.

6 Erasmus refers to several incidents of this which were in the limelight in 1996 (Makgoba affair) and 1998 (Mamdani affair at the University of Cape Town). These received considerable attention in the South African media. Makgoba (1997) has since recorded his experiences of being accused of fleshing out his CV, his near expulsion from a top liberal South African university (the University of the Witwatersrand), and the manner in which none of the reasons given by the 13 white professors of that institution for alleging that he was underqualified and bringing the university into disrepute, could be substantiated. Erasmus also comments on the way in which the incident cited above at another top liberal South African university (the University of Cape Town) echoed the Makgoba affair. Several other scholars have written on the slow pace of transformation, and racial harassment at South African universities. There is a growing body of work which engages with the manifestations of this violence at South African white institutions as larger numbers of Black academics enter these sites. See Mabokela and

King (2001), Mabokela (2000), and Mabokela and Magubane (2003) on the slow pace of transformation; also Khusi (2002).

CHAPTER 4

1 *Cape Times* 11 January 1961. See also the *Cape Argus* of the same day.

2 Jeppie, for example, lists Muhammad Suharto, the Malaysian president's, official state visit to South Africa during which he was awarded the highest state honour by the Republic of South Africa, thus reciprocating the honouring of President Nelson Mandela earlier; Malaysian government-funded/-sponsored initiatives and festivals celebrating the arrival of Islam from South East Asia in South Africa.

3 By 'young Capetonian Muslim scholars' I intend the 'Capetonian Muslim scholars' to qualify both the self-identification and the focus area of scholarship.

4 The chronotope is Mikhail Bakhtin's (1981) theorisation of time and space as intimately connected. See his 'Forms of Time and of the Chronotope in the Novel', in Holquist (1981). See also Peeren (2003).

5 The recent upsurge I refer to relates to non-Jewish explorations, since Jewish diasporas have a long history of coding religion as home space.

6 In her acknowledgement to the first issue of her novel (1998), to which version all bracketed page numbers in the chapter refer, Rayda Jacobs positions her narrative thus:

> A book of historical fiction is an arrogant attempt by a writer in a few hundred pages to recreate and inform. The best you can hope for is a glimpse, and trust that the glimpse will open a much larger window in your mind. I couldn't possibly speak on behalf of those early people, and don't pretend to know what it was like. This book is merely a scratch at the surface.

7 Kananga's representation, along with those of the other African slaves

in the novel, rehearses colonial inscriptions on East/West African and Khoi bodies specifically. I have argued this at length in my ' "Slaves don't have opinions": Inscriptions of Slave Bodies and the Denial of Agency in Rayda Jacobs' *The Slave Book*', in Erasmus (2001c).

8 Baderoon (2002: 6): '[Islamic] refers to the practices of the religion based on its scriptures, and [Muslim] is an adjective to describe the inevitably varied practices and cultures of people who are adherents of the religion. The conflation of the terms leads to an erasure of difference between Muslim communities, and the perception of Muslims as rigid, unvarying, and uninterested in leisure and art.'

9 The *Umma(t)* is the common Muslim religious community globally.

10 Sheik Yusuf, known as the founder of Islam in South Africa, was exiled to Java, imprisoned in Ceylon and later exiled to the Cape after he led and participated in various anti-Dutch rebellions in Macassar and Java. His exile to the Cape by the Dutch East India Company was to isolate him from slaves, but backfired as his location in Zandvliet became a pilgrimage site for western Cape Muslims. His resting place in Faure remains one of 20 holy sites for Capetonian Muslims.

CHAPTER 5

1 See http://www.knet.co.za/capemalay/capemalayhistory.htm; see also http://www.saembassy-jakarta.or.id/shyusuf.html and http://www. owls.co.za/english/bokaap.htm where similar terminology is used.

2 See http://www.knet.co.za/capemalay/capemalayhistory.htm.

3 She has also released the equally famous *The Culture and Cuisine of the Cape Malays* (1995).

4 Iterability as used by Jacques Derrida (1988) suggests a language/ meaning sequence which requires some aspect to remain the same while another needs to differ each time, so that with each 'repetition' there is something recognisable and something new in order to allow a proliferation of meanings.

5 For the online version, see http://www.museums.org.za/sang/exhib/ isintu/sa_art.html, accessed on 10 January 2003.

6 From *Head North: Views from the South African National Gallery Permanent Collection*, which toured BildMuseet, Ume , Sweden, from 25 February to 01 May 2001. Statement available at http://www. museums.org.za/sang/exhib/headnorth/artists.htm#Berni%20Searle, accessed on 10 January 2003.

7 For a very different reading of this image, see Annie Coombes, who reads the imprints thus: 'the ghosts of ecstatic female bodies rise out of red clay dust, the characteristic color of so much South African soil' (2003: 251–252).

8 Bishop Desmond Tutu (1999: 21) cites:

> to equip the Bantu to meet the demands which economic life will impose upon him ... What is the point of teaching a Bantu child mathematics when it [sic] cannot use it in practice? ... Education must train and teach people in accordance with their opportunities in life.

9 From *Head North: Views from the South African National Gallery Permanent Collection*.

CONCLUSION

1 In the doctoral dissertation which has now been extensively revised for this book, I spent some time illustrating this.

2 This dyamic has been explored in great detail in the essays collected in *Agenda* 50: African Feminisms volume 1, edited by Desirée Lewis.

REFERENCES

Abrahams, Cass. 1995. *The Culture and Cuisine of the Cape Malays*. Cape Town: Metz.

Abrahams, Cass. 2000. *Cass Abrahams Cooks Cape Malay: Food from Africa*. Cape Town: Metz.

Abrahams, Yvette. 1997. 'The Great Long National Insult: "Science", Sexuality and the Khoisan in the 18th and early 19th century', *Agenda*. 32.

Abrahams, Yvette. 2000. 'Colonialism, Dysjuncture and Dysfunction: Sarah Baartman's Resistance', unpublished PhD thesis. University of Cape Town.

Abrahams, Yvette. 2004. 'Ambiguity is My Middle Name: A Research Diary', in Reitumetse Mabokela & Zine Magubane. eds. *Hear Our Voices: Race, Gender and the Status of South African Women in the Academy*. Pretoria: UNISA Press.

Abrahams, Yvette & Fiona Clayton. 2004. *The Life and Times of Sarah Bartmann*. Cape Town: Herstory Project for European Project for Human Rights.

Achebe, Chinua. 2000. *Home and Exile*. New York: Oxford University Press.

Adhikari, Mohamed. 2009. *Burdened by Race: Coloured Identities in Southern Africa*. Cape Town: University of Cape Town Press.

Alexander, Neville. 2001. 'The State of Nation-building in South Africa', *Pretexts*. 10.1.

Ali, Farook. 1986. 'Tell the Moslems I'm Proud of Them, Says Mandela', *Sechaba*. March.

Anthias, Floya. 2002. 'New Hybridities, Old Concepts: The Limits of "Culture" ', *Ethnic and Racial Studies*. 24.4.

Anthony, Kenny D. 1999. *History, Memory and Responsibility*, speech delivered on Emancipation Day and launch of design for National Heroes Park, St Lucia, 03 August. Available at http://www.stlucia.gov.lc/primeminister/former_prime_ministers/kenny_d_anthony/statements/1999/history_memory_responsibility_speech_on_emancipation_day_launch_of_design_for_national_heroes_park.htm, accessed 15 October 2002.

Asmal, Kader. 1994. *Making the Constitution*, paper delivered as the 8th Moran Lecture at Trinity College, Dublin, 8 December. Available at http://web.uct.ac.za/depts/sarb/X0032_Asmal_36.html, accessed 24 October 2002.

Baderoon, Gabeba. 2001. 'Art and Islam in South Africa: A Reflection', *Annual Review of Islam in South Africa*. December.

Baderoon, Gabeba. 2002. 'Everybody's Mother was a Good Cook: Meanings of Food in Muslim Cooking', *Agenda*. 51.

Baderoon, Gabeba. 2003. 'Covering the East/Veils and Masks: Orientalism in South African Media', in Herman Wasserman & Sean Jacobs. eds. *Shifting Selves: Post-apartheid Essays on Mass Media, Culture and Identity*. Cape Town: Kwela.

Baderoon, Gabeba. 2004. 'Oblique Figures: Representations of Islam in South African Media and Culture', unpublished PhD thesis, University of Cape Town.

Baderoon, Gabeba. 2007. 'Catch with the Eye: Change and Continuity in Muslim Cooking in Cape Town', in Sean Field, Felicity Field & Renate Meyer. eds. *Imagining the City: Memory, Space and Culture in Cape Town*. Cape Town: HSRC Press.

Bailyn, Bernard. 2001. 'Considering the Slave Trade: History and Memory', *The William and Mary Quarterly*. 58.1. Reprinted online in association with the History Cooperative. Available at http://www.historycooperative.org, accessed 24 October 2002.

Bakhtin, Mikhail. 1981. *The Dialogic Imagination: Four Essays*. Translated by Caryl Emerson & Michael Emerson. Austin: University of Texas Press.

Bassnett, Susan & Harish Trivedi. 1999. 'Introduction', in Susan Bassnett & Harish Trivedi. eds. *Post-colonial Translation: Theory and Practice*. London & New York: Routledge.

Berger, John. 1972. *Ways of Seeing*. London: Penguin.

Bester, Rory. 2003. 'Floating Free', *Berni Searle Catalogue, Standard Bank Young Artist, 2003 Catalogue*. Cape Town: Bell-Roberts.

Bhabha, Homi K. 1990. *Nation and Narration*. London & New York: Routledge.

Bhabha, Homi K. 1994. *The Location of Culture*. London: Routledge.

Bhabha Homi K. 2002. 'Inauguration of Global Literature Forum', paper presented as the inaugural lecture for the interdisciplinary Postcolonial Studies Graduiertenkolleg of the University of Munich. 25 January.

Binder, Wolfgang. 1997. 'Interview with David Dabydeen', in Kevin Grant. ed. *The Art of David Dabydeen*. London: Peepal Tree.

Birbalsing, Frank. 1997. 'Interview with David Dabydeen', in Kevin Grant. ed. *The Art of David Dabydeen*. London: Peepal Tree.

Blumenbach, Johann Friedrich. 1865. *The Anthropological Treatises of Johann Friedrich Blumenbach*. Translated and edited by Thomas Bendyshe. London: The Anthropological Society of London.

Boehmer, Elleke. 1992. 'Transfiguring: Colonial Body into Post-Colonial Narrative', *Novel: A Forum for Fiction*. 26.1.

Boyce Davies, Carole. 1994. 'Introduction: Migratory Subjectivities', in Carole Boyce Davies, *Black Women, Writing and Identity: Migrations of the Subject*. London & New York: Routledge.

Boyce Davies, Carole. 1996. 'Other Tongues: Gender, Language, Sexuality and the Politics of Location', in Ann Garry & Marilyn Pearsall. eds. *Women, Knowledge and Reality: Explorations in Feminist Philosophy*. London & New York: Routledge.

Bradford, Helen. 1996. 'Women, Gender and Colonialism: Rethinking the History of the British Cape Colony and its Frontier Zones, 1806–1870', *Journal of African History*. 37.3.

Brah, Avtah. 1996. *Cartographies of Diaspora: Contesting Identities*. London & New York: Routledge.

Chabot Davies, Kimberley. 2002. '"Postmodern Blackness": Toni Morrison's *Beloved* and the End of History', *Critical Voices*. February. Available at http://www.thecriticalvoice.com/feb2002archive.html. Accessed 20 October 2002.

Chance, Kerry. 2001. *The Right to Narrate: Interview with Homi Bhabha*, Bard College, 3 March. Available at http://www.bard.edu/hrp/resource_pdfs/chance.hbhabha.pdf, accessed on 10 December 2009.

Chrisman, Laura. 2000. *Rereading the Imperial Romance: British Imperialism and South African Resistance in Haggard, Schreiner and Plaatje*. Oxford: Clarendon Press.

Chude-Sokei, Louis. 1997. *'Dr Satan's Echo Chamber': Reggae, Technology and the Diaspora Process*. Mona: University of the West Indies Reggae Studies Unit.

Cliff, Michelle. 1990. 'Object into Subject: Some Thoughts on the Work of Black Women Artists', in Gloria Anzaldua. ed. *Making Face, Making Soul, Hacienda Caras*. San Francisco: Aunt Lute.

Clifford, James. 1997. 'Diasporas', in James Clifford, *Routes, Travel and Translation in the Twentieth Century*. Cambridge, MA: Harvard University Press.

Clifford, James. 2001. 'Indigenous Articulations', *The Contemporary Pacific*. 13.2, Fall.

Coetzee, Carli. 1998. 'Krötoa Remembered: A Mother of Unity, a Mother of Sorrows', in Sarah Nuttall & Carli Coetzee. eds. *Negotiating the Past: The Making of Memory in South Africa*. Cape Town: Oxford University Press.

Coetzee, Carli. 2001. ' "They Never Wept, the Men of My Race": Antjie Krog's *Country of My Skull* and the White South African Signature', *Journal of Southern African Studies*. 27.4.

Coetzee, J.M. 1988. *White Writing: On the Culture of Letters in South Africa*. New Haven: Yale University Press.

Cohen, Robin. 1997. *Global Diasporas: An Introduction*. Seattle: University of Washington Press.

Condé, Maryse. 1999. 'O Brave New World', *Research in African Literatures*. 29.3. This paper was previously presented as the keynote address at the joint meeting of the Comparative Literature Association and the African Literature Association, Austin, Texas, March 1998.

Coombes, Annie E. 2003. *History after Apartheid: Visual Culture and Public Memory in a Democratic South Africa*. Durham: Duke University Press.

Cooper, Carolyn. 2000. [1993]. *Noises in the Blood: Orality, Gender and the 'Vulgar' Body of Jamaican Popular Culture*. Durham: Duke University Press.

Crais, Clifton & Pamela Scully. 2008. *Sara Baartman and the Hottentot Venus: A Ghost Story and a Biography*. Johannesburg: Witwatersrand University Press.

Cullen, Countee. 1925. 'Heritage', in *Colour*. New York: Harper.

Cuvier, Georges. 1817. 'Extrait d'observations faites sur le cadavre d'une femme connue á Paris et á Londres sous le nom de Vénus Hottentote!' *Mémoires du Muséum d'histoire naturelle*. 3. Translated by Mara Vena. Available at www.hottentotvenus.com, accessed 15 July 2003.

Dabydeen, David. 1987a. *Hogarth's Blacks: Images of Blacks in Eighteenth Century English Art*. Manchester: Manchester University Press.

Dabydeen, David. 1987b. *Hogarth, Walpole and Commercial Britain*. London: Hansib.

D'Agostino, Melissa. 2003. 'Muslim Personhood: Translation and Islamic Religious Education Within the Muslim Diaspora of New York City', paper presented at Diaspora and Memory Conference, Amsterdam School for Cultural Analysis, University of Amsterdam, 26–28 March.

Das, Veena. 1995. 'Introduction', in Veena Das, *Critical Events: An Anthropological Perspective on Contemporary India*. Delhi: Oxford University Press.

Dasmariñas, Julius. 2003. 'Of Religion, Migration and Community: The Filipino Catholic Immigrant in New York City', paper presented at Diaspora and Memory Conference, Amsterdam School for Cultural Analysis, University of Amsterdam, 26–28 March.

Davids, Achmat. 1980. *The Mosques of the BoKaap: A Social History of Islam at the Cape*. Athlone: South African Institute of Arabic and Islamic Research.

Dawes, Kwame. 1997. 'Interview with David Dabydeen', in Kevin Grant. ed. *The Art of David Dabydeen*. London: Peepal Tree.

Dayan, Joan. 1997. 'Paul Gilroy's Slaves, Ships, and Routes: The Middle Passage as Metaphor', *Research in African Literatures*. 27.4.

Daymond, Margaret. 2002. 'Bodies of Writing: Recovering the Past in Zoë Wicomb's *David's Story* and Elleke Boehmer's *Bloodlines*', *Kunapipi*. 14.1&2.

Derrida, Jacques. 1988. *Limited Inc*. Chicago: Northwestern University Press.

de Torro, Fernando. 2002. *The Post-colonial Question: Alterity, Identity and Other(s)*. Frankfurt am Main: Vervuert.

Driver, Dorothy. 2002. 'Women Writing Africa: Southern Africa as a Post-apartheid Project', *Kunapipi*. 14.1&2.

Dubow, Saul. 1995. *Scientific Racism in Modern South Africa*. Cambridge: Cambridge University Press.

Easton, Kai. 2002. 'Travelling Through History, "New" South African Icons: The Narratives of Saartje Baartman and Krotoä-Eva in Zoë Wicomb's *David's Story*', *Kunapipi*. 14.1&2.

Erasmus, Zimitri. 2000. 'Hair Politics', in Sarah Nuttall & Cheryl-Ann Michael. eds. *Senses of Culture: South African Culture Studies*. Cape Town: Oxford University Press.

Erasmus, Zimitri. 2001a. 'Introduction: Re-imagining Coloured Identities in Post-apartheid South Africa', in Zimitri Erasmus. ed. *Coloured by History, Shaped by Place: New Perspectives on Coloured Identities in Cape Town*. Cape Town: Kwela & South African History Online.

Erasmus, Zimitri. 2001b. 'Recognition Through Pleasure, Recognition Through Violence: Gendered Coloured Subjectivities in South Africa', *Current Sociology*. 48.3.

Erasmus, Zimitri. ed. 2001c. *Coloured by History, Shaped by Place: New Perspectives on Coloured Identities in Cape Town*. Cape Town: Kwela & South African History Online.

Erasmus, Zimitri & Edgar Pieterse. 1999. 'Conceptualising Coloured Identities in the Western Cape Province', in M. Palmberg. ed. *National Identity and Democracy in Africa*. Pretoria: Human Sciences Research Council.

Fanon, Frantz. 1967. *Black Skin, White Masks*. Translated by Charles Markmann. New York: Groove Press.

February, Vernie. 1981. *Mind Your Colour: The 'Coloured' Stereotype in South African Literature*. Boston & London: Kegan Paul.

Ferrus, Diana. 2002. 'I Have Come to Take You Home', in Shelley Barry, Malika Ndlovu & Deela Khan. eds. *Ink @ Boiling Point: A Selection of Twenty-first Century Black Women's Writing from the Southern Tip of Africa*. Cape Town: WEAVE

Fester, Gertrude. 2000. 'Women Writing for Their Rights', *Agenda*. 46.

Figueroa, John J. 1996. 'The Relevance of West Indian Literature to Caribbean Heritage People Living in Britain', in Colin Brock. ed. *The Caribbean in Europe: Aspects of West Indian Experience in Britain, France and the Netherlands*. London: Frank Cass.

Fraser, Vikki & John Gunders. 1999. 'Editorial: Food', *M/C: A Journal of Media and Culture*. 2.7.

Gamiet, Aysha. 1985. 'Moslems of the Cape: Descendants of Indonesian Freedom Fighters', *Sechaba*. October.

Gerzina, Gretchen Holbrook. 1999. *Black England: Life Before Emancipation*. London: Allison & Busby.

Goniwe, Thembinkosi. 2008. 'Goodbye Post-colonialism and Post-apartheid', unpublished paper presented as part of the Division of Visual Arts Talks (DIVA Talks), University of the Witwatersrand, 11 September.

Gordimer, Nadine. 1991. *My Son's Story*. London: Penguin.

Gordon-Chipembere, Natasha Maria. 2006. 'Even with the Best of Intentions: The Misreading of Sarah Baartman's Life by African-American Writers', *Agenda*. 68.

Gqola, Pumla Dineo. 2001a. 'Defining People: Analysing Power, Language and Representation in Metaphors of the New South Africa', *Transformations*. 47.

Gqola, Pumla Dineo. 2001b. 'Ufanele Uqavile: Blackwomen, Feminisms and Postcoloniality in Africa', *Agenda*. 50: 11–23.

Gqola, Pumla Dineo. 2004. 'Shackled Memories and Elusive Discourses? Colonial Slavery and the Contemporary Cultural and Artistic Imagination in South Africa', unpublished PhD thesis. University of Munich.

Gqola, Pumla Dineo. 2005. 'Memory, Diaspora and Spiced Bodies in Motion: Berni Searle's Art', *African Identities*. 3.2: 123–138.

Gqola, Pumla Dineo. 2007. ' "Like Having Three Tongues in One Mouth": Tracing the Elusive Lives of Slave Women in (Slavocratic) South Africa', in Nomboniso Gasa. ed. *Basus'iimbokodo, Bawel'imilambo/They Remove Boulders and Cross Rivers: Women in South African History*. Cape Town: HSRC Press.

Gqola, Pumla Dineo. 2008. 'Crafting Epicentres of Agency: Sarah Bartmann and African Feminist Literary Imaginings', *Quest: An African Journal of Philosophy*. 20.1/2.

Halbwachs, Maurice. 1980. [1951]. *The Collective Memory*. Translated by LA Coser. Chicago & London: Chicago University Press.

Hall, Stuart. 1990. 'Cultural Identity and Diaspora', in Jonathan Rutherford. ed. *Identity: Community, Culture, Difference*. London: Lawrence & Wishart.

Hall, Stuart. 1991. 'Old and New Identities, Old and New Ethnicities', in Anthony Kind. ed. *Culture, Globalization and the World System*. London: MacMillan.

Hall, Stuart. 1997. 'Introduction', in Stuart Hall. ed. *Representation: Cultural Representations and Signifying Practices*. London: Sage.

Haron, Muhammed. 2001. *Conflict of Identities: The Case of South Africa's Cape Malays*, conference paper presented at the Malay World Conference, Kuala Lumpur, 12–14 October. Available at http://phuakl.tripod.com/eTHOUGHT/capemalays.htm, accessed 20 August 2003.

Harris, Ashleigh. 2006. 'Accountability, Acknowledgement and the Ethics of "Quilting" in Antje Krog's *Country of My Skull*', *Journal of Literary Studies*. 22.1–2.

Hassan, Salah & Olu Oguibe. 2001. ' "Authentic/ex-centric" at the Venice Biennale: African Conceptualism in Global Contexts', *African Arts*. 34.4: 64–75.

Hendricks, Cheryl. 2001. ' "Ominous" Liaisons: Tracing the Interface between "Race" and Sex at the Cape', in Zimitri Erasmus. ed. *Coloured by History, Shaped by Place: New Perspectives on Coloured Identities in Cape Town*. Cape Town: Kwela & South African History Online.

Hesse, Barnor. 2002. 'Forgotten Like a Bad Dream: Atlantic Slavery and the Ethics of Postcolonial Memory', in David Theo Goldberg & Ato Quayson. eds. *Relocating Postcolonialism*: 143–173. Oxford: Blackwell.

Hill Collins, Patricia. 1990. *Black Feminist Thought: Knowledge, Consciousness and the Politics of Empowerment*. New York & London: Routledge.

Hoeane, Thabisi. 2004. 'Under Strain: The Racial/Ethnic Interpretation of South Africa's 2004 Election', *Journal of African Elections*. 3.2, December: 1–26.

Holmes, Rachel. 2007. *African Queen: The Real Life of the Hottentot Venus*. Jeppestown: Jonathan Ball.

Holqvist, Michael. ed. 1981. *The Dialogic Imagination: Four Essays by M M Bakhtin*. Austin: University of Texas Press.

hooks, bell. 1996. 'Feminism as a Persistent Critique of History: What's Love Got to Do with It?' in Alan Read. ed. *The Fact of Blackness: Frantz Fanon and Visual Representation*. Seattle: Bay Press.

Huggan, Graham. 1989. 'Decolonizing the Map: Post-colonialism, Post-structuralism and Cartographic Connection', *Ariel*. 20.4.

Huggan, Graham. 1990. '(Un)co-ordinated Movements: The Geography of Autobiography in David Malouf's *12 Edmond Street* and Clark Blaise's *Resident Alien*', *Australian and New Zealand Studies in Canada*. 3, Spring.

Husseyn, Andreas. 2000. 'Present Pasts: Media, Politics, Amnesia', *Public Culture*. 12.1.

Jacobs, Rayda. 1998. *The Slave Book*. Cape Town: Kwela.

Jeppie, Shamil. 1987. 'Historical Process and the Constitution of Subjects: I D Du Plessis and the Reinvention of the "Malay" ', unpublished Master's thesis. University of Cape Town.

Jeppie, Shamil. 1996. 'Commemorations and Identities: The 1994 Tercentenary of Islam in South Africa', in Tamara Sonn. ed. *The Question of Muslim Minorities*. Atlanta: Scholars Press.

Jeppie, Shamil. 2001. 'Re-classifications: Coloured, Malay, Muslim', in Zimitri Erasmus. ed. *Coloured by History, Shaped by Place: New Perspectives on Coloured Identities in Cape Town*. Cape Town: Kwela & South African History Online.

Kadalie, Bruce. 1995. 'Coloured Consciousness: Building or Dividing the Nation?' *Die Suid-Afrikaan*. 5, December.

Khusi, Ply D. 2002. 'An Afrocentric Approach to Tertiary Education in South Africa: Personal Reflections', in Norman Duncan, Pumla Dineo Gqola, Murray Hofmeyr, Tamara Shefer, Felix Malunga & Mashudu Mashige. eds. *Discourses on Difference, Discourses on Oppression*. Cape Town: Centre for Advanced Studies of African Society.

Kiguwa, Samuel. 2002. 'South Africa in Transition: A Study of the Impact of Cultural Diversity on Nation Building', in Norman Duncan, Pumla Dineo Gqola, Murray Hofmeyr, Tamara Shefer, Felix Malunga & Mashudu Mashige. eds. *Discourses on Difference, Discourses on Oppression*. Cape Town: Centre for Advanced Studies of African Society.

Kingdon, Geeta Gandi & John Knight. 2004. 'Race and the Incidence of Unemployment in South Africa', *Review of Development Economics*. 8.2.

Kitson, Peter J. 1998. 'Romanticism and Colonialism: Races, Places, Peoples, 1985–1800', in Tim Filford & Peter J. Kitson. eds. *Romanticism and Colonialism: 1780–1830*. Cambridge: Cambridge University Press.

Krog, Antjie. 1998. *Country of My Skull*. Johannesburg: Random House.

Krog, Antjie. 2009. *Begging to be Black*. Johannesburg: Random House.

Lakoff, George. 1994. *Conceptual Metaphor Homepage*. Available at http://cogsci. berkeley.edu/metaphors/, accessed 22 August 2003.

Lalu, Premesh. 2008. *The Deaths of Hintsa*. Cape Town: HSRC Press

Lewis, Desirée. 2000. 'Living on an Horizon: The Writings of Bessie Head', unpublished PhD thesis. University of Cape Town.

Lewis, Desirée. 2001. 'Review: The Conceptual Art of Berni Searle', *Agenda*. 50.

Lewis, Desirée. 2002. *African Gender Research and Postcoloniality: Legacies and Challenges*. Conference paper presented at the Codesria Conference on Gender in the New Millenium, Cairo, 7–10 April. Available at http://www.codesria. org/Links/conferences/gender/gender.htm, accessed 20 August 2003.

Lewis, Desirée & 'Molara Ogundipe. 2002. 'Conversations', *Feminist Africa*. 1.1. Available at http://www.feministafrica.org/01-2002/morala4.html, accessed 04 November 2002.

Long, Edward. 1774. *History of Jamaica*. London: T Lownudes.

Low, Gail Ching-Liang. 1999. 'Introduction: The Difficulty of Difference', in Julian Wolfreys. ed. *Literary Theories: A Reader*. Edinburgh: Edinburgh University Press.

Lyon, Anne. 1983. 'Cape Malays/Cape Muslims: A Question of Identity', unpublished master's thesis. National University of Australia.

Mabokela, Reitumetse Obakeng. 2000. *Voices of Conflict: Desegregating South African Universities.* New York & London: Routledge Falmer.

Mabokela, Reitumetse Obakeng & Kimberley Lenease King. eds. 2001. *Apartheid No More: Case Studies of Southern African Universities in the Process of Transformation.* Westport, CT & London: Bergin & Garvey.

Mabokela, Reitumetse Obakeng & Zine Magubane. eds. 2003. *Race, Gender and the Status of Black South African Women in the Academy.* Pretoria: UNISA Press.

Magubane, Zine. 1997. 'Beyond the Masks', *Agenda.* 32.

Magubane, Zine. 2001. 'Which Bodies Matter? Feminism, Poststructuralism, Race, and the Curious Theoretical Odyssey of the "Hottentot Venus" ', *Gender and Society.* 15.6.

Magubane, Zine. 2004. *Bringing the Empire Home: Race, Class and Gender in Britain and Colonial South Africa.* Chicago: University of Chicago Press.

Majaj, Lisa Suhair. 2001. 'On Writing and Return: Palestinian-American Reflections', *Meridians: Feminism, Race, Transnationalism.* 2.1: 113–126.

Makgoba, William. 1997. *Makoko: The Makgoba Affair.* Johannesburg: Vivlia.

Marco, Derilene. 2009. 'A Coloured History, a Black Future: Contesting the Dominant Representations in the Mass Media Through Hip-hop Beats', unpublished master's thesis. University of the Witwatersrand.

Martin, Denis-Constant. 1999a. 'Cape Town's Coon Carnival: A Site for Contestation and Competing Coloured Identities', in Sarah Nuttall & Cheryl-Ann Micheal. eds. *Senses of Culture: South African Culture Studies.* Cape Town: Oxford University Press.

Martin, Denis-Constant. 1999b. *Coon Carnival, New Year in Cape Town, Past and Present.* Cape Town: David Philip.

Martin, Denis-Constant. 2001. 'Politics Behind the Mask: Studying Contemporary Carnivals in Political Perspective', *Questions de Recherches/Research in Question.* 2.

Mashile, Lebogang. 2008. 'A Daughter's Wish', in Lebogang Mashile, *Flying Above the Sky.* Johannesburg: Lebogang Mashile & African Perspetives.

Matlanyane Sexwale, Bunie. 1994. 'The Politics of Gender Training', *Agenda*. 23: 57–63.

Mayekiso, Mzwanele. 1993. 'The Legacy of Ungovernability', *Southern African Review of Books*. November/December.

McFadden, Patricia. 1999. *Homeless in Harare Another Day*. Available at http://www.wworld.org/programs/regions/africa/patricia_mcfadden.htm, accessed 21 July 2003.

McFadden, Patricia. 2000. *International Policies, African Realities: Democracy and Human Realities*, presentation as part the Africa Policy Roundtable Series, July, Washington, DC. Available at http://www.africaaction.org/rtable/pat0002.htm, accessed 08 October 2008.

Mercer, Kobena. 1999. 'Eros and Diaspora', in Olu Oguibe & Okwui Enwezor. eds. *Reading the Contemporary: African Art from Theory to the Marketplace*: 244–275. London: Institute for International Visual Art (inIVA).

Mignolo, Walter D. 1994. 'Signs and Their Transmission: The Question of the Book in the New World', in Elizabeth Hill Boone & Walter D. Mignolo. eds. *Writing Without Words: Alternative Literacies in Mesoamerica and the Andes*. Durham & London: Duke University Press.

Mirza, Safia Heidi. ed. 1997. *Black British Feminism*. London & New York: Routledge.

Mishra, Vijay. 1993. 'Introduction: Diaspora', *SPAN: Journal of the South Pacific Association for Commonwealth Literature and Language Studies*. 34/35.

Morrison, Toni. 1987. 'The Site of Memory', in William Zinsser. ed. *Inventing the Truth: The Art and Craft of Memoir*. Boston: Houghton.

Morton, Timothy. 2000. 'Chapter One: The Confection of Spice: Historical and Theoretical Considerations', in Timothy Morton, *The Poetics of Spice: Romantic Consumerism and the Exotic*. Cambridge: Cambridge University Press.

Moss, Laura. 2006. ' "Nice Audible Crying": Editions, Testimonies and *Country of My Skull*', *Research in African Literatures*. 37.4.

Motsemme, Nthabiseng. 2004. ' "The Mute Always Speak": On Women's Silences at the Truth and Reconciliation Commission', *Current Sociology*. 52.3.

Mudimbe, V.Y. 1999. '*Reprende*: Enunciations and Strategies in Contemporary African Arts', in Olu Oguibe & Okwui Enwezor. eds. *Reading the Contemporary: African Art from Theory to the Marketplace*. London: Institute for International Visual Art (inIVA).

Nattrass, Nicoli & Jeremy Seekings. 2001. ' "Two Nations"? Race and Economic Inequality in South Africa Today', *Daedelus*. 130.1.

Ndebele, Njabulo. 1990a. *South African Literature and Culture: Rediscovery of the Ordinary*. Johannesburg: Congress of South African Writers.

Ndebele, Njabulo. 1990b. 'Liberation and the Crisis of Culture', *Southern African Review of Books*. February/May.

Ndebele, Njabulo. 1994. *South African Literature and Culture: Rediscovery of the Ordinary*. Manchester: Manchester University Press.

Ndebele, Njabulo. 2001. 'South Africans in Search of Common Values', *Pretexts*. 10.1.

Nichols, Grace. 1983. *i is a long memoried woman*. London: Karnak.

Nichols, Grace. 1984. 'Thoughts Drifting Through the Fat Black Woman's Head While Having a Full Bubble Bath', in Grace Nichols. *The Fat Black Woman's Poems*. London: Virago.

Nichols, Grace. 1989. *Lazy Thoughts of a Lazy Woman*. London: Virago.

Nnaemeka, Obioma. 1995. *Sisterhood, Feminism and Power: From Africa to the Diaspora*. Trenton, NJ: Africa World Press.

Nora, Pierre. 1984–1992. *Lieux de Mémoire* (7 volumes). Paris: Edition Gallimard.

Nuttall, Sarah. 2001. 'Subjectivities of Whiteness', *African Studies Review*. 44.2.

Nuttall, Sarah & Carli Coetzee. 1998. 'Introduction', in Sarah Nuttall & Carli Coetzee. eds. *Negotiating the Past: The Making of Memory in South Africa*. Cape Town: Oxford University Press.

Nuttall, Sarah & Cheryl-Ann Michael. 2000. 'Introduction', in Sarah Nuttall & Cheryl-Ann Michael. eds. *Senses of Culture: South African Cultural Studies*. Cape Town: Oxford University Press

Nzegwu, Nkiru. 2000. 'Creating Memory: A Conversation with Carole Harris, a Detroit-based Quilt Artist', *Ijele: eArt Journal of the African World*. 1.1. Available at http://www.ijele.com/ijele/vol1.1/nzegwu2.html, accessed 15 April 2003.

Oakley, Todd. 1998. 'Implied Narratives: From Landor to Vistaril-i.m', conference paper presented at the Historicizing Cognition: Literature and the Cognitive Revolution Forum at the Annual Convention of the Modern Languages Association, San Francisco, 27–30 December.

Oguibe, Olu & Okwui Enwezor. 1999. 'Introduction', in Olu Oguibe & Okwui Enwezor. eds. *Reading the Contemporary: African Art from Theory to the Marketplace*: 8–14. London: Institute for International Visual Art (inIVA).

Peeren, Esther. 2003. 'Towards a Chronotopical Redefinition of Diaspora', ASCA Diaspora and Memory Conference, Amsterdam, 26–28 March.

Pennington, Dorothy L. 1985. 'Time in African Culture', in Molefi Kete Asante & Kariamu Welsch Asante. eds. *African Culture: The Rhythms of Unity*. Westport, Connecticut & London: Greenwood Press.

Pierre, Jemima. 2002. *Diaspora and the Dynamics of Racialization*, lecture presented as part of the Cultural Cross-Currents in the African Diaspora Series at the Carter G. Woodson Institute for Afro-American and African Studies, Virginia University. Available at http://www.virginia.edu/woodson/courses/aas102%20(spring%2001)/articles/pierre_lecture.pdf, accessed 20 November 2002.

Poitevin, Guy & Bernard Bel. 1999. 'People's Memory, Remake of History', in Bernard Bel, Biswajit Das, J. Brouwer, Vibodh Parthasarathi & Guy Poitevin. eds. *Communication Processes*. Available at http://www.iias.nl/host/ccrss/cp/cp2/cp2-Politics.html#Heading6, accessed 25 November 2002.

Posel, Deborah. 2001. 'What's in a Name? Racial Classification in Apartheid South Africa and Beyond', *Transformation*. 47.

Prins, Deirdre. 2000. 'Timelines', unpublished poem.

Prins, Jo-Anne. 2002. 'Mediating Difference: Politics of Representation in Antjie Krog's Chronicling of the Truth and Reconciliation Commission in *Country of my Skull*', in Norman Duncan, Pumla Dineo Gqola, Murray Hofmeyr, Tamara Shefer, Felix Malunga & Mashudu Mashige. eds. *Discourses on Difference, Discourses on Oppression*. Cape Town: Centre for Advanced Studies of African Society.

Probyn, Elspeth. 1999. 'Indigestion of Identities', *M/C: A Journal of Media and Culture*. 2.7.

Ramaswamy, Sumathi. 1998. 'Body Language: The Somatics of Nationalism in Tamil India', *Gender and History*. 10.1.

Reddy, Thiven. 2001. 'The Politics of Naming: The Constitution of Coloured Subjects in South Africa', in Zimitri Erasmus. ed. *Coloured by History, Shaped by Place: New Perspectives on Coloured Identities in Cape Town*. Cape Town: Kwela & South African History Online.

Reynolds, Andrew. ed. 1994. *The Role of the White Right*. Cape Town: David Philip.

Ross, Robert. 1983. *Cape of Torments: Slavery and Resistance in Southern Africa*. London: Kegan Paul.

Ruden, Sarah. 1999. '*Country of My Skull*: Guilt and Sorrow and the Limits of Forgiveness', *Ariel*. 30.1.

Ruiters, Michele. 2009. 'Collaboration, Assimilation and Contestation: Emerging Constructions of Coloured Identity in Post-apartheid South Africa', in Mohamed Adhikari. ed. *Burdened by Race: Coloured Identities in Southern Africa*. Cape Town: University of Cape Town Press.

Ruiters, Michele René. 2006. 'Elite (Re-)constructions of Coloured Identities in Post-apartheid South Africa: Assimilations and Bounded Transgressions', unpublished PhD thesis. Rutgers, The State University of New Jersey.

Rushdie, Salman. 1983. *Shame*. London: Jonathan Cape.

Said, Edward W. 2000. *Out of Place*. New York: Vintage.

Samuelson, Meg. 2007. *Remembering Nation, Disremembering Women? Stories of the South African Transition*. Scottsville: University of KwaZulu-Natal Press.

Sarker, Sonita. 2002. 'Moving Target', *Women's Review of Books*. February.

Saunders, Christopher. 1988. *The Making of the South African Past: Major Historians on Race and Class*. Cape Town: David Philip.

Sen, Sharmilla. 2002. 'Foreign Accents: Notes Upon My Return to the Diaspora', *Women's Review of Books*. February.

Setshwaelo, Marang. 2002. 'The Return of the "Hottentot Venus" ', *Blackworld*. 14 February. Available at http://www.blackworld.com/articles/daily/index_20020214.asp and also at *Race Sci: History of Race in Science*, http://web.mit.edu/racescience/in_media/baartman/baartman_africana.htm. Both sites accessed 04 September 2003.

Smith, Gail. 2002. 'Fetching Sarah', unpublished paper.

Smith, Valerie. 1998. *Not Just Race, Not Just Class*. London & New York: Routledge.

Spearey, Susan. 2000. 'Displacement, Dispossession and Conciliation: The Politics and Poetics of Homecoming in Antjie Krog's *Country of My Skull*', *Scrutiny2*. 5.1.

236

Steyn, Melissa. 2001. *Whiteness Just Isn't What it Used to Be: Whiteness in a Changing South Africa.* Albany: SUNY Press.

Strauss, Helene. 2006. 'From Afrikaner to African: Whiteness and the Politics of Translation in Antjie Krog's *A Change of Tongue*', *African Identities.* 4.2: 179–194.

Strauss, Helene. 2009. ' "...[C]onfused about Being Coloured": Creolisation and Coloured Identity in Chris van Wyk's *Shirley, Goodness and Mercy*', in Mohamed Adhikari. ed. *Burderned by Race: Coloured Identities in Southern Africa.* Cape Town: University of Cape Town Press.

Taliep, Ismoeni. 1992. 'Coloured or Muslim? Aspects of the Political Dilemma of the Cape Muslims, 1925–1956', unpublished Honours thesis. University of Cape Town.

Tamale, Sylvia. 2002. *Gender Trauma in Africa: Enhancing Women's Links to Resources.* Conference paper presented at the Codesria Conference on Gender in the New Millenium, Cairo, 7–10 April. Available at http://www.codesria. org/Links/conferences/gender/gender.htm, accessed 20 August 2003.

Thelen, David. 2002. *Challenges the Truth and Reconciliation Commission Poses to the Modern Discipline of History and its Civics.* Paper presented at the University of South Africa's History Seminar Series, Pretoria, and at Wits Institute for Social and Economic Research, University of the Witwatersrand, Johannesburg. Available at wiserweb.wits.ac.za/PDF%20Files/wirs%20-%20 thelen.PDF, accessed_10 November 2002.

Thomas, Helen. 2000. *Romanticism and Slave Narratives: Transatlantic Testimonies.* Cambridge: Cambridge University Press.

Tobias, Saul.1999. *History, Memory and the Ethics of Writing: Antjie Krog's* Country of My Skull, available at www.trcresearch.org.za, accessed 18 February 2005.

Tutu, Desmond. 1999. *No Future Without Forgiveness.* Cape Town: Trafalgar.

Upham, Mansell. 2000. *Selective Memory/Selective Quoting.* South Africa L-Archives, hosted by Rootsweb. Available at http://archiver.rootsweb.com/th/ read/SOUTH-AFRICA/2000-07/0963230149, accessed 20 July 2003.

van der Spuy, Patricia. 1996. ' "What, then, was the sexual outlet for black males?" A Feminist Critique of Quantitative Representations of Women Slaves at the Cape of Good Hope in the Eighteenth Century', *Kronos.* 23.

Van der Walt, André. 2000. 'Dancing with Codes: Protecting, Developing, Limiting and Deconstructing Property Rights in the Constitutional State', Konrad Adenauer Stiftung Seminar Series, Johannesburg.

Van Rooyen, Johan. 1994. *Hard Right: The New White Power in South Africa.* London: IB Taris.

Veale, Tony. 1996. 'Creativity as Pastiche: A Computational Treatment of Metaphoric Blends with Special Regard to "Cinematic" Borrowing', unpublished mimeo. University of Dublin.

Walvin, James. 1982. *Black Personalities in the Era of the Slave Trade.* London: Blackwell.

Walvin, James. 1986. *England, Slaves, and Freedom, 1776–1838.* Basingstoke: Palgrave MacMillan.

Ward, Kerry. 1995. 'The 300 Years: The Making of Cape Muslim Culture', *Social Dynamics.* 21.1.

West, Cornel. 1993. *Race Matters.* New York: Vintage.

White, Charles. 1799. *Account of the Regular Gradation in Man and in Different Animals and Vegetables.* London: C Dilly.

Wicomb, Zoë. 1996. 'Postcoloniality and Postmodernity: The Case of the Coloured in South Africa', in Herman Wittenberg & Loes Nas. eds. *AUETSA 96: Proceedings of the Conference of Association of University English Teachers of South Africa.* Bellville: University of the Western Cape.

Wicomb, Zoë. 1998. 'Shame and Identity: The Case of the Coloured in South Africa', in Derek Attridge & Rosemary Jolly. eds. *Writing South Africa: Literature, Apartheid and Democracy, 1970–1995.* Cambridge: Cambridge University Press.

Wicomb, Zoë. 1999. 'Five Afrikaner Texts and the Rehabilitation of Whiteness', *Social identities.* 4.3.

Wicomb, Zoë. 2000. *David's Story.* Cape Town: Kwela.

Williams, Patricia J. 1991. *The Alchemy of Race and Rights.* Cambridge, MA & London: Harvard University Press.

Williams, Susan H. 1999. 'Truth, Speech and Ethics: A Feminist Revision of Free Speech Theory', *Genders.* 30.

Worden, Nigel & Clifton Crais. 1994. *Breaking the Chains: Slavery and its Legacy in the Nineteenth Century Cape Colony.* Johannesburg: Witwatersrand University Press.

REFERENCES

Young, Jean. 1997. 'The Re-objectification and Re-commodification of Saartje Baartman in Suzan Lori Parks' Venus', *African American Review*. 5.

Zegeye, Abebe. 2001. 'A Matter of Colour', *South African Historical Journal*. 44.1: 207–228.

FILMS

Maseko, Zola. Dir. 1998. *Hottentot Venus: The Life and Times of Sara Baartman*. Johannesburg: First Run/Icarus.

Maseko, Zola. Dir. 2003. *The Return of Sara Baartman*. Johannesburg: First Run/ Icarus.

INDEX

CPSIA information can be obtained
at www.ICGtesting.com
Printed in the USA
LVHW011338271118
598414LV00002B/480/P